In My Rear View Mirror . . .

Sal Marchiano

To order additional copies of this book, contact:
Xlibris Corporation
1-888-795-4274
www.Xlibris.com
Orders@Xlibris.com
38326

CONTENTS

ICONS

STEW ZOO

REFLECTIONS

To my daughter, Susie Q.,
I love you.

ACKNOWLEDGEMENTS

My sincere thanks to Eric Vaughn-Flam for realizing this project, and to Tommy Culla, Bob Taute and Barry Werner for their editing. Research was easier thanks to witnesses, Ray Abruzzese. Joe Aceti, Peter Beilen, Joanne Cerreta, Marvin Cohen, Ed Croake, Joe Delapina, Fred Dryer, Tad Dowd, Teddy Drucker, Ruta Gerulaitis, Hank Goldberg, Liz Goldberg, Martha Haines, Jim Lampley, Phil Linz, John Martin, Larry McTague, Arthur Mercante, Nick Mormando, Tommy O'Neill, Timmy Secour, Bobby Van, Jimmy Walsh, and Richard Weisman. Dan Baliotti, Mel DeGiacomo and George Kalinsky were generous with their photographs. Much gratitude to Howard Halpern who showed me the way, to Don Imus who came through in the clutch, to Les Davis and Joe Valerio for their friendship, loyalty and counsel and to Karen Scott and Richard Liebner for their support.

INTRODUCTION

Much occurred in New York City in the late '60s as that ghetto of a decade came to an end. A cultural phenomenon developed among young people while three of their professional sports teams won first-time championships within two years. The new birth control pill liberated women from the fear of pregnancy. Promiscuity was the rage, and the singles bars on Manhattan's East Side were mating grounds for professional athletes as well. Tommy O'Neill, a manager of Mr. Laffs on First Avenue, wisecracked, "Hookers can't make a living here, the girls are giving it away."

Many experimented with drugs and the popular music was anti-establishment because the young people were morally split on the Vietnam War.

As a native New Yorker, I was familiar and knowledgeable about the ineptitudes and struggles of the Jets, the Mets and the Knicks before their ascendancies from September 1968 to May 1970. Schooled in radio and wire service work, I was fortunate to be a sports anchor and reporter for WCBS-TV during that period and at WABC-TV in the 1970s when Muhammad Ali and Joe Frazier battled three times, Secretariat won the Belmont Stakes for a sweep of the Triple Crown and the Yankees took two World Series. These are my behind-the-scenes memories and "in the moment" profiles about those seminal sports events and the games that were played after hours too.

I am privileged to say that I reported on what I believe to be some of the top moments in sports over the past five decades. They are in chronological order:

◊ **Shea Stadium Inaugural Game** April 17, 1964, Flushing Meadows, New York. Mets lost to Pittsburgh 4-3, 48,776 . . . WJRZ Radio, Newark New Jersey.

◊ **1964 World Series** . . . Yankees-Cardinals, won in 7 games by St. Louis . . . WJRZ Radio, Newark, N.J.;

◊ **Ali-Liston II** . . . Lewiston, Maine, won by Ali, May 25, 1965, (United Press International Audio);

◊ **1966 Major League Baseball All Star Game** won by the American League 2-1 . . . the new Busch Stadium, St. Louis, Missouri, (UPI-Audio);

◊ **Super Bowl-I,** Green Bay over Kansas City, January 15, 1967, Los Angeles Coliseum (WCBS-TV and CBS News);

◊ **U.S. Open at Baltusrol**, Springfield, N.J, won by Jack Nicklaus, June, 1967 (WCBS-TV and CBS News);

◊ **1967 Major League Baseball All Star Game** won by the National League 2-1 on Tony Perez' 15th inning home run and the winning pitcher was Tom Seaver of the Mets, Anaheim, California (WCBS-TV and CBS News);

◊ **1968 World Series** won by the Detroit Tigers over the St. Louis Cardinals in 7 games (WCBS-TV and CBS News).

◊ **Super Bowl III** . . . . the Jets' upset of the Baltimore Colts for their first NFL and only championship, January 12, 1969, Orange Bowl, Miami. (WCBS-TV and CBS News);

◊ **1969 World Series** . . . . the Mets upset the Baltimore Orioles in five games for their first championship, (WCBS-TV and CBS News);

◊ **The Knicks win their first NBA championship** defeating the Los Angeles Lakers in seven games . . . . May, 1970, Madison Square Garden. (WCBS-TV and CBS News);

◊ **Ali-Frazier I**, Madison Square Garden, Joe Frazier retains his world heavyweight championship by a 15 round decision, March 8, 1971, (WABC-TV, ABC News);

◊ **1972 U.S. Open** at Pebble Beach, California, won by Jack Nicklaus . . . . (ABC News/WABC-TV);

◊ **The Knicks win their second NBA championship** against the Los Angeles Lakers, May, 1973, (WABC-TV and ABC News);

◊ **Secretariat's Triple Crown**, winning the Kentucky Derby, the Preakness Stakes and the Belmont Stakes, spring 1973 . . . . (WABC-TV and ABC-News);

◊ **Ali-Frazier II**, Madison Square Garden. Ali wins NABF heavyweight title by 12 round decision. Jan. 28, 1974 (WABC-TV, ABC News);

◊ **The New York Nets first American Basketball Association Championship**, May 1974 . . . . MVP Julius Erving, followed by a second championship in 1976 (WABC-TV and ABC NEWS);

◊ **Mickey Mantle and Whitey Ford inductions into Baseball Hall of Fame**, Cooperstown, N.Y. . . . . . August 12th 1974 . . . . (WABC-TV);

◊ **The Thrilla In Manila**, Oct. 1, 1975, Ali retains world heavyweight title KO 14 (ABC Sports/ABC News/WABC-TV);

◊ **1977 U.S. Open** Tennis . . . . Guillermo Vilas defeated Jimmy Connors in the final. Connors hit the last ball, an unforced error, in championship play at Forest Hills . . . . September, 1977, (WABC-TV/ABC News);

◊ **1977 World Series**, the Yankees defeat the Los Angeles Dodgers in six games (WABC-TV, ABC News);

◊ Affirmed nipping Alydar at the wire in the stretch run of the **Belmont Stakes for the Triple Crown**, June 10, 1978 at Belmont Park, (WABC-TV and ABC News);

◊ **Muhammad Ali regaining his World Heavyweight Title** from Leon Spinks . . . . W I5, September, 15, 1978 . . . New Orleans (WABC-TV, ABC News);

◊ **The Yankees' playoff win** in Boston for the American League East championship (Bucky Dent's homer) October 2, 1978, Fenway Park. (WABC-TV and ABC News);

◊ **1978 World Series**. The Yankees beat the Los Angeles Dodgers in six games (WABC-TV, ABC News);

◊ **The 1980 NHL Stanley Cup Final**. The Islanders defeat of the Philadelphia Flyers in six games for their first of four straight Stanley Cups . . . . May, 24, 1980 . . . . WCBS-TV/WABC-TV;

◊ **Larry Holmes' KO of Muhammad Ali** in 11 rounds for the world heavyweight championship, Oct. 2, 1980, Las Vegas, (ESPN);

◊ **Sugar Ray Leonard regains World Welterweight title** from Roberto Duran ("No Mas, No Mas") KO 8 . . . . Nov. 25, 1980 . . . . New Orleans (ESPN);

◊ **Sugar Ray Leonard retains World Middleweight title** against Thomas Hearns KO 14 . . . Las Vegas . . . . September 16, 1981 . . . (ESPN);

◊ **Muhammad Ali's last fight**, a 10 round decision loss to Trevor Berbick, Nassau, the Bahamas, December 11, 1981(ESPN);

◊ Blow-by-blow of **Marvin Hagler's successful defense of his World Middle Weight Championship** over Roberto Duran, 15-round unanimous decision, November 10, 1983, Las Vegas.(Pay Per View);

◊ **Joe Namath's induction into the Pro Football Hall of Fame**, (also O.J. Simpson) August 3, 1985, Canton, Ohio . . . . (WNBC-TV);

◊ **Game-6 . . . 1986 World Series** . . . against Boston, the Mets scored 3 runs in the 10th inning to even the best of seven at three apiece

(Mookie Wilson's trickler through Bill Buckner's legs, allowing Ray Knight to race home with the winning run) October 25, 1986(WNBC-TV);

◊ **Game-7**, two nights later, the Mets won the World Series October 27, 1986. Shea Stadium (WNBC-TV);

◊ **Walt Frazier's induction into the Basketball Hall of Fame**, Springfield, Ma., May 5, 1987 . . . . (WNBC-TV);

◊ The Giants beating Buffalo in **Super Bowl-XXV**, January 27 1991, Tampa, Florida. (WNBC-TV);

◊ **The Rangers first Stanley Cup win in 54 years**, defeating Edmonton, June 14, 1994, Madison Square Garden. (WPIX-TV);

◊ **Cal Ripken Jr. in his 2,131st consecutive game** breaks Lou Gehrig's "Iron Man" record . . . . Sept. 6, 1995, Baltimore, (WPIX);

◊ **1996 World Series** . . . . The Yankees defeated Atlanta, starting a run of seven divison titles, six pennants and four world championships in eight years with manager Joe Torre . . . (WPIX-TV);

◊ **The 2003 American League Championship Series** and the Yankees edging the Boston Red Sox in the 7th and deciding game on Aaron Boone's 11th inning home run. Oct. 16, 2003 (WPIX-TV);

◊ The Boston Red Sox becoming the first team in baseball history to rally from a 3-0 deficit in the postseason to defeat the Yankees for **the American League Championship,** sweeping the last four games. October, 2004 (WPIX TV).

ICONS

THE MICK

In early April 1963, the Yankees were working out at the Stadium, the day before their home opener. I held my microphone in my right hand and my tape recorder in my left hand and I introduced myself to Mickey Mantle. Could I ask him a couple of questions for WJRZ Radio in Newark, New Jersey? The Mick gave this rookie radio guy a once over and nodded yes. The interview went well until I posed a third question. He blurted "You asked me your TWO fucking questions!" He turned and walked back to the batting cage, his no. 7 in my face. I had learned my first lesson in dealing with sports heroes. Don't overstep your bounds or you'll lose access.

Mantle was a 19-year-old rookie with the Yankees who originally was a shortstop and wore no. 6. After a dozen dizzying years with baseball's premier team in the nation's no. 1 city, the handsome home run hitter was no longer the shy and puzzled country bumpkin from Commerce, Oklahoma. The Mick used aloofness as a shield against most of the media and the public. When Mantle allowed someone inside his circle, he could be a caring and loyal friend and great fun to be with. Because of his small town background Mickey was ill suited to be a cultural hero, but he was an icon to sports fans. Even followers of opposing teams had to grudgingly give him his due.

The Mick could back up his movie star looks. Tutored by his father and grandfather to swing the bat from both sides of the plate, Mantle was arguably the greatest switch-hitter in the history of the game. Listed as 5-11 ½ inches and 195 lbs., he was really about 5-10, blessed with an athletic body that was the rare combination of speed with power.

Mickey enjoyed his teammates company very much and the Yankees' clubhouse was his inner sanctum. After the trade of second baseman Billy Martin in 1957, he lost his best buddy during the season. He hung out with

Whitey Ford on the road. At home, Whitey was very married, so Mickey was on his own. His wife, Meryln, hardly ever came to New York, raising their four sons in Dallas, Texas, during the season, while he lived at the St. Moritz Hotel on Central Park south. He considered himself a transient New Yorker. In the off season, he preferred to be home in Oklahoma, hunting and fishing, where no one made a fuss over him. But, he morphed into The Mick and grew accustomed to off-season visits to New York City, alone.

Mickey Mantle—at spring training, Ft Lauderdale Florida, 1967

He was extremely generous with his younger teammates, picking up their tabs for food and drink.

Bobby Murcer, who starred for the Yankees in the 1970s, recalls how Mickey made him feel welcome when Murcer reported to the Yankees' spring training complex in Fort Lauderdale, Florida, in 1966. Some of the other Yankees were mocking the 19-year-old rookie from Oklahoma. Mantle remembered how difficult it was when he was a teenager in pinstripes. Murcer says Mantle made it a point to put his arm around Bobby, in the middle of the clubhouse, shouting to all who could listen that the kid was also from his home state of Oklahoma and everyone should be nicer to him.

Murcer recalls that Mickey threw a nasty knuckleball and delighted in playing catch with rookies and befuddling them with his dancing ball. One of them was Jake Gibbs, the Yankees' first $100,000 "bonus baby." It was no joking matter when Gibbs broke his nose trying to catch the Mick's knuckler.

It took years for Mantle to overcome his shyness, and he struggled with his loneliness. Imagine the Mick lonely. But, like DiMaggio and Ruth before him, Mickey was highly recognizable and attracted too many people in restaurants and bars. Men were impressed and women attracted to the blond, muscular centerfielder on the most glamorous team in sports. Mickey was wary of strangers, so he appeared aloof and sullen. After games, he went to restaurants and clubs that assured his privacy. In New York, he preferred stay-up-late places like Toots Shor's, Manuche's, Danny's, The Little Club, and the Harwyn Club. He and Billy Martin hung out on the East Side of Manhattan at Dorie's and The Recovery Room, which was special because it was a block from the hospitals and filled with nurses.

Very late at night, P. J. Clarke's was his favorite saloon. At Clarke's, they roped off an area in the backroom so Mickey could have something to eat and drink without interruption. As much as he bounced around in Manhattan, he enjoyed himself more on the road because he had more anonymity. A bartender at the Hudson Bay on Second Avenue and 76th Street named Chipmonk had to telephone Billy Martin many times to pick up Mickey who used to drink himself into a stupor at the back table in the corner by the window. Mickey drank too much alcohol and he had a temper, but he wasn't a violent man. There was ample proof of Mickey losing his cool in the Yankees' dugout, cussing and raising hell after tough at bats and his cool treatment of fans in public places. But, he had to endure the constant demands of strangers for a handshake, an autograph and a picture. The Mick was a "down-home" guy from Oklahoma who didn't take notoriety seriously, unless he benefited in some way.

Former flight attendant Martha Haines claims she had a relationship with Mickey for nearly 25 years. She had met him in Atlanta in 1965, while in college and they became reacquainted in New York because of Alex Hawkins who was a wide receiver for the Atlanta Falcons. Martha described Mickey as happy when he wasn't drinking, and kind and sweet and very protective of her.

"One time, we went to a resort in Pennsylvania, to play golf. As I tried to sit in the golf cart, a guy put his hand under my rear end. Mickey grabbed him by the shirt and threw him about 20 feet. One night, we went to the Stork Club in New York with a bunch of people. A girlfriend of mine, who flew for United Airlines, was vulgar at the table. Mickey excused himself to go to the men's room and he didn't return. A waiter asked me if I was 'Big Red' and passed along the message from Mickey to meet him at his hotel."

Haines had a concurrent eight-year relationship with Spiro Theodore Agnew, the former Vice President of the United States under Richard Nixon. They traveled together often to England and Greece. All in all, Martha traveled around the world with Agnew seven times. "Mickey knew about Ted, but Ted didn't know about Mickey, who would always telephone me and cry out, 'HOW'S SPY-RO?' Mickey used to ask me to break dates with Ted to be with him. It was easy because I could always say the airline called for an assignment. I didn't want to marry either one of them, both had families."

"Mickey was always a gentleman and pretty much a loner. He drank too much alcohol because he didn't think he would live long and he wanted to have a good time while on earth. In 1952, as his major league career was blossoming, Mickey's father died at 39 of Hodgkins disease, which infects the lymph nodes, spleen and liver. Mickey was fatalistic because most of the men in his family passed away young. So, when he got drunk at the end of the night, I would take care of him. In 1995, when he was suffering from cancer at home in Dallas, I spoke with him a couple of times on the telephone and he said, 'don't worry, I'll get through this thing and we'll have fun again.' I knew that wasn't going to happen. He died at 63, two months after he had a liver transplant."

When the retired Mickey Mantle was hired by Sportschannel in New York to work the Yankees telecasts, it was announced at a standing-room-only news conference at Yankee Stadium. After he answered several questions, I asked Mickey if his new job analyzing baseball games would include interviewing ballplayers. He said he didn't know and looked to someone at his side, who nodded yes. My follow up question was "What would you do if a player ignored you, the way you used to ignore us?" Mantle shot back, "I'll rip him the next day in the booth, the way you used to rip me." There was an explosion of laughter from the reporters. It was pure Mickey humor. That's when he could be downright charming.

Months later, during a Mother Day's broadcast, Mantle's partner mentioned the holiday and asked Mickey what he gave his wife, who had borne him four sons. The Mick said on TV, "Nothin' . . . . she ain't my mama."

Yankees owner George Steinbrenner tolerated the Mick despite his poor behavior and teasing. Former Yankees catcher Fran Healy recalls that Mantle heard from a classmate of Steinbrenner at Williams College that George fumbled the football a lot. The Mick's nickname for his boss was "Hands Steinbrenner."

He could be crude, as well as cold. I once overheard him in the dugout during a pre-game media baseball game in 1964 promoted by Ballantine Beer. Three cheerleader type girls in tights represented the company's slogan of "Purity, Body and Flavor." Those words were on their tight tank tops. The girls used the dugout runway to leave and Mickey propositioned Purity and Body, suggesting they go back to the Yankees locker room to take a shower together. They ran away, giggling.

In December of 1972, when Mickey received a memo with an attached questionnaire from Yankees public relations man Bob Fishel, asking all players to describe "their most outstanding event at Yankee Stadium," his reply was handwritten.

New York Yankees Inc.

BUSINESS AND TICKET OFFICES   293-4300
YANKEE STADIUM, BRONX, N.Y. 10451   293-6000

Dear Mickey,

As you probably know, 1973 marks the 50th anniversary of Yankee Stadium and we are going to have a season-long Golden Anniversary celebration. We hope to mark the occasion on our Old Timers Day, Saturday, August 11, as well as on individual dates during the season.

We thought it would be interesting to learn from you what you consider your outstanding event at Yankee Stadium. In many cases the answer is obvious, but because we are writing a large number of your former team mates, we are asking you to answer this question for us.

1973 will be the final season at Yankee Stadium as we know it. We will be located at Shea in 1974 and '75 while Yankee Stadium is completely rebuilt to reopen in 1976.

Thanks for your cooperation. We are looking forward to seeing you in 1973 and wish you a happy holiday season.

Very truly yours,

Bob Fishel

December 14, 1972/m

I consider the following my outstanding experience at
Yankee Stadium:

_____

I got a blow-job
under the right field
Bleachers. by the yankee
Bull pen.

_____

This event occurred on or about: (Give as much detail as you can)

It was about the third
or fourth inning. I had
a pulled groin and couldn't
fuck at the time. She was
a very nice girl and asked
me what to do with the
cum after I come in her
mouth. I said don't ask
me, I'm no cock-sucker.

*
Signed *Mickey Mantle*

* The All-American. Boy

"I got a blow job under the right field bleachers by the Yankee bull
pen... It was about the third or fourth inning. I had a pulled groin
and couldn't fuck at the time. She was a very nice girl and asked
me what to do with the cum after I came in her mouth. I said 'I
don't ask me, I'm no cock-sucker.' Signed: Mickey Mantle The All
American Boy."

Whitey Ford told me that one winter, the Mick was in New York alone and he ran into one of his all-time favorites, sultry actress Angie Dickinson, in the St. Moritz lobby. Mickey introduced himself and she agreed to join him for dinner the next night. They went on the town and had a ball. Late in the evening, in her suite at the St. Moritz, Mickey had too much to drink and he barfed on the movie star. She was horrified and ordered him to leave.

Mickey went to his suite and removed his soiled clothes and, emptying his jacket pocket, he found a bracelet she asked him to save because the clasp had broken during their date. Mickey figured this would be a good way of getting back into her suite, He telephoned her. "It's Mickey."

"What do you want?"

"I have your bracelet."

"Mail it."

The romantic notion of Major League Baseball and its larger than life stars left me my first year as a radio sports reporter covering the Yankees. It was 1963 during batting practice at the Stadium, the afternoon before opening day. Mickey was outside the cage waiting for Roger Maris to finish. Here they were, "the M&M Boys" who had combined to wallop 257 home runs in the past three seasons, Maris with 133 and Mantle with 124. Two years earlier, in 1961, Maris broke Babe Ruth's record of 60 in a season with 61 homers. Taking batting practice, Maris laced a rocket of a line drive down the right field line. Before Yankee Stadium was refurbished and altered in the early '70s, the box seats, along the right field foul line, jutted out. The line drive hit a spectator who went down like he was shot. There was a brief hush, but the guy jumped up happily, waving the souvenir that apparently hit him somewhere else but blessedly not in the head. At the batting cage, Mickey yelled to Maris, "Just another fucking, hard-headed New Yorker."

On June 8, 1969, the Yankees retired Mickey's no. 7 during special ceremonies at the Stadium, between games of a doubleheader against the Chicago White Sox. Mayor John Lindsay issued a proclamation designating that Sunday, "Mickey Mantle Day." On the field, the Mick was flanked by his teammates from a dozen Yankees championship teams. Mel Allen announced that Mantle's no. 7 uniform would be sent to the Baseball Hall of Fame in Cooperstown, New York.

He had retired the previous spring. In his 18 years with the Yankees, the Mick had played in 2,401 games, belting 536 home runs with 1,509 runs batted in. His most memorable season was in 1956 when he was 24 years old. Mickey bashed 52 home runs, knocked in 130 runs and batted .353. He was first in all three categories and the Triple Crown earned him the American League's Most Valuable Player Award. Also, in 1956, Frank Gifford of the New York Giants was the Most Valuable Player in the National Football League. Gifford told me Mickey delighted in the fact that they shared the same locker, during different seasons, in the clubhouse at Yankee Stadium.

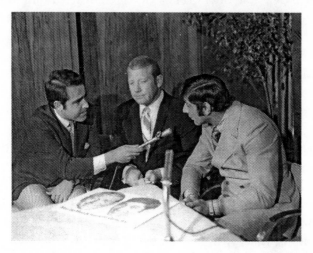

Interviewing Mickey Mantle and Joe Namath NYC 1969

Because of the Yankees' dominance and national television, Mantle's natural charisma made him one of the most recognizable figures in all of sports. Now, on "Mickey Mantle Day," he wasn't wearing his familiar no. 7, but a dark blue business suit with matching tie and shirt. He had a neat haircut, the sun glinting off his blond hair. At the home plate ceremony, thanking the sellout crowd, he looked presidential. Then, he took a ride around the perimeter of the outfield in a golf cart, the standing ovation cascading down from the third deck and across the bleachers to the oval at home plate where he ended his ride. Mickey waved one last time, and disappeared into the dugout.

Under the stands, the press room was packed as Mickey entered. The veteran reporters were stunned. The Mick was wiping tears from his eyes as he was led to a chair to meet with them. Mantle slowly said, ". . . they love me, they really love me" There was a long silent pause, before Milton Gross spoke. The well-known and hard-hitting columnist from the New York Post broke the quiet, "Mickey, you're a schmuck." There was a gasp from the baseball scribes, but no reaction from Mantle. "They've always loved you," Gross continued, "You should be running for mayor, but you've been too much of a redneck to know better. If you had used the opportunity, you wouldn't have the money problems you have now." Mickey took it, with no response. He stopped crying. After a while, somebody changed the subject.

While retired from baseball, Mickey accepted an invitation from a jock-sniffer-buddy to play golf with other celebrated athletes at Casa de Campo in the Dominican Republic. One late afternoon over cocktails, Mickey was sitting with Don Drysdale and "Tammy," a voluptuous woman from New York, whose assignment was broadly termed "public relations." After everyone had too much to drink, Mantle and Drysdale argued as to who was better in bed. Tammy interrupted and suggested they flip a coin to determine who would go first in proving their sexual prowess. Mickey guessed right on the flip of the coin and headed off with Tammy. Forty minutes later, they staggered back to the table where Drysdale was waiting for his chance. Tammy said, "Don, you lose." Mickey had told her to say that.

One hot summer day in the 1990s, Steinbrenner welcomed reporters to his suite at the Regency Hotel for separate interviews about the state of baseball. Whether writers or broadcast reporters, we each had to take a number for the order and we waited in front of the Regency on Park Avenue. The press wasn't welcome in the Regency lobby; however, no one could stop me from using the hotel bar and enjoying its air-conditioning. The bar had a side entrance and exit on the 63rd Street side. I sat alone and The Mick walked in from 63rd Street. He wore a Red Sox cap, beige polo shirt, blue shorts and sneakers. He wouldn't remove his sunglasses because he didn't want to be recognized. He had a woman in tow and both were nervous. Mickey was using the bar entrance as a shortcut to the elevator bank in the lobby. I stopped him and informed him that most of New York's sports reporters were around the corner. He and his new friend bolted out the door, back into the heat on 63rd Street, the Mick looking ridiculous, and not just for wearing a Boston cap. One Sunday night in the '80s, after my sportscast on WNBC-TV, I received a telephone call from a buddy who said he had to tell somebody what was happening. One of this guy's girlfriends was a young prostitute and she telephoned to cancel getting together with him because she got a job with a girlfriend to party "with some old ballplayer" at the Regency Hotel. She had no idea of his fame. My buddy said he was so shocked, he couldn't say the old ballplayer's name on the telephone. He simply said, "It's no. 7." When I hung up, I had to tell someone. I called an ex-New Yorker in Los Angeles, Marvin Cohen, a huge baseball fan. I went through the story, ending with "Marvin, I don't want to say the name but it's no. 7." Marvin didn't miss a beat, answering, "Ed Kranepool?"

JOE NAMATH'S DECISION

July 20, 1969 ended what President Richard Nixon described as "The greatest week in the history of the world since creation."

On that Sunday, a pair of American astronauts of the flight of Apollo-11, stepped slowly down the ladder of their fragile four-legged lunar module and planted the first human footprints on the surface of the moon. An estimated four billion people around the world watched Neil Armstrong and Edwin Aldrin Jr on television and heard Armstrong say "That's one small step for man, one giant leap for mankind."

Later that evening, on the campus of Hofstra University, in Hempstead, New York, I'm among a knot of reporters watching a chauffeured black limousine arrive at Tower C of the dormitories. Joe Namath steps out, carrying a black attaché case and a clothes bag. He's reporting to the New York Jets' training camp, two days late. He refuses comment and takes an elevator to his 10th floor room.

Legendary sports columnist and former war correspondent Jimmy Cannon is 60 years old. He had started in the newspaper business at 14 as a copyboy for the New York Daily News. He covered the Lindbergh kidnapping in the '30s. The crusty Cannon is in foul mood this humid summer evening. He had given up his Sunday for this story and Namath had passed by without a comment. Cannon mutters to me, "We have men on the moon and I'm covering a fucking quarterback."

Why all the fuss about a 26-year-old professional football player? Because the charismatic Namath had been making headlines like furniture collects dust. Seven months earlier, on a bitterly cold and very windy December afternoon at Shea Stadium, Namath was injected with pain killing medication in both knees at halftime, and he out-dueled Oakland's Daryle Lamonica, as the Jets won 27-23 for the AFL championship. It capped the Jets best-ever season. Then, the glittering star of New York sports boldly stated, "I guarantee" a Jets upset victory over Baltimore Colts in Super Bowl III. On January 12, 1969, in Miami's Orange Bowl, that's exactly what the 17-point underdog Jets accomplished. The AFL's Jets upset the NFL's Colts, who had lost one game all season, 16-7.

Colts coach Don Shula had warned his team about overconfidence. He reckoned that Namath, who had been the Jets' quarterback for four years, was smart with a powerful right arm. Shula was wary about his quarterback, Earl Morrall, who had filled in well for the injured Johnny Unitas, but for only four months. The Jets intercepted four Colts passes while allowing 145 yards rushing. The offense handled Baltimore's constant blitzing because of Namath's ability to read the extra rushers and, thanks to his lightning quick release, he found open receivers. The Colts double-teamed future Hall of Fame wide receiver Don Maynard, who was hiding a hamstring injury and didn't catch a pass. Namath connected with his other wide receiver, George Sauer eight times for 133 yards. He tossed to his backs, Matt Snell and Bill Mathis for a total of seven passes for 60 yards and tight end Pete Lammons twice for 13 yards. After a scoreless first quarter, the Jets scored 16 straight points. Snell roared in from the 4-yard line and Jim Turner kicked three field goals. The Jets ran the ball mostly weak side, exploiting Baltimore's veteran right end Ordell Braase, who was playing his last game. The Jets switched their mammoth right tackle Winston Hill to left tackle and he teamed with halfback Emerson Boozer to block Braase. Snell totaled 121 yards rushing, mostly to his left. Guard Dave Herman was switched to Hill's right tackle spot and, despite being undersized in his match-up, he did a tremendous job blocking Baltimore's All Pro defensive end Bubba Smith. It was a total team victory.

The Jets became the first American Football League team to win the Super Bowl. After two straight defeats, the AFL established its credibility and forced a merger and realignment of teams. "Broadway Joe" trotted off the field with his right index finger aloft. He had completed 17 of 28 passes for 206 yards and no interceptions. The game's Most Valuable Player wore a steel-and-rubber brace to support his chronically sore right knee. Afterwards, it took some convincing from the Jets' public relations director, Frank Ramos, to get Namath to talk with the press, most of whom gave the Jets no chance. I interviewed Namath for CBS News and asked him if he felt like "the King of the Hill?" Joe insisted it was a total team victory.

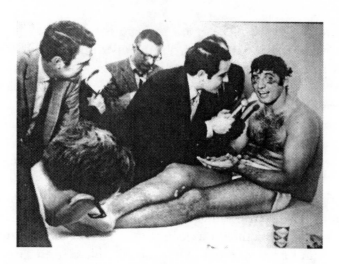

Joe Namath—after the NY Jets victory in Super Bowl III, Miami, 1969

He was awarded the Hickock Belt as the outstanding professional athlete of the United States. The Jets' improbable Super Bowl triumph insured places in Pro Football Hall of Fame for Coach Weeb Ewbank, Maynard and Namath.

The next morning, I flew from Miami to Jamaica with my wife, Bernadette. For the next week, we enjoyed the Miranda Hill Resort in Montego Bay, eating off gold plates and swimming in pools decorated with rose petals, because I won $5,000 betting on the Jets.

I covered the Jets all season for WCBS-TV and while the network was aligned with the older and more established NFL, it was obvious to me that the AFL was not inferior. In fact, the younger league had many players of all-pro talent, if they wore NFL uniforms. The Jets stormed through their league, winning the AFL championship against the powerful Oakland Raiders, 27-23.

I grew to know Namath better because his attorney, Jimmy Walsh, agreed to take me on as a client. Joe allowed me into his inner circle and I was his house guest in Beverly Hills, California. I learned that Joe wasn't a braggart, but a down-to-earth, nice guy. For someone who was a national sports celebrity since his days at the University of Alabama, I found Joe to be quite humble, even as he signed autograph after autograph and posed for pictures with his fans, over and over again.

Joe is comfortable with fame. He doesn't dwell on the negative either. Hanging out with his buddies runs a close second to his female encounters.

He insists on addressing older folks as "m'am" and "sir" and says "thank you" a lot. He doesn't curse or tell vulgar jokes in the presence of women and is courteous to all. Except, one night at Broussard's restaurant, in New Orleans, when a guy asked him for an autograph while Joe was eating, after he signed autographs for 40 minutes in the bar. Joe treated him like an Oakland Raider and the guy ran out of Broussard's.

Joe has a yen to act and sing. He gained experience by making guest appearances on television variety shows and endorsing products on TV commercials. Johnny Carson let him substitute for him on "The Tonight Show."

Joe is also investing in businesses. He says calmly, "I'm trying to become the best at what I do."

Above all, Joe is passionate and very knowledgeable about football. In the days leading up to Super Bowl III, Joe was absolutely confident about beating the Colts because he and his wide receivers could exploit Baltimore's safety blitz. He thought the Colts were predictable and slow, while the Jets were a quick and well-balanced team. "We're not second rate players in a second rate league. We're not overmatched. The other day, coming back from practice in the car, Billy Mathis, Big Boy Pete Lammons, Babe Parilli and I were laughing because Lammons said if we don't stop looking at the Colts films we're gonna get overconfident."

For the first and only time in my life, I made a large wager on the game. Joe didn't know he was associating with a gambler. Actually, Joe unknowingly did the same with others. Everyone who asked him about the Super Bowl received the same answer, "We're gonna win . . . I guarantee it." Three days before the game, Joe said it publicly while accepting a Player of the Year award from the Touchdown Club at the Miami Springs Villas. It was his answer to a heckler. The next morning, Ewbank, the Jets 61-year-old coach, fumed at his quarterback, asking "Joseph, why did you say that?" Namath apologized, but added "I said what I felt. If the Colts need press clippings to get fired up, they're really in trouble."

On Friday night, the NFL hosted its party at the plush Eden Roc Hotel on Miami Beach. Mexican food was on the menu and Jack Benny was the entertainment. During the cocktail party, Colts owner Carroll Rosenbloom loudly boasted, within earshot of everyone, that he had bet 250-thousand dollars on his team. The NFL beat reporters were there, enjoying the tacos and frozen concoctions, but no one quoted Rosenbloom.

Many fans gambled on Namath's guarantee, so did some of his Bachelor's III customers, and at least one reporter.

After the upset win that shook up the NFL, Namath spent most of his time at his winter home near Miami, where he played a lot of golf and fished often. He took a trip for the U.S. Army, visiting hospitals in Hawaii, Okinawa and Japan.

What he saw in those hospital wards sickened him. He met and tried to encourage American soldiers younger than him who were maimed and burned. He realized how lucky he was to be 4-F, physically unfit for military service. The right knee he injured while playing for the University of Alabama had kept him out of the hellhole that was Vietnam.

Joe's hometown of Beaver Falls, in Western Pennsylvania, honored him with "Joe Namath Day." He was in California to make his movie acting debut in "Norwood," a Paramount production starring Glen Campbell and Jim Darby.

He was back in New York on Tuesday evening, June 3 1969, for a coronation-like, black tie affair at the Waldorf-Astoria. The New York chapter of the Pro Football Writers Association attracted about 650 people for its annual awards banquet. Joe was given the George Halas Award, as the AFL Player of the Year. Ewbank was cited as the Man of the Year in Pro Football. Earl Morrall of the Baltimore Colts was the NFL Player of the Year.

In a private chat with Commissioner Pete Rozelle, Coach Ewbank and club president Phil Iselin, Jack Danahy, the NFL's chief investigator, wiped the smile off Joe's face in an accusatory tone. Danahy and his staff had determined that Bachelor's III, was frequented by known gamblers and Namath was guilty by association. According to the standard pro football contract, players "must not associate with gamblers or other notorious characters." Rozelle ordered Namath to divest his half interest in his Manhattan bar, Bachelor's III, the next day for his own good and the good of football. Rozelle said if Joe didn't follow his order, he would be suspended in two days. Joe was shocked and infuriated, and he agonized. His magic carpet ride of a championship season was over and back to earth.

As for the issue of the moment, is Joe guilty by association because some gamblers were on the Bachelor's III premises? Not in Namath's mind, heck, even Rosenbloom hoisted a few drinks in Joe's joint on Lexington Avenue.

America's Football Hero soon found this "association thing" is attached to celebrity in pro sports, which must have the trust of the public or the money machine stops.

Four years earlier, in January of 1965, Namath signed with the AFL New York Jets for the record sum of $427,000 over 3 years. St. Louis of the NFL had drafted Namath with their 13th pick while the Giants selected Auburn running back Tucker Fredrickson as the NFL's top draft choice overall. Part-owner David "Sonny" Werblin had been a major show business agent and he reckoned Joe had natural charisma, confidence and star quality. That's what his team needed in competition for the entertainment dollars in New York against the established Giants. That's what the American Football League needed. Werblin had been the agent on TV network deals for westerns and variety programs. NBC had taken a chance on the AFL. Namath and a winning New York franchise attracted advertisers as well as viewers all over the country. Fans wanted to see this "Broadway Joe" with the white shoes and his laser bolt passes and his cocky attitude. Namath's athleticism and personality was "product" and Sonny knew that in show business, including the television industry, talent is what sells.

Namath's heritage was Hungarian. He was born May 31, 1943, in the steel mill town of Beaver Falls.

"I had God-given athletic ability and the desire to improve, but I was lucky. After high school in Beaver Falls, I didn't even want to play football. I wanted to play baseball. Roberto Clemente was my favorite player. I tried to mimic him because he looked like he was always in control. As for football, I was a Colts fan and, in my senior year in high school, I wore Johnny Unitas' no. 19. I went to Pittsburgh to try and sign up for the Air Force to stay out of the Pennsylvania steel mills where my father had worked. My folks wouldn't let me do it. As a matter of fact, if I hadn't hurt my knee my senior year at Alabama, I would have been in Vietnam. My draft status was 4-F. I don't know what would have happened after that. I was lucky in that regard and, also, I had great teachers and coaches who helped me to learn and pursue the right course."

"I never dreamt of signing for that much money coming out of college and I was thankful for that and worked hard to try and earn it. My first real job was working for the City of Beaver Falls Recreation Department. I earned a dollar an hour, forty hours a week. I would get my paycheck for $34.00 in change. I'd fill up my car with gas for 4-dollars and give the rest to my mom. She'd give me a couple of bucks to go out at night."

While the quarterback for the Crimson Tide, Namath performed with a swagger. He was brash and cocky and his teammates rallied around him. Legendary Alabama coach Paul "Bear" Bryant demoted Joe from the team for breaking curfew in his junior year, but gushed, "He's the greatest athlete I ever coached or ever saw."

"I never planned on wearing white football shoes. Coach Bryant let me slide at Alabama when I taped my worn shoes. Some teammates teased me that Coach Bryant was gonna get on me. But, he didn't say a word. The shoes were tearing and they looked pretty cool. The first game I didn't tape my shoes, I tore ligaments in my right knee. So, when I got to the Jets I still taped my shoes. One day, there was a surprise in my locker. I never saw a pair of white football shoes before, but someone was smart enough to make them."

Joe's staggering salary put him on the cover of Sports Illustrated. He was framed in a Jets uniform against the bright lights of Broadway. "We came in from practice one day," Joe recalls, "and copies of the magazine were sitting on the stools in front of our lockers. Sherman Plunkett was our left offensive tackle and elder statesman on the team. He's sitting across from me and looking at the magazine cover. I'm a rookie and it's embarrassing to me. The veterans still hated me for making much more money. Sherman, who weighed more than 300 lbs., looks at me with a big smile and says, 'Ol' Broadway . . . . Broadway Joe.' I was never called that before. It stuck and I liked it but I never called myself that."

The Jets recouped his pay within weeks because season-ticket holders increased from 15,000 to 18,000.

Until he signed with the Jets, Joe had never been to New York. Werblin introduced him to a handful of trusted friends, including thoroughbred racing expert Joe Hirsch who wrote for the Morning Telegraph. Hirsch introduced him to Tad Dowd, a manager-publicist who had helped the careers of singers Tom Jones and Mary Wells. After Joe's first training camp with the Jets, he was eager to do some socializing and Tad introduced him to Bobby Van who had run successful New York restaurants and bars called Table Talk, the Rolling Stone and Dudes and Dolls. At the time, Dudes and Dolls was the first "go-go dancing" joint in New York and one of the young dancers was Goldie Hawn who ended up a very successful actress, winning the Best Supporting Actress Oscar for "Cactus Flower," in 1969.

To please Joe, the Jets traded with Buffalo to acquire his former Alabama teammate Ray Abruzzese. Joe lived with Abruzzese and Hirsch. Manhattan nightlife was very exciting in the late-60s and Joe was one of the most eligible bachelors in town.

"I dig people who are free and who don't necessarily have to be doing anything ritzy. My intimate friends are nice people . . . no rats . . . regular people who like other people, who've got humor and don't bother anybody else. Yeah, I dig girls, especially the pretty ones. They're the only ones I like.

Sometimes, I'll dress up in a suit and eat at a fancy restaurant. Other times, I'll wear a pair of jeans and tennis shoes and take a drive in my Jaguar. I love my golf clubs and my pool cue"

Van recalls, "Joe said, he wanted to own a bar one day." In 1968, Van and Abruzzese took over a bar, called The Margin Call, on Lexington Avenue between 61st and 62nd Streets, near Bloomingdale's Department store. Werblin didn't want Joe involved. At one point, his Jets teammate Johnny Sample wanted to invest. But, Namath became a partner with Abruzzese and Van.

Bachelors III sat only 65 people. It was a long, narrow, and dark with wood paneling and sports pictures on the walls. The bartenders were females. Behind the juke box hung a Leroy Niemann painting of Joe that had to be bolted to the wall to avoid theft. When Joe arrived, he liked to socialize at the bar and sign autographs before he sat at a round table for dinner. His customers were respectful, so arguments were infrequent and fights rare. The menu was simple, mostly grilled food like steak, burgers and chicken served at the handful of tables. Premium liquor cost $1.50 a shot and beer was a dollar. Every night by 11, was packed with people and there was no cover charge.

Van remembers, "It was a people place, guy meets girl. If we knew Joe would get involved, we would have gotten a bigger place. With standing room at the bar, we would squeeze in 120 customers. The Copa was hot at the time, so was Danny's Hideaway, Jilly's, the Gaslight and the Playboy Club. There was room for another nightspot on the east side in midtown Manhattan and, every night, the Playboy Bunnies came to our place, after work, because there was a lot of loose money around. It was a comfortable feeling and Joe was an accommodating host."

In the autumn of 1968, as the Jets made their run, eventually winning the Super Bowl in January of 1969, you couldn't get into Bachelors III. The sidewalk was jammed with customers. Van says, "It was a zoo, we couldn't do anymore business. It was a nightly stop for Johnny Carson, after he hosted "The Tonight Show." Actress Angie Dickinson and singers Dionne Warwick and Paul Anka were always there. Out of town athletes like Ken Stabler, O.J. Simpson, Dan Reeves, Fran Tarkenton, Jack Lambert and Pete Maravich were steady customers. Bachelors III sponsored a softball team in the Broadway Show League, so many actors and actresses frequented the place. Bing Crosby came in one night, 'to find out what this place is about'. The famous singer drank at the bar with Namath. Vince Lombardi was there with friends, a couple of times. Mickey Mantle and Joe Pepitone visited with Joe. Frank Sinatra used to come in and so did Janis Joplin."

Van says the rock star bragged she bedded down with Joe. When her name used to come up, Joe would laugh and ignore the subject. If they did get together, did two icons of the '60's counterculture understand the meaning or was it just one of those things?

Joe Dellapina, the manager of Bachelor's III, remembers, "I handled all the money and paid all the bills. We had no hidden partners and there was never an investigation of our business, even by the State Liquor Authority, which at the time, was very tough on businesses. The guilt by association thing was a bad rap. Yeah, the wise guys came in and Joe said hello to everybody. My mother heard about the controversy on Italian radio and said to me, "If all those people are so bad, why aren't they in jail."

Three days after Rozelle's order to divest, on Friday, June 6, 1969, "The guy of the moment in sports" calls for a news conference at Bachelors III at 9:30 am. He enters at 10. The bar is jam-packed with sportswriters and sportscasters, floodlit by lights for the dozen TV film cameras. Sitting in a booth, Joe is flanked by New York's leading television sportscasters, Frank Gifford of channel-2 on his right, and, on his left, by Kyle Rote of channel-4 and Howard Cosell of channel-7.

Namath begins calmly but it's clear he's emotionally upset. "At the commissioner's office on Wednesday, I was shown nine pictures of guys. I didn't know any of their names, but I recognized a few of them as having been in my place. It would be pretty stupid of me to fool around with anybody in gambling. I'd be putting my life and my future in jeopardy."

After he says "I'm not a gambler," with tears streaking down his face, Namath announces his retirement, rather than bend to the commissioner's order. "I want to play football. It's not fair."

Namath's tearful "Goodbye" was the lead story on the evening TV and radio newscasts. The next day, the tabloid newspapers follow with bold headlines. Sports columnists have enough material for weeks and Broadway Joe, "the Quitter," is an easy target.

It's no stunt. Namath is angry enough to quit pro football and his livelihood, on principle, rather than sell his interest. Jimmy Walsh estimates Namath's financial loss at about five million dollars. Joe says, "You can meet a lot of undesirables in bars."

When the 61-year-old Ewbank hears about it, he barks, "This is what I have to put up with."

Rozelle counters with resolution. It is his responsibility to keep the NFL clean and some of Namath's customers have dubious backgrounds and habits. Therefore, guilt by association.

NFL Commissioner Pete Rozelle, NYC, 1980.

Abruzzese recalls, "We had the element there, wiseguys from downtown, Brooklyn and East Harlem. But, we also had guys from Wall Street, doctors and lawyers. The guy they were suspicious about, because they wiretapped our three pay phones, was identified as Tommy 'the Hammer' Mannino. Well, 'The Hammer' happened to be our carpenter." A cute story, but, like most popular New York city nightclubs of the time, some desperadoes were steady customers.

Among the wiseguys and Mafia wannabes, who were regulars at Bachelors' III, was a swarthy Italian with Dean Martin looks, who had two nicknames, "Angelo Cheesecake" and "The Jet." He was friendly with Joe, even though they almost had a brawl the first night they met in Jilly's. It was a misunderstanding about a woman and put aside. Joe and "The Jet" were courteous to each other. Otherwise, Joe had little to do with this noted hoodlum who paid for his drinks and happily handed out big tips.

There's a certain buzz at Bachelors' III when Joe is in the place. He works the room with warm greetings. Surely, jokes are shouted out about the point spreads and Joe just laughs them off. His bar is open to the public, it isn't a private club. He can't answer for the integrity of his customers.

The issue of guilt by association preoccupied sports fans and much of American culture. Johnny Carson joked about it in his opening monologue of "The Tonight Show." Even from outer space, Neil Armstrong and Buzz Aldrin asked Mission Control in Houston, "What's happening with Joe Namath and Bachelor's III?"

For the greater part of two months, in the spring of 1969, the center of the sports universe was Bachelors III at 798 Lexington Avenue between 61st and 62nd Street. A short walk away, 410 Park Avenue between 54th and 55th Streets, the address of the National Football League and the office of Commissioner Pete Rozelle. About a dozen blocks further up the East Side, Joe lived in the Newport East apartments at 370 East 76th Street.

Broadway Joe on Lexington Avenue, NYC, 1969.

In June, and most of July, 1969, the rest of pro football waits to see if its most attention-getting star player is history. Other interested parties are NBC-TV and the sponsors of the football telecasts.

Namath maintains his innocence and insists he wasn't seeking publicity. He believed he was right. Rozelle never accused Joe of any wrongdoing, but the commissioner was concerned with the image of pro football. In 1963, he had suspended outstanding players Paul Hornung and Alex Karras for betting on themselves. Rozelle maintained that guilt by association is damaging to a person, and ultimately, to the NFL.

"Guilt by association" . . . . hounded Namath.

He was also perceived by many as counter-cultural and rebellious because of his long hair, and casual mod attire, along with his white football shoes when everyone else's was black.

Spring becomes summer, in 1969, and the currents of Manhattan's nightlife are especially murky in a bar, a half block from his apartment on 76th Street and First Avenue. It's a dive with low class customers called The Open End, and Joe is killing some time. In the dark hush of this gin mill, the celebrity quarterback, who's lost his job, won't have to smile nicely for the "in crowd" and sign autographs. Jasper is one of Joe's favorite bartenders, a short guy with fast hands and a good sense of humor, he's pouring Namath's favorite scotch, Johnny Walker Red, on the rocks.

Joe sneers, "I can't buy our coaches or our commissioner saying you have to shave your mustache, or you have to cut your hair. Why? Because it's too long? Too long for what? Ridiculous. My dress isn't contrived, the hats, the flowery shirts, the bell-bottoms. It's my style for now. That's not making a statement, but I'll say this, we have Vietnam going on and there's a big question of why we're there and who's telling the truth. 'B-S' comes from our government and people are fed up with it. Many are rebelling simply by giving honest feelings about things."

Joe was vilified by most sportswriters for quitting football. He was familiar with the slings and arrows from the press box.

"I just simply stopped reading about myself. That was the cure all, last season. I was going to practice one morning and I saw something in the paper that really teed me off. I get to the meeting and I'm thinking about what I read. So, I decided to stop reading the stuff.

Namath believes his critics factored his lifestyle into his evaluation as a football player. "Winning is the thing. Unless there's something wrong with you, there's nothing else left in life. No matter what you do for a living, when you're doing well, you've got to be in a better frame of mind. Besides, the better I do, the more people will shut up, people who are looking to rap me. The same people don't rap so much when I'm doing good things."

Jasper puts fresh ice in a tumbler and pours another Johnny Walker Red. The Open End is where guys try to forget the gals that got away. Joe knows his apartment and his bed are only a few steps away. With each tumbler of scotch, Gasper is helping this troubled young man get through the night.

Joe is represented by attorneys Mike Bite and Jimmy Walsh. They meet to no avail with Rozelle, along with Joe, in New York, on June 26. Two weeks later, there's a flurry of activity and the ordeal reaches a boil. On Sunday, July 13, the defending champion Jets report to training camp without their most valuable player. The next day, another meeting with Rozelle brings no resolution. Pressure from the public, the press and NBC is mounting.

One night, Joe is hanging out in a bar, across the street from his apartment, called The Gordian Knot. I ask him for a private conversation in the kitchen. I said CBS News had given me the green light to spend anything or go anywhere to get the scoop. Joe tells me he'd like to help me out but he doesn't know what's going to happen.

On Wednesday, July 16, Joe goes to Hempstead to brief his teammates and unhappily tells them there's no solution in sight.

Rozelle alienated a large group of the public that rooted for Joe, perceived as anti-establishment, and, therefore, an underdog. However, the commissioner was confident a large segment of the public understood his motives. Rozelle was backed by most of his bosses, the 26 NFL franchise owners. Under his savvy guidance, the owners were never more prosperous. Rozelle was a visionary who shrewdly negotiated the big ticket contracts with the TV networks, convinced the franchise owners to share the millions of dollars equally and forged the merger between the AFL and the NFL. Television's progression from black and white into color made football more of a spectacle and America wanted more, and in record numbers. Millions of dollars were at stake, as the renegade quarterback of the championship team was embroiled in an ethics debate with the establishment.

Joe Willie Namath isn't some crew-cut jock in khakis and white bucks holding hands with the Sweetheart of Sigma Chi. He isn't Pat Boone, the acceptable all-American boy. He's Jerry Lee Lewis, self-styled and so passionate, a sex symbol to many women. The antihero with long hair, a Fu Manchu mustache, white football shoes instead of the standard black, throwing touchdown passes, and interceptions too, winning games and flashing a warm smile, with flashing green eyes, that wins over women. Joe isn't reluctant to admit "I prefer my Johnny Walker Red and my women blondes and brunettes." Most guys wish they were like him.

In the late '60s and early '70s, in a whirlwind of social and political upheaval, Joe is the brightest star in sports, forever more, like DiMaggio and "Willie, Mickey and the Duke," linked to New York, the center of the entertainment universe. He doesn't subscribe to the theory that athletes, to be successful, must have the social life of a clam. His loner style makes him the most glamorous of heroes. He is a fantasy for good and bad girls alike. He enjoys his freedom and marriage is a far off notion. His parents had divorced after 27 years, when he was twelve years old, and that hurt enough for him to hold off an absolute commitment to one woman.

Joe would never admit it, but more than one of his pals were eyewitnesses the night in Bachelor's III when he was challenged to trading liquor shots by rock star Janis Joplin and actor Michael J. Pollard. After a fierce competition, Pollard had to be carried out. According to Bobby Van, Janis and Joe took it to the next level, sex between two cultural symbols of the swinging 60s . . . the rock star and the quarterback.

Publicist Tad Dowd recalls: "In 1968, Joe grew a Fu Manchu mustache to amuse himself. I convinced Harry Harris, the sports photographer for the Associated Press, to take a picture of Joe's new look with a couple of girls next to a Christmas tree because the holiday was coming up. AP ran it and newspapers all over the country published the picture. Two weeks later, Harris called me and said, because of many requests; he'd like to take a picture of Joe every two weeks to see how his mustache was growing. So, we did it. The Schick Razor Blade Company offered Joe $10,000 to shave his mustache in a Christmas-time television commercial. He did it and got even more publicity. I looked like a public relations genius. But, it was Joe's charisma. Today, the same offer would be $3 million dollars."

When the Jets travel to road games, their hotel lobbies are jammed with people who idolize him and want him to pose for pictures and get personalized autographs. His guest appearances on the Tonight Show with Johnny Carson and his TV commercials, endorsing shaving cream, Brut, a men's fragrance and even a female product like panty hose had made him a household name. Joe looks like a televised male centerfold as he pitches Beautymist Panty Hose for $1.69.

One time, at an airport, in San Juan, Puerto Rico, I witness a young couple ask Joe for an autograph addressed to their newborn infant son, the mother is holding. He agrees and asks for the boy's name. They say they haven't picked one yet because the infant has just been adopted. Joe asks them for their last name and they said "Ittleson," Joe writes, "To the little Ittleson . . . Joe Namath."

Traveling with him was like shadowing a rock star. When people spot him, they smile and call his name. He's a football hero and readily accepted as one of them. They want to meet him and touch him, plead for an autograph and a picture. The Jets plot secret ways of getting him in and out of stadiums, like in an equipment truck or armored car while fans crowd the Jets team buses for a glimpse of him. He had to take the telephone off the hook in his hotel room and eat out at midnight to avoid the crowds. Girls knock on his hotel door in the middle of the night.

"People ask me what's it was like to be a sex symbol and that's clumsy for me. It's embarrassing because it's private business, private life. It's never anybody else's business but mine and hers, first of all."

Namath crossed the line from sports star to national celebrity and he was typecast as a rebel and anti-establishment because he wore white football shoes, grew facial hair and wore flamboyant clothes and a fur coat. He was the ultimate bachelor and his East Side apartment featured a llama fur rug, a mirrored ceiling in his bedroom, and an illegal small swimming pool, which turned out to be the cause of his eviction from that building because the floor was not engineered to bear its weight.

Joe was from a blue collar background. His dad worked in steel mills for forty years. Joe worked at a paper mill and saw football as a financial means to escape that and enjoy life. Now, at age 26, he was faced with life without football and a huge cut in income.

On Thursday, July 17, 1969, Bite and Walsh devised a compromise. Joe would come back if he could sell his half interest in Bachelors III in New York, but keep his ownership in the franchising of Bachelors III in development. Rozelle agreed, as long as the NFL approved his partners. On Friday, July 18, 1969, at another jammed packed news conference, Rozelle announced, "I'm happy to announce Joe will be back with the Jets. He and I have privately reached total accord. He is selling his interest in Bachelors III and we consider the entire matter closed."

Cleverly, Namath sold his half interest to his roommate, Ray Abruzzese. Subsequently, Namath's financial group owned successful franchise Bachelors III in Tuscaloosa, Alabama, near the state university, and in Boston and Fort Lauderdale. The Florida project turned out to be the most lucrative because the land was owned and the partnership held onto it for decades, during which Fort Lauderdale became more valuable. There were never any raids or arrests in Bachelors III in New York and never any proof of wrongdoing on Joe's part.

When Namath heard Rozelle's acceptance of the terms, he was in California, acting in "Norwood," produced by Paramount Pictures. He happily finished his role and flew to New York.

Close to midnight, Sunday, July 20, Namath turned out the lights, and got into bed in room 1008 in Tower C of Hofstra University. He was back with his Jets teammates, back in football, and out of the swirl of controversy that hounded him for two months. Laying there in the light of the moon and silence around him, Joe could sleep without a care for the first time in months. The end of his "retirement" seemed like small potatoes compared to American astronauts spending a day and a half on the moon.

As Nixon's "Greatest week in the history of the world since creation" was coming to a close, there was a new, disturbing development that would crowd the historic astronauts, and Jimmy Cannon's "fucking quarterback," for newspaper space and television/radio time.

Ted Kennedy, the Democratic U.S. Senator from Massachusetts had a huge problem, while trying to follow his assassinated brother, John, to the presidency of the United States. Two nights earlier, late Friday, Kennedy was involved in an automobile accident with a fatality, in Edgartown, Massachusetts. A young woman, Mary Jo Kopechne, drowned when Kennedy mistook a curve on a dark road and drove the car into the water under a bridge. Kennedy escaped the submerged vehicle, but she did not. Inexplicably, Kennedy failed to report the tragedy to the local police for nine hours, till mid-day Saturday.

This epic Sunday night in world history, Republican President Nixon already had operatives in Edgartown, investigating this "death by association."

TUG McGRAW GROWS UP

Some athletes say one moment, one play, one match-up can change an entire playing career. For Tug McGraw, a pitching situation in an important game charged him with newfound confidence as a major league pitcher and enhanced his outlook on life. The spirited lefthander who was good enough to pitch 19 years in the majors, saving 180 games, while winning 96 and losing 92 games, coining the expression, "Ya gotta believe" as a rallying cry for the 1973 New York Mets, didn't come to his baseball moment of truth until four years earlier, at a critical moment, in the first ever National League Division Series. Tug's maturing process, from the friendly streets of a northern California town, through the minor leagues, serving in the U.S. Marine Corps, and into the buzz of New York City, reached its natural evolvement.

After the 162-game schedule for every franchise in the two leagues, four teams were competing for the National and American League championships. It was the afternoon of October 5, 1969, at Atlanta Fulton County Stadium in Atlanta. The Mets had just spent the summer sweeping past the Chicago Cubs into first-place, ending the futility of the losing New York franchise born only seven years earlier. Baseball fans in New York were still shocked by the departures of the Dodgers and Giants to the West Coast. Reluctantly, they embraced an expansion team of retreads that lost 120 games in its maiden season in 1962. But, the fans, nicknamed "the New Breed," were patient and supportive like in the old days, with the hope that the team would improve. Now, in 1969, the Mets had grown up, finishing first, going 100 and 62, an improvement of 27 games over 1968. The Mets were in the first-ever divisional, best-of-five game NLCS. The Atlanta Braves hosted the first two games.

That season, the Mets had beaten the Braves 8 of 12 games, taking four at home and winning four in Atlanta. The Mets continued their dominance in the postseason, winning the opener, and building an 8-0 lead in the second game. But, Mets starter Jerry Koosman began giving up runs. Home run king Hank Aaron blasted a three-run homer in a five-run fifth, chasing the lefthander. The Mets had added a pair of runs to lead 11-6 when McGraw was summoned out of the bullpen to start the Braves 7th. He was 25 years old, struggling with the notion of confidence, even after his first season as an effective relief pitcher.

Six months earlier, on the last day of spring training, Mets manager Gil Hodges had summoned McGraw to his office in St. Petersburg, Florida, the Mets' winter home.

McGraw had been a Mets' project, signed out of Vallejo, California, as the caboose to the signing of his older brother Hank, who was a high school All-America catching prospect. Mets scouts gave McGraw little chance of making the major leagues as a starter because he was only six-feet, 170 lbs. Hank McGraw never escaped the minor leagues and Tug proved the scouts wrong. He even beat the Los Angeles Dodgers' future Hall of Famer Sandy Koufax in a 1965, rookie-year match-up in New York. However, over his first three seasons with the Mets, as a starter he won only 4 games and lost 19. In 1968, military reserve duties caused him to be late for spring training. To catch up, he threw too hard too early, hid the injury, and missed the entire year with arm pain. When McGraw showed up in February of 1969, he unleashed his screwball, which he had learned from former Yankee pitcher Ralph Terry. He was allowed to throw the odd pitch only in the minor leagues. From a lefthander, the screwball moves away from a right-handed hitter and into a left-handed hitter. Not everyone can throw it because the inward motion of the arm, at release, is unnatural and therefore puts great stress on the bones, ligaments and muscles. At that point in time, the only other screwball pitcher in the National League was Jim Brewer of the Dodgers. McGraw caught Hodges' eye as his screwball overwhelmed batters during exhibition play.

Just before the Mets broke camp, Hodges made McGraw an offer. The Mets manager knew he had strong starting pitching in Tom Seaver, Jerry Koosman, Gary Gentry, Don Cardwell, Jim McAndrew and a young flame thrower named Nolan Ryan. McGraw said, "The Mets were growing pitchers like roses." Hodges said if McGraw became a relief pitcher it would suit the Mets needs and insure his spot on the roster. He said Tug was an average starter but he could be excellent in the bullpen and, therefore earn more money. Hodges believed no team could win a championship without effective relief pitchers. He disdained the term "mop-up man." Hodges made

McGraw believe relief pitching wasn't a secondary job. McGraw eagerly agreed and says. "He shuffled me off to the bullpen, making me feel like the king of the world."

The imposing Hodges had been a hero first-baseman with the Brooklyn Dodgers, the fabled "Boys of Summer," as documented by their historian, Roger Kahn. He was a quiet leader who never panicked and instilled confidence in his players. "He was the first guy in my baseball life to teach me responsibility and accountability," says McGraw.

"If he thought you weren't playing up to your potential, he would want to find out why. He was the kind of man you always wanted to please. He was a parent or uncle to some, a drill sergeant to others, and a policeman to some. But, to me he was the manager who got me to where I wanted to go, to a consistent level of performance. When I walked on the field, I trusted myself and my teammates were glad to see me pitching. That came from Gil Hodges."

There was no "miracle" to the 1969 Mets, who had never been higher than 9th place. McGraw says, "We were a good blend of exuberant young and veteran players, led by a strong manager who kept us focused. Starting in spring training, Gil would walk up and down the bench asking you questions about the game. He didn't mind if you were goofing off on the dugout bench, he didn't mind if you were laughing or carrying on, he wanted you to understand what was happening on the field."

McGraw was a positive influence in the clubhouse, very friendly, attentive to all and interested in the lives of the stadium crew, like the groundskeepers. He had a quick wit and seemed to be always smiling. Tug energized his teammates with his happy-go-lucky attitude, until he pitched. That's when they felt his intensity. He seemed fearless on the mound, slapping his glove on his right thigh after closing another game, as his trademark sign of victory. He was a happy extrovert who liked to say "I'm a flake, not a screwball." In "baseball-speak," a "flake" was an off-beat guy and acceptable. A "screwball" was dangerous to be around.

McGraw liked to "power shag" during batting practice. He tried to catch every fly ball, even diving for some, as one of the ways to stay in shape. Hodges pulled him aside and said he would hold him accountable if he injured himself in practice because that wouldn't help the team. It would result in a huge fine and a demotion to the minor leagues. He wanted McGraw to stay healthy and not take unnecessary chances in batting practice. But, he told Tug he would expect that same enthusiasm during a game.

**Tug McGraw, after clinching the National League Pennant,
Shea Stadium NYC, Sept 1973.**

McGraw recalls. "Gil didn't scream or holler. He just drew a picture with words. He let you figure it out for yourself."

And, in a turbulent decade, there was a lot to figure out. McGraw, like other young people in the '60s, was struggling with the confusion of the times. America was locked in the Vietnam War that was growing more unpopular everyday. The country's young people were morally split on military obligations and many refused to risk their lives in a conflict on the other side of the world that didn't threaten America. Many youngsters were experimenting with drugs and much of the music was anti-establishment. The most popular song in 1969 was "The Age of Aquarius" by the Fifth Dimension. The "peaceniks" danced to the Fifth Dimension's lyric ". . . let the sunshine in." Television's big hit was "Laugh In," an irreverent and satiric comedy program. The Oscar for best motion picture went to "Midnight Cowboy," a grim depiction of two rural male hustlers who fail in New York's bright lights and shadows. It was the first and only time an X-rated movie received the honor.

The new birth control pill had liberated women from the fear of pregnancy. Promiscuity was the rage and the singles bars on Manhattan's East Side spawned similar mating-grounds pubs all over the country. Indiscriminate sex ruined marriages and relationships and The Stones cranked out a bluesy, national moan: ". . . . Honky-Tonk women give me the Honky-Tonk blues."

Tug made all the stops along the National League trail. In New York, Mr. Laffs was his main watering hole, as it was with dozens and dozens of pro athletes. It was partially owned by Phil Linz, a teammate of McGraw's on the 1967 Mets. Tug recalled, "After a game, all we wanted was a buzz and a one night stand. Being a Mets player was a big deal to the chippies and some times I was propositioned."

This small-town guy had become a sports celebrity in the country's largest city. As a boy, his mother suffered from rage and required hospitalization and shock treatments. She moved to San Francisco nearly two hours away and the marriage ended. Tug shared the loss and a hardscrabble life with his two brothers and father who worked at a water treatment plant.

Wary of the uncertainties of marital ties, Tug tried to sort out the sexual temptations in the singles bars and at the ballpark to stay mentally and physically fit for the life of a professional baseball player. It seemed everyone wanted to party to avoid thinking of the lives being lost in Vietnam. Young people his age were getting high on alcohol and marijuana. Sexually eager girls hung out near the Mets' right-field bullpen at Shea Stadium, hoping to meet him and the other players. The Mets bullpen was adjacent to a toilet that originally was built for public use. A door with a lock was attached and it opened from the inside. Tug recalled, "Just before games and sometimes during the first inning because starters rarely got knocked out in the first inning, girls we knew would give us the secret knock and we'd let them in and have sex. We were never found out."

Coming after the New York Jets' astonishing upset of the Baltimore Colts in Super Bowl III for the World Championship, in January, there were two major diversions in 1969. In July, two American astronauts, Neil Armstrong and Edwin Aldrin Jr., became the first humans to walk on the moon. The country was brimming with pride and elation. If we could go to the moon, why not the faraway stars? In August, "Woodstock" was the spontaneous communal music and songfest where thousands of "flower children" spent a rainy four-day weekend on an upstate New York farm listening to rock n' roll, getting whacked on drugs and cavorting in the mud. "Dropping out," leaving school and/or a job, was increasingly popular. "Hippies" formed communes and draft dodgers headed for Canada.

After meeting a stewardess in Mr. Laffs named Phyliss and marrying her, McGraw resumed acting responsibly, "One day at a time, following the

Golden Rule approach to things." It was his natural inclination no matter what was in vogue. "I grew up in a town where you knew everybody and, as a child, people did care about you. In Vallejo and Napa, the elders cared very much about the kids and what they did. When so many people care about you, it makes you care about yourself. We were accountable for our actions and, maybe, that's why Gil was so good for me."

"Bob Boone, the Philadelphia Phillies' great catcher, once said, 'The most important thing you have to learn about playing major league baseball is what you do when you're not at the ballpark'.

McGraw adds, "We often underrate the effect of our lives away from the ballpark. The tough, social decisions I made were the result of the way I was brought up, starting with my dad and family, then the community and then Hodges. Gil took me aside and counseled me about my sometimes excessive alcohol habit. Every once in awhile, it got out of hand and he reminded me about responsibility to myself and everyone dear to me."

During the spring and summer of '69, McGraw's screwball was his redeemer. Tug says, "I couldn't wait to get into the ballgames." He and the veteran Ron Taylor became potent and complimentary lefty-righty closers. McGraw pitched 100 and 1/3 innings, saving 12 games, winning 9 and losing 3. Taylor hurled 76 innings, saving 13 games, winning 9 and losing 4. In the season of the Mets emergence, McGraw and Taylor figured in 43 of the team's 100 victories.

Despite his pitching success, McGraw wrestled with his self-confidence until he toed the rubber in the bottom of the 9th in Atlanta with a Mets' five-run lead. Tug threw four straight balls to Felix Millan, leading off. Then, three straight balls to Tony Gonzalez, before Gonzalez stroked a curveball for a single. Braves were on first and second bases with none out and up stepped Hank Aaron, one of the most feared sluggers in baseball history, with a chance to cut the Mets' lead to two runs. In a game and a half against the Mets, Hammerin' Hank had walloped a pair of home runs and a double for five runs batted in.

Catcher Jerry Grote crouched behind the placid-faced Aaron who was waving the bat that had terrorized National League pitchers for almost two decades. He wore Atlanta's home white uniform with the blue-and-red "Braves" scrawled across his chest and his familiar no. 44 on his strapping back. That season, Aaron smacked 44 home runs, one less than San Francisco's Willie McCovey, the league leader.

**Hank Aaron—champion home run hitter of the Atlanta Braves
at Shea Stadium 1971.**

In the dozen regular-season games against the Mets, Aaron had belted 5 homers. Grote was an excellent catcher and savvy about hitters and pitching sequences. He was a thinking-man's backstop who collaborated with the ace of the staff, Tom Seaver, every fifth day. That season, Grote caught the USC-educated Seaver, a smart power pitcher who won 25 games, lost 7 with 18 complete games and an earned run average of 2.21. Grote also caught Jerry Koosman every fifth day. The barrel-chested lefthander was 17-9 with 16 complete games and an earned run average of 2.88. Erect as if still in the military, McGraw stood with his cleats together on the pitching rubber, gripping the baseball behind his back, staring at home plate, 60 feet, 6 inches away. He wore the Mets' gray road uniform with the printed "New York," in blue with orange trim, on the front of his jersey and his no. 45 on his back. Grote flashed his sign for the first pitch and McGraw shook him off.

"Aaron was a nemesis, but I decided to go with my own mind, even though Grote was strong willed and didn't like pitchers changing his mind."

McGraw sensed Aaron would be guessing screwball. Tug had enough confidence in his fastball to outfox one of the greatest fastball hitters in major league history.

"Grote and I were off on every pitch and he was pissed. I threw two fastballs for strikes, wasted a screwball outside for a foul ball and locked him inside with a fastball for a called strike three." McGraw then got Rico Carty to bounce into a game-ending double play. Aaron was still looking for the screwball as McGraw raised his left fist into the air and slapped his glove on his right thigh. Tug was engulfed by his happy teammates who were up two games to none in the best of five series for the National League pennant.

"It was one of the few times I threw a fastball by Aaron and not too many pitchers were able to do that. It was one at-bat for Hank Aaron but for me it gave me the confidence to take charge on the mound. I knew my tools on the mound and how to use them. It changed my whole relationship with the catcher. I didn't have to always rely on someone else. I even had a talk with Grote about it and he said he was finally glad I had a head on my shoulders."

McGraw blanked the Braves over the last three innings of an 11-6 win. Then, at Shea Stadium in New York, the Mets completed their three-game sweep of Atlanta for the National League Championship. With momentum under their wings, the Amazin' Mets then defeated the favored Baltimore Orioles in five games to win the World Series. McGraw's only post-season appearance was his three-inning scoreless stint for a save against Atlanta when he made a decision to rely on himself. Something he really knew all along.

McGraw went on to close out the Philadelphia Phillies' only world championship. After 19 years in the major leagues, he was a television sportscaster in Philadelphia, promoted a bank, wrote three children's books and earned a living as a public speaker and consultant.

After surgery for a malignant brain tumor, and nearly a year of treatment, Tug died of cancer at age 59, January 5, 2004. His son, Tim McGraw, is a major country music star.

DAVE DEBUSSCHERE AND THE BALL

It's late in the afternoon of May 8, 1970, and Dave DeBusschere steps into the 33rd Street employees' entrance at Madison Square Garden, out of the midtown traffic noise, and into the quiet of an arena that will be bedlam within a couple of hours. The Knicks' 6 foot, 6 inch, All-Star forward walks past a security guard and a couple of workers who all wish him and the Knicks good luck that night against the Los Angeles Lakers in the 7th and deciding game for the championship of the National Basketball Association. The workers ask "What's with Willis?" DeBusschere shrugs and remains silent as he slips onto an elevator that takes him to the 5th floor, where the 19,000 seat arena is in semi-darkness. DeBusschere is backstage in "The World's Most Famous Arena" and he strides past a couple of hockey nets, stacked sideboards and several rows of portable seats. The New York Rangers' ice re-making machine stands quietly in a corner. The only sounds are from the distant vending stations as attendants prepare for the event that has the city of New York in a buzz.

As usual, DeBusschere is early; he won't break his pre-game routine just because it's the most important game he's ever played. His wife, Geri, and a handful of their friends will come to the Garden later. His steps are hollow sounding as he approaches the Knicks' dressing room on the left hand side of the long corridor.

DeBusschere is not the first to arrive. Willis Reed was there for hours, treated by trainer Danny Whelan for a hip injury that might keep him out of the game. Since the morning, Whelan treated the Knicks center with whirlpool, ultrasound, hot packs and massages. Reed had a high tolerance for pain but this one wouldn't go away and he couldn't move his legs naturally. He took time out to telephone his daughter Veronica who turned 5 years old that day. He wished her a happy birthday and she asked him if he was going to play. He said yes.

Reed had a problem that preoccupied New York sports fans. All day, they read about it in the newspapers and heard about on all-news radio WINS at 15 minutes after the hour and 15 minutes before. All day, fans telephoned Madison Square Garden with their inquiries and, in some cases, remedies for Willis. The questions all over the five boroughs and neighboring Connecticut and New Jersey were . . . . "Will Willis play? If he can, how much?"

In the opener of the best of 7 series at the Garden, Reed blistered Los Angeles with 37 points and the Knicks won 124-113. But, the Lakers took game 2 105-103 for a split in New York. In Los Angeles, at the Forum, DeBusschere's jumper with 3 seconds left gave the Knicks a two-point lead. Jerry West snared an in-bounds pass and heaved a 63-foot prayer of a shot that hit nothing but net just before the buzzer. The shocked Knicks and the jubilant Lakers went to overtime. Somehow, the Knicks won 111-108. Game 4 also needed overtime and the Lakers evened the series at two apiece 121-115.

Back in New York, early in the 5th game of the series, Reed was enduring arthritic pain just below his left knee, when he dribbled the ball past Wilt Chamberlain and suddenly felt a new jolting pain. Favoring his left leg, Reed put too much weight on his right and he collapsed. Reed needed help to rise and he couldn't continue. The 6 foot, 10 inch Reed was well-muscled with a strong determination and tolerance to pain, but he grimaced as he leaned on the smaller Whelan and dragged his right leg to the dressing room. Willis had pulled a ligament in his right hip. The NBA's Most Valuable Player, who beat out Jerry West and Lew Alcindor in the players' voting, was the Knicks' heart and soul and their captain. They had to go on without him.

Versatility, intelligence and a commitment to defense were the trademarks of Red Holzman's talented team. Even though they were down by 20 points in the first half, the Knicks beat the Lakers without their big man, pressing reserves Nate Bowman and Bill Hosket into action to help neutralize the giant Wilt. DeBusschere switched from covering Elgin Baylor to help out with Chamberlain.

Coach Holzman was a short man and looked conservative in his gray suits, with oxford dress shirts, button down collars and rep ties, but he was cunning and a strategist. Holzman was a former New York City College player who played on the Rochester Royals NBA championship team in 1950-51. He told his players to swarm on defense. They forced 30 turnovers, 10 in the last quarter. The standing room only crowd chanted the now familiar "Dee-fense" and roared with every Lakers mistake. The Garden huffed and puffed with boisterous human emotion in the last quarter, when the Knicks outscored the Lakers by 14 points to win 107-100.

The Knicks led 3 games to 2, a victory away from clinching their first ever championship, but their solid-as-a-rock center and captain was laying on the trainer's table with two painful legs.

Reed: "It turned out that the fifth game was the most important. We won a game we should have lost. We avoided being down 3-2 and headed back to L.A. for an almost certain clinch by the Lakers."

Reed traveled with the team to Los Angeles for game 6 and team Dr. James Parkes gave him heat treatment and massages that didn't work. Reed couldn't play and the Lakers weren't the "nervous nellies" they were in New York. The Knicks couldn't clinch the franchise's first championship, dating back to 1946. They were trampled 135-113. Chamberlain poured in 45 points and hauled down 27 rebounds. Chamberlain, West and Elgin Baylor were within a victory of their first NBA championship, too.

As Manhattan's evening rush hour traffic peaked and the sidewalks around the Garden were jammed with people, there was heightened anxiety for the Knicks and their fans. The 7th and deciding game approached and Madison Square Garden began to fill.

DeBusschere was alone with Reed at the trainer's table. "There was no one else there at the time. Willis said, 'Damn, Dave, it hurts. I got pain on the right side and my left leg. They're gonna give me a pain killer injection.' I said 'it's your life . . . you do what you have to do, but if you take a shot from the doctor and give us 10 minutes, I think we can beat these guys."

Reed answered, "I think I can play, but I don't know how well. I went on the court this afternoon and shot the ball a little bit. But, I got a lot of pain."

DeBusschere crossed the austere dressing room. Each player had a 4 foot wide locker with one shelf. The red nameplates on the gray walls were small with white letters. Each player had a stool. Dave was alone in his thoughts as his teammates began to arrive. The long season, which began in training camp in the late summer, through the grind of the 82-game schedule, then the playoffs, would end this night in May. Would there be a happy ending? He glanced around the room . . . Bill Bradley, the thinking man's player from Princeton . . . . Walt Frazier, the clothes horse "Clyde" from Southern Illinois who was a complete player . . . . Dick Barnett, the former Laker whose lefty "fall-back-baby" jumper was a constant threat . . . Cazzie Russell, the sharp-shooting guard from Michigan . . . the backups known as "The Minute Men," Nate Bowman, Dave Stallworth, Mike Riordan, Donnie May,

Bill Hosket and John Warren. All of them understand their roles and were committed to defense.

The injured Phil Jackson loaded his camera with film. The lanky and unorthodox defender, out of North Dakota State, was the Knicks best sixth man. But, he was off the roster, rehabilitating his back after surgery. Jackson was keeping busy, collecting a photo essay of the team, from his inside view.

In various stages of undress, the Knicks watched a videotape of their lopsided loss in game 6. Dave had seen enough of Baylor, but there would be one last match up.

Dave was 29 years old and felt older. Holzman had rested the starters somewhat before the playoffs, but he was aching. After the grueling season and life on the road, it was a relief to compete in the best-of-seven game playoff series against the same team. His body was tired from the rigors of the long season and he had constant leg cramp problems. He would have to defend against the silky-smooth, sharp-shooting Baylor and keep him within reason. But, it was easy to get inspired for the challenge. This game was the climax to the Knicks' rise to prominence and his athletic career.

David Albert DeBusschere was born October 16, 1940 in Detroit, Michigan. His grandparents had immigrated from Belgium to Canada, and then the United States, to avoid World War II. Like others who escaped tyranny in Europe at the time, self-reliance was the family trait. They lived on the East Side of Detroit, where many immigrants and itinerate factory workers raised their families. Dave's father and his uncles began a beer importing business, dealing with Canadian brewers. But, the powerful truckers who were Jimmy Hoffa's unionized Teamsters put them out of business.

So, Dave's father took over a neighborhood tavern, The Lycast Bar. It was located a block and a half from the Chrysler Automotive plant on the East Side of Detroit, close to where they lived. The customers were a mix of races, nationalities and personalities. It was a blue-collar crowd and they were raunchy shot-and-beer guys from all three shifts, from morning into the night. They were burdened with boredom because of their repetitive work, as sedans rolled off the Chrysler assembly lines. Hard drinking helped them endure the sameness of their lives. Dave's father was their affable host and he was as common and hard working as them. After school and on weekends, Dave worked at the Lycast, helping his father unload crates of liquor and kegs of beer and keeping the place clean as possible. The lanky teenager did his work methodically in the shadowy saloon, paying little mind to the barfly talk which was as constant as the twirling cigarette smoke and the country and western tunes on the jukebox. All over the Motor City, there were similar taverns like the Lycast, close to Ford and General Motors and the dozens of manufacturing plants related to the auto industry. Liquor, cheap food and union trades talk were the attractions, but not to Dave whose focus was athletics and females.

Sports intrigued the teenager. Dave loved to play baseball in Michigan's hot and humid summers and basketball in the frosty winters, when the wind whipped off Lake St. Clair in icy sheets. There were girls to meet and school grades to maintain, and beer to drink and chores to perform, but all of that were interruptions in his desire to compete and improve in baseball and basketball. He played against tough black guys in both sports. Dave grew up easily with black people around him and competed with them naturally in sports. Friendship ended on the schoolyard basketball court because he had to be aggressive and rebound the ball to keep playing. Losers had to give up the ball and the court to others who were waiting to play. No one except the winners owned the ball. The only way to continue playing was to keep the ball. There were no referees, no stoppages of play, no scoreboard or clock, just the basic rules, the ball and the baskets. Dave learned about controlling his body, keeping himself between the backboard and his man, boxing out (blocking his opponent) and timing the missed shot and leaping for the carom off the rim or backboard.

When he was alone on those courts, he practiced dribbling with either hand and took thousands of jump shots, concentrating on his form. Springing from his feet with his body erect, he was mindful of flicking the ball at the right moment from above his head with the proper arc and spin off his right hand fingers with his eyes riveted on the rim. He was so familiar with the feel of the basketball, it was an extension of him, seized when rebounding, directed when passing and caressed when shooting.

All through that experience, Dave went about his business quietly, letting his play speak for himself. His behavior and selfless team-always style was patterned after his father's basic immigrant-belief that hard work and cooperative effort were rewarded. Dave earned respect from the black guys who played with much determination. (Years later, he was asked to be inducted as the first white man in Detroit's Black Sports Legends Hall of Fame. In his acceptance speech, DeBusschere said "Now, I know how Jackie Robinson felt" and more than 600 people at the dinner roared with laughter.)

"I became good at basketball because of the competition I played against. We had games that were vicious. They were older guys and you learned to keep your mouth shut and play hard because you wanted to get picked to play."

**Dave DeBusschore of the NBA Champion New York Knicks shooting
over Baltimore's Earl Monroe at Madison Square Garden May 1970.
Photo by George Kalinsky**

The post-war late '40s and '50s in Detroit were happy times. Americans were buying Motown's cars and the automotive industry and its related businesses kept workers busy and earning. With three, eight-hour shifts everyday at the car-making plants, Detroit hummed with activity, optimism and relative new prosperity. Its sports heroes were the legendary Joe Louis, the world heavyweight champion, nicknamed "The Brown Bomber," Lions quarterback Bobby Layne, one of the most colorful characters in the National Football League and the baseball Tigers' Al Kaline. "Mr. Hockey" in Detroit was Gordie Howe of the Red Wings. Along with his high scoring linemates, Sid Abel and Ted Lindsay, they were called the NHL's "Production Line." Defenseman Red Kelly and goalie Terry Sawchuck were also All-Stars and the Red Wings won 4 Stanley Cups in 6 years, 1950, '52, '54 and '55.

Dave's teenage years were about school, sports and the Lycast Bar. He was in the second class of the new Catholic Austin High School and stood 5 feet, 11 inches. He started to grow quickly while in his freshman year at Austin. He played hard every minute on the court and his overall play was so excellent, he was promoted to the varsity right away and that wasn't commonplace. He

led Austin to the Michigan championship in basketball and pitched on the
Detroit high school baseball championship team. By the time Dave graduated
high school, he was 6 feet, 6 inches and he stayed home to play baseball and
basketball at Detroit University. He was extremely talented in both sports
and cared little for football.

As the best athlete on the Detroit University basketball team, he averaged
25 points a game, playing in the NCAA tournament once and the NIT twice.
Pitching for the Titans, Dave competed in three NCAA tournaments.

Baseball scouts watched him pitch in a dominant way and in his senior
year the 20-year-old was signed by the Chicago White Sox. He accepted a
signing bonus of $75,000. In the spring, while still a senior at the University
of Detroit, the White Sox flew him to Chicago, Indianapolis and Kansas
City to pitch. "It was a lot of fun for a kid in high school to be signed by
a big league team. But, part of the deal, when I signed, was to graduate
and that's what I did." Indianapolis was the White Sox Triple-A team.
Alternating between both over two years, DeBusschere was 25- 9. The
White Sox rated his potential exceptional enough to protect Dave instead
of Denny McLain in the draft. Years later, McLain won 31 games in one
season for the Detroit Tigers.

New York Yankees slugger Mickey Mantle once asked Dave if he had ever
faced him in a game. Yes, he did and DeBusschere joked that the Mick didn't
hit a home run off him, but he walked a lot.

At the same time, the Detroit Pistons of the National Basketball
Association made DeBusschere their territorial first round pick in the
collegiate draft. In his first season, 1962-63, DeBusschere was voted to
the all-rookie team. He handled the ball well for a big man, was savvy
enough to shoot off picks, slid past his man for offensive rebounds and
had uncommon maturity.

For the next four years, Dave pitched for the White Sox as a fifth starter
and in long relief and played a lot of minutes as a forward on the Pistons.
Professional sports seasons didn't overlap, so he had some time off and he
was single. Traveling had become familiar and he enjoyed experiencing the
rest of the country and the people he met. Above all, he was self reliant and
accustomed to sports notoriety.

In 1964, Fred Zollner, who owned the Pistons, asked him to coach as
well. "It was inevitable that I had to make a decision about continuing a
dual athletic career. I felt the area of responsibility was larger in basketball. I
was more advanced in basketball than in baseball. I decided to concentrate

on one. Later, I wondered how it might have turned out because I thought I was a decent pitcher."

So, DeBusschere stopped pitching and he became the youngest coach in the history of the NBA at age 24, only 18 months out of college.

"In hindsight, it was probably a mistake. It hurt my playing because I had to be aware of everything that was going on. My mistakes piled up and veterans like Ray Scott and Bailey Howell were judging me because I was telling them 'do as I say, not as I do.'"

The Pistons were too young and too inexperienced and DeBusschere's coaching record was 79-143 with no playoff appearances. The 1966-67 season, the Pistons hired Donnis Butcher to replace him as coach. "It was a relief to not coach anymore. I didn't have enough experience and maturity to handle it."

In 1968, former Rochester Royals' great Paul Seymour took over the Pistons operation and on December 19th, he traded DeBusschere to the Knicks for center Walt Bellamy and guard Butch Komives.

DeBusschere proved to be the last important part in the Knicks' total team concept because he could rebound the basketball, play tough defense against the NBA's top forwards and score on them as well. His favorite offensive maneuver was to run the baseline, pick up a screen and shoot a jumper from the side. Around the NBA, it was inarguable that DeBusschere couldn't be intimidated. With no. 22 as his new strong forward, Holzman moved Reed from forward to center. Bowman moved to the bench as Willis' backup, and with the shot-crazy Komives removed, Frazier started at guard.

"I had been married in June and traded in December. I met Geri in a Detroit bowling center. She was working for American Airlines and originally from New York, so she was delighted to be going back home. I was happy too. Playing against New York, I felt they were on the verge of becoming extremely successful because they were young, strong and very talented. I would have picked the Knicks myself, if I could. So, I was fortunate to be traded to New York."

With Holzman stressing defense, role-playing and unselfishness, the Knicks team chemistry took hold.

"If every player in the NBA is required to be the coach, that his job is to win the game, the players learn to be unselfish and work to win the game. It was a great experience for me because we couldn't play for ourselves. Red insisted we play together, sacrifice to make up for others' mistakes and simply win the game. It's an attitude that must come from the individual and then blended into the team concept. Early on, I made a mistake in a game and during the next time out, I went to the huddle and said, 'My fault guys, I'm sorry for that mistake.' Phil Jackson pulled me aside and said 'no one else ever said that. We don't have to say that to each other. We are aware we all make mistakes. Your job is to correct them, not apologize.' That was a nice comment. In other words, face up to your mistake and don't let it happen again."

The Bill Russell Boston Celtics finished fourth in 1969, but they won their 11th championship in 13 years after eliminating the Knicks in the Eastern Conference finals. But, Red Auerbach's storied Celtics had grown old, Russell retired and the Knicks were the new best thing in the NBA. Reed said, "Next year, we're going to win this thing." Holzman took note of the Celtics' way of playing team basketball and he preached to his Knicks the time tested truth that the whole is equal to the sum of its parts.

"We have the right guys, in that they understand their roles and accept unselfishness. (Jack Ramsey who coached the champion Portland Trail Blazers later told DeBusschere he used to run films of the Knicks for his players to study their execution at both ends of the floor. Ramsey said the Knicks were the best passing team in pro basketball.)

Over a 17 month period, from January of 1969 to the May of 1970, New York's sports fans enjoyed a rollicking good time. The possibility of a first-ever Knicks championship was added to the Mets' first-ever World Series victory in the previous October and the Jets' first-ever Super Bowl championship in the previous January. The Knicks won 27 of their first 30 games and their home games became events and tickets were at a premium. They set an NBA record, winning 18 consecutive games. In the middle of it, DeBusschere broke his nose against the Lakers and had to wear a mask while playing until it healed. The Knicks' winning streak was topic-A among sports fans. Movie stars liked Woody Allen, Dustin Hoffman, Robert Redford and Barbra Streisand were visible at courtside. So was comedian Bill Cosby who was the star of NBC's "I Spy" dramatic series. Of the 41 home dates, the Knicks sold out 26 times, totaling a franchise record 761,226 customers, averaging 18,566 filled seats a game. Holzman, who employed no assistants, had a good working relationship with general manager Eddie Donovan and president Ned Irish, who had successfully showcased college basketball games at Madison Square Garden and created the National Invitational Tournament. "Fuzzy" Levane scouted players and Frankie Blauschild was the traveling secretary. Jim Wergelies handled the media. Danny Whelan was the only trainer. The operation was lean but run well because of their vast experience in the sport.

Dave's great play and good looks attracted the Knicks fans, especially the women who were coming to home games in greater numbers. DeBusschere was getting cards and letters from females. As for the matinee idol stuff, "It was nice to be recognized and I was definitely flattered. I never experienced this kind of adulation on our team, collectively and individually. It was a mania and crazy and part of the times. The country, as well as the city of New York, was split into factions. We were at war in Vietnam, people were choosing alternate lifestyles, women were more liberated, but New Yorkers agreed on rooting for their beloved Jets, Mets and Knicks."

"Most New Yorkers know the sport of basketball better than the others because they played the game in the school yards and the YMCAs. The electricity in the Garden was unbelievable. Their reactions were immediate and loud. The chant "Dee-fense" started at Knicks games at the Garden. The fans were starved for a winner. Our guys were very bright and we became the best passing team ever in pro basketball and New Yorkers appreciated that skill because we exemplified that tradition."

"Red wasn't a genius with x's and o's. He was a genius at recognizing the individual personalities and their skill levels. He understood their makeup. Frazier needed a lot of attention, but Red hardly talked to Bradley and me. Sometimes he became so gruff and shouted 'watch the damn ball' and 'don't turn your head on defense'; 'get back on defense', 'block out', so much during games, we actually would ask him to calm down. All the players trusted Red. The only rivalry I noticed was between Bill Bradley and Cazzie Russell because they had phenomenal collegiate careers, played against each other in a classic NIT final, won by Michigan. But, Bill was voted the MVP. They came into the league together with the same team. They were fighting for that fifth spot and then, Cazzie broke his ankle and Bill made the best of the opportunity."

From the beginning as a Knick, Dave roomed with Bradley, the son of a Missouri banker, who was an All-American from Princeton University and a Rhodes Scholar. Bradley's signing with the Knicks for the unheard of figure of $125,000 drew much publicity, which was something he wasn't comfortable with. The New York tabloids nicknamed him "Dollar Bill." Dick Barnett wisecracked, "I thought when he took off his shirt in the locker room, he would have a big 'S' underneath." Bradley disdained attention away from basketball and refused to endorse products, turning down a handful of offers in excess of $50,000. "I wanted to keep experience of basketball as pure and unpolluted as it can possibly be."

After graduating from Princeton, Bradley spent two years as a Rhodes Scholar at Oxford in England. He was interested in effecting social changes as a lawmaker someday, but it was too early for politics. While he enjoyed academia, he realized how much he missed basketball. Bradley's acceptance of a contract with the New York Knickerbockers was big news. On December 9, 1967, he debuted at the old Garden against the Pistons and DeBusschere. It was one of the four sellouts that season and the fans cheered loudly when he sank his first shot. Bradley made a glamorous entry into the National Basketball Association, but wasn't an instant impact player as a professional until he eased into the acknowledgement of his strengths and weaknesses.

Despite Bradley's reputation as a college All-American, there were doubts about his professional capabilities. He was too short at 6-5, didn't jump high enough to be a dominant forward and wasn't quick enough to be a guard. But, Bradley's intelligence enabled him to be the classic small forward, constantly on the move for open shots or feeding an unguarded teammate. The team grew confident in his ability to get open and shoot the basketball. "I'm a good player who fits in with a good team and does the essential things for the team to win. I have never maintained I'm the greatest to play the game. I am also not a model for anything. Parents are the best models for their children. I don't want to be a celebrity. I just want to play the game. Basketball is not a metaphor for life. It's a metaphor for ultimate cooperation."

DeBusschere and Bradley formed a friendship. "Bill is so well-rounded and he's taught me a lot. He introduced me to new interests, like art. We've gone to museums and we even bought art work together. Stuff I would have never done on my own. On the road in our room many people telephone Bill to invite him to functions and speak. I mind my own business. We have respect for each other's privacy. It works out well."

Bradley described DeBusschere as "the best defensive forward in the NBA." Dave had to guard and leap against standout forwards like Bob Pettit, Elgin Baylor, Gus Johnson, Billy Cunningham, Connie Hawkins, Rick Barry, Chet Walker and Spencer Haywood. At 235 lbs., DeBusschere couldn't keep up with John Havlicek of the Boston Celtics. Bradley drew that tough assignment and they had nose to nose wars on the court.

Dave relished playing defense and rebounding the basketball.

"I love playing against those guys. I try to take away their obvious strengths and make them do what they don't like. For example, if they like to move to their left for a jump shot, I overplay and don't allow that. If they're comfortable to the right, I don't allow that. When you get someone frustrated a little, they lose their natural flow. I learned in the schoolyards how to rebound and it's simple, you have to keep your man from getting inside of you. On a shot, your first movement is to step to your man and screen him and then look for the ball. Bradley isn't considered a terrific rebounder but he keeps inside his man. Willie and I say to Bill, 'screen out your man and we'll take care of the rebounding.' Willie and I go for the ball hard. We're very strong guys. Once, the ball was in our hands, it was ours."

Reed said of DeBusschere, "Ounce for ounce, pound for pound, there's never been a tougher guy at power forward with his skill level . . . . a tremendous outside shooter, rebounder and defender who could handle the ball. Our G.M. Eddie Donovan, promised a championship and the trade for Dave put everything together. DeBusschere was a natural at power forward. I was switched to center and Bradley could look for shots off our picks. Clyde got more minutes and the way he penetrated, I got the ball for easy lay-ups at least three times a game. We went from a team of two big guys, me and Bellamy, to a balanced starting five that could defend, pass and shoot the basketball."

The Knicks won 60 regular season games without a serious injury. In the Eastern Division semifinals, the Baltimore Bullets leaned on Earl "The Pearl" Monroe, who scored 39 points in the opener but the Knicks won by three points in overtime. Bullets guard Kevin Loughery, a hard nosed New Yorker who played at St. John's University, competed but was sub par with broken ribs because of a collision with Wilt Chamberlain in a regular season game. In the fifth game of the series, a 2-point win by the Knicks at home, Reed scored 36 points with 36 rebounds against Wes Unseld, who was the Rookie of the Year and the NBA's Most Valuable Player, the season before. DeBusschere's match-up at forward was with Gus Johnson, the consensus best combination of power and speed in the league. DeBusschere positioned himself a bit back defending against his drives, allowing Johnson long range jump shots. Johnson also loved to defend and they went at each other intensely and in silence. Trash-talking was not their style. The Knicks won the 7th and deciding game by 13 points. Johnson scored 23 points with 14 rebounds. DeBusschere totaled 28 points with 13 rebounds. Reed held Unseld to an ignominious two points.

The Bullets' elimination from the playoffs further frustrated their loyal fans who had seen their beloved Orioles suffer an upset by the Miracle Mets and their cherished Colts shocked by the Jets, whose quarterback Joe Namath, had correctly guaranteed a New York victory.

In the Eastern Division finals, the Knicks blew out the Milwaukee Bucks in five games despite the imposing presence of center 7-foot, 1-inch, Lew

Alcindor who would later take the Muslim name Kareem Abdul-Jabbar. At 6-9, Reed was 5 inches shorter than Alcindor, but Willis outplayed the 23-year-old rookie, scoring a series high 35 points in the second game. Alcindor was a New Yorker who led the UCLA Bruins to 3 National Championships. He was booed by Knicks' fans who didn't forgive him for leaving to play his college ball in Los Angeles, after starring at Power Memorial High School in Manhattan. DeBusschere's match-up was Bob Dandridge and he took away his fade-away jump shot by playing Dandridge tightly, looking for help from Reed when Dandridge drove to the basket. After they clinched in Milwaukee and left Alcindor in their wake, the Knicks had to contend with three future Hall of Famers in the championship round.

The firepower of Jerry West and Elgin Baylor and the rebounding of Wilt Chamberlain forced the Knicks into a 7th and deciding game.

The Knicks trotted onto their home court in their white satin warm-up gear. Most of the fans were already there, standing and cheering. Even before the opening tap, the Garden crowd was shouting. Most buzzed about the absence of Reed. Willis stayed behind in the locker room. The pain in his right hip was excruciating and it took Dr. Parkes a long time to inject Willis with cortisone, an anti-inflammatory drug and the pain killer, carbocaine. He used a long spinal needle because Willis was so muscled. Would the pain killer obscure his injuries and cut short his career? Dr. Parkes assured Reed there would be no permanent damage if he played.

From rural Louisiana, the burly Reed had grown up picking cotton and hauling hay for less than ten dollars a day. His father didn't earn enough to pay for a college education. But, Willis made it to Grambling University because of a full athletic scholarship and ten dollars a day. With little national attention while at Grambling, he wasn't selected in the first round of the 1964 NBA draft, involving the existing nine teams. The Knicks selected Jim "Bad News" Barnes as their first round choice. After the reigning champion Boston Celtics selected Mel Counts of Oregon State as the last pick of the first round, the Knicks chose Willis.

The Knicks signed Reed to a one-year non-guaranteed contract for $11,000. Before leaving home in Louisiana, Willis told his father, "I'm gonna have to take somebody's job." Unexpectedly, Reed became the Knicks most important player.

Reed swung between center and forward as the Knicks went through growing pains. Veteran Johnny Green and Bob Boozer tried to blend with Reed, and the other rookies, Barnes, Butch Komives and Emmette Bryant. Eventually, they were replaced by Bradley, DeBusschere and Frazier. Reed could defend against the league's dominant centers and his ability to handle the ball and shoot, fit easily with his teammates.

In January of his rookie year, Reed was voted to the NBA All Star game which he said was "thrilling." Growing up in Louisiana, he watched the nationally televised NBA Game of the week on Saturday afternoons on his family's black and white television set. His favorite player was Bill Russell of the champion Boston Celtics. In St. Louis, before the All-Star game, Reed encountered Russell in the hotel elevator. Russell said, "Hey, rookie, where you eating tonight?" A year after playing college ball at Grambling, Reed had dinner with his idol.

Reed led the Knicks in scoring his rookie year. He played with a passion for the game and his enthusiasm and determination affected everyone on the team. Willis was a rock solid player and so respected by his teammates, he was named captain and that made him very proud.

All of that was prelude to this very special night. No matter what, he had to play tonight.

I was covering the game for WCBS-TV. Frank Gifford and I were behind the press table at center court talking with the Knicks public relations director Jim Wergelies. He was having a tough time finding us seats because there was an overflow of reporters assigned to the game. Madison Square Garden filled quicker than usual with Knicks' fans schmoozing about the game. Suddenly, as both teams practiced their shots, Reed walked steadily out of the runway on the 33rd Street side of the arena. The people across the way saw him first in his white satin warm up suit and there was a burst of cheering from the 31st Street side. Gifford and I looked behind us and Reed veered left, passed the press table, joined his teammates, grabbed a ball and took a jump shot. Cheering swept across the Garden. It was time to decide the NBA championship and Willis was on the court.

Bradley recalls, "Nobody really knew whether he would play or not when we left him on the trainer's table in the locker room. We knew his injury was extremely serious. I had no idea whether he would play while I warmed up. When he came out, it was a major high for the players, as well as the fans. We didn't know what he did in the locker room, but he played on courage. It was one of the greatest sports moments in New York, because here was a man who was prepared to put his whole career on the line for his teammates."

George Kalinsky, Madison Square Garden's resident photographer, was asked by Wilt Chamberlain if Reed would play. Only minutes ago, Kalinsky had seen Dr. Parkes inject Willis in his thigh and he figured he was going to try, but he didn't tell it to the Lakers center. Kalinsky positioned himself on the edge of the court and was in perfect position to take a photograph of Reed joining his teammates. "The crowd noise as he walked onto the court was the most electrifying, passionate crowd noise I ever heard."

It was the most dramatic moment in the Knicks' 24 year history. Marty Glickman described it on HBO cable and Marv Albert talked about it on local radio. All over the city, in homes and bars, in taxi cabs and backstage at Broadway theaters, even at Shea Stadium where the Mets were playing, Willis Reed was on everyone's lips. The captain was on the court at the Garden. Could he help the Knicks?

DeBusschere: "I didn't look at Willis. I looked down the court at the Lakers. Every one of them stopped shooting and stared at Willis. Chamberlain, West, Baylor and the rest of them looked dumbfounded. I said to myself, 'we got 'em, we got 'em.' Reed took his warm up shots flatfooted. He told me he didn't want the Lakers to see his lack of mobility."

Reed: "I didn't look at the Lakers. I concentrated on trying to play and look as normal as I could. I realized if I kept my leg straight, I could move around. But, I couldn't flex the right leg because of the hip muscles that were hurting. I wanted to shoot the ball without limping. I think I pulled it off."

Public address announcer John F.X. Condon had to stretch his vocal chords to get above the crowd noise and announce the starting lineups. When Condon finally reached Willis' name, Knicks fans bellowed "LETS GO KNICKS' so much, his voice was obscured.

This one game for the championship was televised live nationally on the ABC network, hosted by Chris Schenkel with Jack Twyman doing the analysis. The referees were the much experienced Mendy Rudolph and Richie Powers.

Reed and Chamberlain met for the opening tap at center court and the Garden crowd didn't sit down. The fans exploded with extra cheering when Los Angeles lost the ball, and in transition, Reed sank a jump shot from the top of the key. Chamberlain countered, and then, Willis made a spin move in the lane with his back to Chamberlain, turned and sank another basket.

Chamberlain was making his own comeback from an injury. Wilt had knee surgery for torn tendons the previous autumn and he played in only a dozen games for the Lakers. This spring night, Chamberlain was upstaged by Reed.

Reed: "Red always says, 'pass to the open man . . . I don't care who shoots the ball.' On the first one, off a turnover, I was the last man down the court because I was dragging the leg. Wilt runs back to the lane to protect the basket, as usual. Clyde comes up with the ball and I'm the open guy . . . he gives me the ball and I sink it. On the second basket, Dick Barnett gave me the ball in the lane and I scored. Maybe it was our time, maybe the ball was supposed to go in. Who knows? If those two shots didn't go in, may be we might have not won."

Willis sacrificed for his teammates and they responded with gusto. DeBusschere felt the Lakers were left at the gate. "We started out with a burst. Willis sank the first basket of the game against Chamberlain and did it again. We had a 5-2 lead. The Garden crowd howled. Holzman quickly replaced Reed with Bowman, knowing he had to get as much as possible from Willis, using him sparingly. Wilt missed a couple of free throws and Keith Erickson walked. The Lakers were down. We pressured the ball and took the Lakers out of their half court game, which was Wilt's strength. He couldn't get enough touches. The quick pace bothered them. Before the game was five minutes old, I hit an off-balanced one-hander from the left baseline and we were ahead 15-6."

The Knicks ran away from the Lakers with a 38-point first quarter and 31 in the second. The Lakers were forcing their shots and lost the ball 15 times to the Knicks' 7 turnovers. By halftime, the Knicks had raced to a 27-point lead, 69-42. Reed took another injection of pain killer during the break and played a few minutes in the third quarter for a total of 27 minutes. Los Angeles trailed 79-54 going into the last quarter. The Garden crowd of more than 18-thousand roared in anticipation. The Knicks won 113-99 despite only those 2 baskets and 3 rebounds from Reed and despite 21 points and 24 rebounds from Chamberlain.

Earlier in the series, Walt Frazier was asked to concentrate on his defense, but with Reed playing courageously on one leg, Holzman unleashed the flamboyant "Clyde" who answered like a champion and Dick Garrett of the Lakers couldn't contain him. Frazier played the game of his life, scoring 23 points by the half, finishing with 36 points with 19 assists, and 7 rebounds. Frazier was 12 of 17 from the field and sank all twelve of his free throws. He stole the ball eight times and held Garrett to eight points. This was Frazier's finest game as a pro and the Knicks were rewarded for scouting him while he led Southern Illinois to the NIT championship as a junior at the Garden and wisely drafting him in 1967.

DeBusschere scored 18 points with 17 rebounds and only one personal foul while Baylor managed 19 points and 5 rebounds. The NBA's best passing team totaled 30 assists while the Lakers had 17.

Time ran out on the Lakers, as the Garden crowd counted down the seconds to the Knicks' first championship. After a Lakers' basket just before the final buzzer, DeBusschere in-bounded the ball from beneath the basket to Dick Barnett on the left baseline. Barnett looked up at the game clock and passed the ball back to Dave close to the basket. The ball was in DeBusschere's hands as time ran out. There was a roar from the standing and bellowing Garden crowd. Within seconds, the Knicks and Lakers ran off the court and the cheering subsided to a buzz about what just occurred on the now empty hardwood court. There was no postgame ritual celebration for the spectators.

The Knicks' game-in, game-out cooperation and mutual trust was finally rewarded. They celebrated alone for a few minutes before opening the door to the media. Along with the other reporters, I rushed in with my WCBS-TV film crew. The players were wet with sweat and champagne.

DeBusschere was in the center of the room saying, "We just ran off the court and into our locker room. I stuffed the game ball into my bag. We're the champions of the NBA. The first one for New York. I've been hugging everybody in the locker room, especially Willis. Only the players, our coach and our trainer could feel our sense of accomplishment. Sharing this with a group of great guys, in a town of great fans, is something special. We're a part of sports history. I'm proud and happy."

Reed was back on Danny Whelan's table, very much in pain, but he had a wide smile. "Winning for the first time is a great achievement. What a sense of satisfaction. In college, you want to win the national championship and in the pros you want to win the title. After losing to the Celtics last year, we realized we had come back in better shape and better prepared. We had a Cinderella season, winning 18 straight, selling out the Garden, getting on covers of magazines and winning the championship."

Reed was told about a team party, later on, at the Four Seasons. He said he'd come for a few minutes, but he had to get to bed because of the pain in both legs.

Bradley stood in front of his locker and summed it up in scholarly fashion to reporters, "We're committed to movement on the court, the fast break and players trying to help themselves get the easiest possible shot. Now, we're sharing the ultimate moment of any athletic career. There are so many bonds in here and what we share transcends normal relationships. There's a great sense of accomplishment. My face aches because I'm smiling so much."

I was trying to get as many reactions on film as possible. Across the locker room, our camera focused on Cazzie Russell who interrupted his merriment and savored the moment. "We play together to utilize everyone's talent. Each guy has a particular specialty and it's blended together. That's why we won 18 straight games and the championship."

Our next stop was Red Holzman's tiny office. He was drenched with champagne and his hair askew as he sat, talking with the beat writers. We filmed Red as he said "They're easy to coach because they're so smart and unselfish. When you get these two things in basketball, which is almost never, it makes coaching easy. We aren't that big but Reed, Bradley, DeBusschere and Frazier really do their jobs. Willis is our main man. Without him, it's difficult."

In a corner of the Knicks locker room, there were bright lights and Howard Cosell interviewed some of team for ABC's post game coverage. On the wall behind them was a sign the Knicks looked at all season, "Hard work overcomes mistakes" At one point, in the giddy interview, Cosell was positioned between DeBusschere and Bradley, and from behind, Nate Bowman poured champagne on Cosell's head almost knocking off his toupee.

In this sweet championship moment, Dave DeBusschere, the quiet shot-and-beer kid from the East Side of Detroit, who learned on the schoolyard courts that the only way to keep playing was to win and keep the ball, was taking long swigs from champagne magnums. He shouted his joy, so happy he couldn't stop laughing. He felt he earned the right to own the ultimate game ball. He KEPT it in his Garden City, Long Island, home for the rest of his life.

The Knicks won another championship in the 1972-73 season with essentially the same players and the additions of Jerry Lucas and Earl Monroe. After 12 years in the NBA, averaging 16 points and 11 rebounds a game, DeBusschere retired following the 1974 season. He was voted to the NBA's all-defensive team the last six years of his playing career. The Knicks retired his no. 22 and it hangs from the rafters of Madison Square Garden. DeBusschere became Vice President and General Manager of the New York Nets of the American Basketball Association. The following year, he stepped up to the commissioner of the ABA and helped forge a merger with the NBA, after the 1975-76 season. In 1982 he returned to the Knicks as executive vice president of basketball operations and stayed until the start of the 1986-1987 season. In 1982, DeBusschere was elected to the Naismith Memorial Basketball Hall of Fame. Other inductees included his coach Red Holzman and teammates Willis Reed, Bill Bradley and Walt Frazier. In 1996, DeBusschere was named to the NBA 50th anniversary team, along with Baylor, Chamberlain and West.

DeBusschere died suddenly of a heart attack, at age 62, on May 14, 2003. He was survived by Geri, his wife of almost 35 years and his children, Michelle, Peter and Dennis. In his eulogy at the end of a Requiem Mass, Bradley said he thought of DeBusschere, "As my older brother. We will miss you no. 22. May God grant you a peaceful journey."

VINCE LOMBARDI IN THE MORNING

It was the beginning of a rainy week in January of 1968, five days before Super Bowl II at the Orange Bowl in Miami. The day before, the Green Bay Packers arrived from their icy "Titletown, USA" in Wisconsin where it was 24 degrees below zero. It was 80 degrees in Fort Lauderdale as the National Football League champions thawed out and flexed their muscles on the baseball field of the New York Yankees minor league ballpark where the Bronx Bombers spent their February and March every year in spring training.

It was late morning and the grass had drained well. There were long chalk markers every five yards in the outfield but not enough for a regulation football field. There was only one set of goalposts. The entire Packers team and assistant coaches were moving about, but one lone man stood out.

With hands on hips, head coach Vince Lombardi watched over and barked at his defending world champions. He wore football cleats and gray sweat pants like them and an oversized dark green windbreaker. His Packers green and gold cap was askew on his head and he looked at his world through black horn-rimmed eyeglasses. Lombardi's football pedigree extended back to the mid-1930s when he was a 170-pound guard on Fordham University's famed "Seven Blocks of Granite" defensive line, coached by "Sleepy" Jim Crowley who was a protégé of Knute Rockne, the legendary coach at Notre Dame.

At this point in time, The Pack was the most respected team in sports and Lombardi had become mythic. His "Packahs" were a study in teamwork and excellence. Starting with an NFL championship in 1961, The Packers were ending a run that included winning 6 divisional, 5 National Football League Championships and 2 Super Bowls.

In 1959, Lombardi had taken over a perennial losing franchise in the boondocks of Wisconsin and turned it into the class of the league. The NFL was enjoying ever increasing national popularity and the Packers were the first TV stars. They had been so successful; most sports fans throughout the country were familiar with their names. Even an offensive lineman like guard Jerry Kramer could co-author a diary type book with Dick Schaap and the result was a runaway best seller.

I was on assignment for CBS News, out of New York, and it was a treat to be so close to the champions and watch them practice. There was no wasted time in Lombardi's practices. The team moved at a quick pace and was business-like. There were some yelps and playful insults but there were no delays. Quarterback Bart Starr was military alert in his movements while he either handed the ball off or backpedaled to throw a pass. The players were in good spirits, enjoying the warm weather of South Florida.

Chuck Mercein was yelled at by Lombardi only moments after the backup fullback stepped onto the practice field. Mercein was mistakenly told by teammate Ben Wilson that they would workout in shorts without helmets. Lombardi screamed at Mercein, "Where's your helmet? Get back inside and get it." Mercein said, "I was in his doghouse for a mental mistake, coming off my contributions in a game-winning drive for the NFL title."

During practice, Mercein trotted slowly and moved about gingerly because of heel and knee soreness and pain in his bandaged left tricep. He was recovering from a severe hematoma (bleeding) because he was kicked early in the famed "Ice Bowl" game. The Packers had just beaten the Dallas Cowboys for the 1967 NFL championship. It was played in 13-below-zero temperatures with a stiff wind making it feel more like minus-35.

Lombardi had signed Mercein just before the post season competition as insurance. Mercein, originally drafted by the New York Giants out of Yale, had been released following a feud with coach Allie Sherman. In Mercein's first start, against the Los Angeles Rams in the divisional title game, a week before the NFL championship, he scored once and blocked well for halfback Travis Williams. The Packers won 28-17.

Against Dallas, in icy Green Bay, Mercein made critical plays in what proved to be a championship drive by Green Bay. With 4:50 left and trailing 17-14, the Packers staged a 68-yard march in front of 50-thousand fans at Lambeau Field and millions watching on CBS.

Mercein said, "Ray Nitschke was waving, on the sideline, and yelling to the offensive unit on the field, 'don't let me down, don't let me down'. He looked frightening with his enraged eyes and yapping mouth with few teeth. In the huddle, Bart Starr was calm. He said, 'let's get this done'.

Starr led the Packers on the most critical drive of their championship run. On the 2nd play, Mercein gained a 1st down with a 7-yard run. A few plays later, Starr flipped a swing pass into the left flat. Mercein caught it on the run and gained 19 yards to the Dallas 11-yard line. "The field felt like stucco. I couldn't make a cut inside. Because of my momentum and the uncertain footing, I had to run out of bounds. In ordinary conditions, I may have scored."

Starr called a "54-give" on the next play. It was a trap. Guard Gale Gillingham pulled, leaving an opening for defensive tackle Bob Lilly who anticipated a sweep and followed Gillingham, while Mercein burst through the hole for eight yards to the 3-yard line.

Time was running out. Rookie Donny Anderson, on the next two plays, slipped twice. The second handoff by Starr was a tad late and low. But Green Bay had picked up a first down and the ball was less than a yard away from the endzone.

In the huddle, Starr called a "31-wedge." Mercein was thrilled. He would get the ball and barrel into the hole between center and guard. Starr didn't want to risk a fumble, so he faked his own teammates, as well as the Cowboys. Sixteen seconds away from defeat, on third down with no timeouts remaining, and two feet from the Cowboys goal line, Starr, on the quarterback sneak, plowed behind Jerry Kramer's block for a 21-17 victory. Behind Starr, at the point of attack, Mercein raised his arms to show the officials he wasn't pushing Starr into the end zone, which is illegal.

Now, two days later, working out in balmy Fort Lauderdale, in t-shirts and shorts, the Packers limbered up easily. Nitschke, their ferocious linebacker, walked with a slight limp. His toes suffered frostbite during the "Ice Bowl" game.

Lombardi demanded dedication, intensity and sacrifice from every player from training camp to the last practices before the Super Bowl. He purposely fatigued his men from the start of a practice. He forced them to exert themselves to finish a practice. Games were easier than a Lombardi-run drill. Subsequently, his teams were stronger in the fourth quarters of games. Lombardi's skill was extracting the most out of every guy. He could be extremely critical. But, off the field, there was a sense of compassion and many of the Packers said they loved the man who browbeat them so much. Mercein was one of them.

"Lombardi treats none of his players like a star, but he is fair. He stresses that everyone should feel like part of the team, so everyone is a cog in the machine. He's a tough guy, but I have no problem with him and feel no intimidation. My parents were strict disciplinarians. My mother is Sicilian, so I'm familiar with his style. Lombardi is trying to get the most out of us. I'm afraid of making mistakes because he's like a parent to me. I don't want to let him down. He's a stickler for good form and he expects everyone to execute perfectly. His manner of coaching makes us play more alertly."

There was speculation that Lombardi was coaching his last game. He refused to comment about the possibility. Green Bay beat-writers advised newcomers to stay off the subject, otherwise, his team would be distracted. The old man could lose his temper and stop talking. Copy was needed to fill the week even if he handed out crumbs in his daily briefings.

A Packers public relations guy had instructed us that the film crews and the reporters had to stay in the foul territory side of the right field line. We could do our filming long range. The Packers drilled toward leftfield and then back in our direction.

After awhile, the offensive unit practiced the famed sweep over and over again. Here it was . . . the sweep . . . . Lombardi's favorite play over and over again . . . . maybe for the thousandth time . . . maybe two-thousandth time. Moving to the right, tight end Marv Fleming, right tackle Bob Skoronski, followed by right guard Jerry Kramer, center Ken Bowman, left guard Gale Gillingham, and left tackle Forrest Gregg. A whole lot of meat on the hoof, moving quickly and in ill humor on game days. In the drill, they created what Lombardi called "an alley" for the ballcarrier, either Donny Anderson or Ben Wilson.

Lombardi watched carefully, measuring their spacing, their individual arcs and synchronized movement. The sweep was power football and it embodied Lombardi's entire coaching doctrine, "Dancing is a contact sport, football is a hitting sport." The linemen worked as one unit, executing so well, with the attitude, "Here it is, try to stop us." At the point of attack, the ball carrier accelerated to the open gap and the end result became known in football as "Running to daylight."

Through their championship run, Skoronski had replaced Fuzzy Thurston, Bowman had replaced Jim Ringo and Fleming replaced Ron Kramer. However, the offensive line remained a powerhouse, each member a driving piston in the machine. At that point in time, the Packers were to football what General Motors was to the auto industry.

At this practice, the Packers worked toward us and then back out to leftfield, but in time, the cameramen were itchy to get closer . . . . they crept past the foul line . . . the cameramen and soundmen only feet away from the Packers . . . all of them except for my cameraman and soundman. I told them not to move. Soon enough, Lombardi realized he had unwanted visitors into his inner sanctum. He whirled and bellowed . . . "WHAT DO YOU WANT TO DO, STICK THOSE THINGS UP MY ASS . . . . GET THE HELL OFF THE FIELD AND GET OUTTA THIS BALLPARK." The film crews scattered like startled birds.

After practice, Lombardi gave me the only interview because we had followed the rules. He was preoccupied and gave me a cursory hello and handshake. I thought I would ingratiate myself by mentioning that I was also a graduate of Fordham University. He spit out "good" and motioned with one hand toward the camera, as if to say, "Let's get this over with."

Once the camera was rolling, Lombardi answered my questions with a toothy smile, brimming with confidence but not elaborating on much either. He talked while holding his Packers cap with both hands behind his back.

Asked about the first day back in cleats, Lombardi felt his team was sluggish, particularly the offense. But, he expected a correction in contact drills beginning tomorrow and all practices from this point on would be closed. He praised the Raiders and their young coach John Rauch and said he was impressed with Oakland's speed on defense. Lombardi said his Packers were physically and mentally ready for Sunday's Super Bowl game. When it was over, I wished him luck and he whispered "Thanks."

Packer's QB Bart Starr, Ft. Lauderdale Florida 1968

After I interviewed Bart Starr I caught up with Lombardi at his press briefing with the print reporters. In his remarks about the American Football League champions, he elaborated about their quickness on defense, especially their cornerbacks and linebackers who he said could cover receivers better than most in his league. Everyone was sitting at a table in a small room. Some sandwiches and soda and coffee had been put out for the press. All the while Lombardi spoke, his right hand played with a salt shaker. He kept rolling it between his fingers keeping it upright enough not to spill any salt. He did this while answering the questions, treating this as an interruption in his preparations for the championship game.

Five days later, in the Green Bay locker room, right after warm-ups for Super Bowl II, Lombardi walked over to Mercein who sat on a stool and gently said that he was starting Ben Wilson because he felt Chuck was too banged up. But, he said "Keep ready, in case we need you." Chuck was disappointed because his parents and friends were in the crowd, but he understood.

Green Bay scored on its first three possessions and defeated Oakland 33-14. More than 75,000 fans at Miami's Orange Bowl watched the Packers dominate the Raiders who were 14-point underdogs. The Packers committed only one penalty, while their balanced attack gained 160 yards rushing and 162 yards passing. They converted on 5-of-16 third down situations and a 4th down try. Wilson rushed for 62 yards and Anderson for 48 and a touchdown. Herb Adderly intercepted a pass and returned it for a touchdown. Bart Starr and Boyd Dowler hooked up on a 62-yard touchdown play and Starr was voted the Most Valuable Player for the second straight Super Bowl because he was 13 of 24 for 202 yards, one TD and no interceptions. The game drew football's first $3-million-dollar gate. It was Lombardi's last as Green Bay coach and marked the end of a great dynasty which resulted in 96 wins, 34 loses and 6 ties.

Two and a half weeks later, Lombardi announced it was no longer practical to continue as both general manager and coach, so the new head coach of the Green Bay Packers was Phil Bengtson. After coaching his team to its third consecutive title, Lombardi was tired, privately suffering digestive problems.

Two years later, in 1970, after one season as coach and general manager of the Washington Redskins, Lombardi died of cancer. The following year, Lombardi was inducted into the Football Hall of Fame posthumously.

My lasting impression was observing Lombardi at his life's work, which was the sum total of his upbringing, environment, schooling and religious values. On a practice field, among his men, coaching and teaching them, which is really another way to say, prevailing his will on them. Essentially, he constantly challenged his players to maximize their individual potential. It was simple math. The whole is equal to the sum of its parts.

On an otherwise hot and humid Florida morning, with championships won and reputations made, when minds could easily wander, I saw the legendary Vince Lombardi and his champion Packers, with a certain determination for excellence; doggedly work on their skills, to the very last public practice.

SINATRA'S PAL JOEY

Frank Sinatra was leaning on the ring apron, peering through his camera, snapping photographs of Muhammad Ali and Joe Frazier inside the Madison Square Garden ring, as they waited impatiently with their handlers on Monday night, March 8, 1971. The cheering from the sold-out crowd sounded like a sustained ocean's roar.

Each fighter was undefeated and the world heavyweight championship was at stake. This first encounter, in what eventually became an historic boxing trilogy, was eagerly anticipated. The historic Garden, the site of so many boxing classics, was filled to capacity. Crouched behind the famous singer, a large man, also in a business suit and tie, didn't need any more problems on this special night, but he made an exception for his idol. Joe Acquafreda was the head of security for Madison Square Garden. He was responsible, with the help of plainclothesmen and uniformed specials, for keeping the peace outside the brightly-lit ring.

The world famous arena was not only jammed, but packed with famous people, including the Apollo-14 astronauts, Captains Alan Shepard, Edgar Mitchell and Stuart Roosa who had received New York City's gold medal from Mayor Lindsay on the City Hall steps that morning. Fans turned their heads when Joe DiMaggio arrived and when Joe Namath took his seat. The world famous soccer player Pele was just another celebrity. So was the internationally known surrealist artist Salvador Dali who twirled his elaborate mustache with a mischievous look. Jazz legends Count Basie and Duke Ellington smiled warmly. Miles Davis did not. Popular singers Bing Crosby, Sammy Davis Jr., Diana Ross, Aretha Franklin and Andy Williams signed autographs. Barbra Streisand and Dustin Hoffman sat in separate seats. Knicks All-Star guard Walt "Clyde" Frazier strolled in, sporting a tilted black fedora. The crowd was so well dressed; it looked like a fashion show. Many wore full-length furs and they were the men. The Ali-Frazier fight was a hot ticket. At the entrances of "The world's most famous arena" gate-crashers were trying to get inside. They had somehow slipped past the NYPD checking for tickets a block away from the Garden. Counterfeit tickets had been scalped in Harlem. Ringside seats priced at $150.00 were being scalped for $1,000.00 each. It was billed as "THE" fight and it was sold out within four days. The demand for tickets was so excessive the Garden could have been filled many times over. Acquafreda had much to worry about, but shadowing Frank Sinatra and making sure no one bothered him was a special pleasure. LIFE Magazine had called the day before with a request for special accommodations and a credential for their celebrity photographer. LIFE was turned down by John F.X. Condon, the Garden's point man with the press. Condon was over-subscribed at more than 700 credentials. Even for Sinatra and LIFE magazine, it was too late for a press pass and a position on the ring apron. Acquafreda asked for help from the closed circuit broadcast crew and Sinatra was allowed a ringside credential and position from their allotment. Sinatra sat to the left of actor Burt Lancaster who worked the broadcast. Only five cars were allowed to park on the ramp inside Madison Square Garden and one of them was Sinatra's limousine. Acquafreda advised Sinatra to arrive during the day and personally greeted Sinatra and escorted him and his security guy Ralph Serpico to a private room. Joe arranged for food, liquor, and a portable bed if Sinatra wanted to nap. The Garden's house photographer, George Kalinsky, was asked by Sinatra, "Please, give me a lesson in boxing photography." Kalinsky spent a couple of hours with Sinatra who was so grateful he took George for a late afternoon meal at his favorite restaurant, Patsy's, on West 56th Street.

Joe Acquafreda looked like an oversized Dean Martin, a handsome centurion with a quick smile. Two months shy of his 38th birthday, Joe was a powerful man who knew how to use his hands. He was born and bred in the Bronx. He never finished high school, painted city bridges and owned two trucks for his delivery service before he moved on to the bowling business. Acquafreda had managed bowling centers and was originally hired by the Garden to supervise its bowling complex before he was promoted to supervise the security for the 18,000 seat arena in mid-Manhattan. He was a sharp dresser, always well-groomed, in shirt and tie and adorned with eye-catching jewelry. Acquafreda was a powerfully built man who had no fear. He was a natural protector of others, and at the same time, affable and downright sweet. Sinatra liked his style and attitude.

While Ali was forced into boxing exile for three and a half years, Frazier captured the vacant world heavyweight title. Jimmy Ellis was the winner of the World Boxing Association tournament. Frazier had knocked out Buster

Mathis in the 11th round for the New York State heavyweight crown, giving him cachet as champion. The Ellis-Frazier showdown lasted only four rounds. After two knockdowns in the 4th round, Ellis couldn't answer the bell for the fifth round. Frazier was the undisputed world heavyweight champion but, he would never be accepted universally until he defeated Ali in the ring.

Ali's refusal of military service cost him time, money and his title. During the Vietnam War, in April of 1967, Ali claimed he was an Islamic preacher and his religion forbade him from killing another human being. Claiming conscientious objector status, he famously declared: "I ain't got no quarrel with the Vietcong. No Vietcong ever called me nigger." Ali was convicted of draft evasion and sentenced to five years in prison and fined $10,000. Ali's attorneys appealed and he avoided a prison term. However, boxing officials stripped him of his championship. (Three months after this encounter, with Frazier, his appeal went before the Supreme Court which ruled in his favor 8-0 with one abstention). Ali's comeback had a logical collision with the hard-hitting Smokin' Joe Frazier from Philadelphia. They signed to fight six months earlier, so there was plenty of time to promote it. The coming event took on huge proportions beyond the ring. While they were not only boxing for a world championship and much money, people perceived Ali as anti-establishment because he was anti-war, and Joe as pro-establishment, for the war. What resulted was a promoter's dream.

Each would earn a record $2.5 million dollars. For the first time in boxing history, two undefeated heavyweights were meeting for the championship of the world. Ali was undefeated in 31 professional fights while Frazier was 26 and 0. Frazier was 4 inches shorter than the 6 foot, 3 inch Ali, who enjoyed a six and a half-inch reach advantage. Frazier was a straight-ahead slugger, who took punches in order to get inside and unleash his powerful left hook. Ali was a quick-footed big man who could slip and slide punches while throwing quick shots. Ali had the rare combination of speed and power.

The morning of the fight, Frazier weighed 215 lbs. to Ali's 205 lbs. Muhammad delighted the press corps and the promoters with an outburst, spewing predictions and poems. Ali had teased Smokin' Joe in pre-fight news conferences. Joe was a Baptist whose lineage went back to slavery in South Carolina. His father was a sharecropper. He considered Ali middle-class and seethed when Ali referred to him as an "Uncle Tom," a term describing a subservient black man. Ali also denigrated him as "ugly and dumb." Joe's response was to call him Cassius Clay instead of his adopted Muslim name.

**Ali at the weigh-in and physical examination at Madison Square Garden
March 8, 1971. His trainer Angelo Dundee behind him, an unidentified
physican and James Dooley, Chairman of the New York State
Athletic Commission.**

In 1971, America was divided on the war. Ali's stance infuriated the
patriotic and appeared to be a sign of growing Black Power. Ali was a symbol of
black pride and the counterculture and, wrongfully, Frazier was considered by
many as a black fighter representing White America. Ultimately, the popularity
and monetary success of the promotion was linked to the nation's political
strife over a conflict on the other side of the world. A conflict more and more
Americans, besides their heavyweight champion, wanted no part of.

In their bombastic news conferences, Ali fueled the anticipation of his
showdown with Frazier by insulting his opponent beyond the ring.

ALI: "This ain't publicity, we don't like each other."

FRAZIER: "I want you like a hog wants slop."

ALI: "I been fightin' regular."

FRAZIER: "Yeah, but who?"

ALI: "You can't dance."

FRAZIER: "I can fight, though."

ALI: "I'm gonna make you more ugly than you is."

FRAZIER: "I'm gonna whup you like you stole something."

ALI: "I predict an easy victory in fifteen rounds. I'm gonna kick your ass."

FRAZIER: "I'm gonna tell you what you're gonna do . . . you might kiss my ass."

Ali's poem to stoke the promotion became a classic newsreel clip, played over and over again on television newscasts.

> *Joe's gonna come out smokin'*
> *But I ain't gonna be jokin'*
> *I'll be pickin' and pokin'*
> *Pouring water on his smokin'*
> *This might shock and amaze ya*
> *But I'm gonna destroy Joe Frazier*

While each champion needed the other as an opponent, Ali's denigration of Frazier was especially infuriating to Joe. During Ali's boxing exile, he earned money as a public speaker, Frazier said, "I put love in his hand," meaning he gave Muhammad money to help make ends meet. Privately, they had been friendly, but Ali went too far in his public insults of a very decent man. Joe felt betrayed. Ali would tell reporters, off the record, that his harangues were for the betterment of the promotion, but, Muhammad was promoting himself.

Madison Square Garden guaranteed five million dollars to be split by both fighters. Alvin Cooperman, who ran the arena, knew that the profit would come from the closed-circuit telecast. All that evening, Cooperman's worry was about losing electrical power in the building. It didn't happen. But, a week later, a New York Knicks-Utah Jazz NBA game was blacked out in the fourth quarter because of a malfunction deep in the bowels of the Garden. Fortunately, this momentous night, there were no such problems.

As fight time approached, the loud chatter of the crowd made one strain to hear a companion's voice. It took ring announcer Johnnie Addie ten minutes to introduce the celebrities at ringside. Then, Addie announced the roll call of former champions in attendance. One by one, they climbed into the most famous boxing ring in the world. Among them, Jack Dempsey, Gene Tunney, Joe Louis, Floyd Patterson, James Braddock, Sugar Ray Robinson, Rocky Graziano, Jake Lamotta and Willie Pep. The Madison Square Garden crowd was electric with excitement, cheering passionately for each champion.

After the national anthem and introductions, the Garden crowd of 20,455 settled back. The ring was vacated except for the fighters and the referee. Would it be over in a flash? Would they disappoint? The 27-year-old Frazier was in green and gold brocade trunks and the 29-year-old Ali in red velvet trunks. Their boxing gloves were wine-colored. What we witnessed was an epic 15 round fight laden with tension and excitement throughout for the undisputed world heavyweight championship.

The only other man inside the ropes was the authoritative "Lord of the Ring," the handsome and square-jawed referee, Arthur Mercante. His stance was erect at 5 feet, 7 inches, 160 lbs., extremely fit in black gym shoes, gray slacks and business shirt with a tight dark bow tie. The referee for this world championship fight was a one-time Golden Glover from Brooklyn who had been a boxing instructor in the U.S. Navy's fitness program during World War II. Now, at 51 years old, Mercante was the most recognized referee because of enormous experience at Madison Square Garden and clubs like St. Nicholas Arena in Manhattan, Sunnyside Gardens in Queens, and Brooklyn's Ridgewood Grove and Eastern Parkway Arena. He had officiated the nationally televised, Gillette Razor Blades' "Friday Night Fights" at the Garden, and the Wednesday night, Pabst Blue Ribbon Beer series. Mercante was no stranger to the responsibility of championship fights.

While Ali and Frazier were splitting $5 million, the New York State Athletic Commission was paying Mercante a mere $750 and its officials didn't inform him of that until the 6pm rules meeting that night at the Garden. "I would have done it for nothing" Surprisingly, it was Mercante's best pay night in the ring, topping the $300 he earned working the second Floyd Patterson-Ingemar Johansson world heavyweight championship fight. Their 1959 match was at Yankee Stadium. The undersized Patterson was knocked down seven times and lost the world heavyweight championship he had captured at age 21, the youngest to do so. Their 1960 rematch was held at the Polo Grounds.

In the 5th round, Patterson threw one of the most lethal left hooks to the head ever seen and Johansson went down, his right leg quivering as Mercante yelled the full ten count over the champion from Sweden. Almost a year to the day, Brooklyn's Floyd Patterson avenged his defeat to Johansson and became the first boxer to regain his world heavyweight crown. Mercante raised Patterson's right arm in triumph.

Eleven years later, under the Madison Square Garden's spoked dome when the house lights went down there was collective breathless anticipation at the opening bell as Mercante motioned Ali and Frazier from their corners. The early pace was quick and hard-hitting. Mercante circled with his trademark quick feet, brushing the ropes with his back until he sliced in to break a clinch. Mercante said the fighters taunted each other. Ali kept insulting Frazier, using curse words. Despite Mercante's orders to stop, Ali wouldn't.

Mercante recalled, "I put my index finger and my thumb and pointed them at Ali's mouth and I said 'stop talking'. According to the rule book, you can take a point away for causing havoc in the ring. I heard Ali say: 'you know, you're in here with God, tonight'. Frazier very quickly said 'If you're God, you're in the wrong place tonight, man."

Bookmakers made Ali a 6-to-5 underdog. It proved to be Frazier's night because Ali had misjudged his own strength and Frazier's. After a furious pace in the early rounds, Ali became content with hanging on the ropes flat-footed, taking blows to wear out Frazier. But, Joe's ceaseless punching impaired Ali's ability to counter and eventually drained Ali's strength. Frazier bloodied Ali's nose in the 4th round. Frazier kept coming forward with his familiar cross handed approach and dip, always looking to unleash his most potent weapon, his left hook.

In the middle rounds, Frazier pounded Ali's body and his upper left arm to sap the strength from Ali's whiplash jab. Ali wasn't winning, but his machine-gun combinations in the 9th round were a reminder to Joe to be wary. In the 10th, Mercante darted between the two as they grappled to separate the clinch. Later commenting, "Frazier was like a bull and resisted my push. My pinkie finger caught Joe inside the lower lid of his eye. He shouted to his corner, 'I got two guys beatin' up on me in this ring.' I said to myself, oh my God, if this guy sits down and the house lights go up and he loses his championship, this will be the greatest controversy ever. But, Joe continued to fight and didn't complain anymore. After the 10th round, I went to his corner. Yank Durham was Joe's trainer and I apologized. He said it was forgotten and with a wave of his hand, he wisecracked 'just watch where you put your hands.'"

On the ring apron edge, Sinatra was still clicking away and things were going smoothly. Joe Aquafreda left his idol during the rounds to check with his security lieutenants, hustling back for quick exchanges about the fight with

Sinatra between rounds. Joe delighted in offering boxing expertise. The famous singer didn't have to bother with the mechanics of sports photography. LIFE Magazine had a guy feeding Sinatra newly loaded cameras. To his immediate right was actor Burt Lancaster, in earphones working as a TV analyst. Sinatra and Lancaster had starred in the film, "From Here to Eternity." Sinatra won the Academy Award ("Oscar") for best supporting actor.

Ali tried to buy time in the 11th, staying in a corner and counter-punching Frazier's assault. It didn't work. Frazier staggered him twice in the 11th round with his potent left hook, making him wobbly. Ali spun him with his arms, trying to smother Joe's punches. Just before the bell, Ali was away from the ropes. Frazier pounded Ali while he backed up. If not for the ropes, Ali's red trunks would have dusted the canvas. In the 15th and last round, Frazier added luster to his apparent lead by knocking down Ali with a thunderous left hook to the right side of Ali's face. Muhammad's white shoes, with red tassels, pointed sideways for the first time. But, Ali quickly lifted himself off the canvas and, in one of the corners, leaned against the ropes with both gloves on the top strands. "My God," said Mercante, "I just got to three when he was up." Ali took the mandatory 8-count from the referee on unsteady feet. However, Mercante points out, ". . . for the last 30 to 45 seconds of that last round, Ali came on strong." They traded punches till the last bell and then, an enormous eruption of cheering and the house lights were up again.

The closed-circuit telecast to an estimated 300 million viewers in the United States, Canada and 15 other countries, replayed Frazier's sweeping left hook and Ali's fall to the canvas 16 times, with commentary from Don Dunphy, actor Burt Lancaster and Archie Moore, the former world light-heavyweight champion.

The emotionally exhausted Garden crowd hushed as ring announcer Johnny Addie intoned the outcome. Frazier won by unanimous decision, stopping Ali's 31-fight winning streak. After a burst of cheering, there was a loud buzz, as the spectators began to argue. Scoring by rounds, Mercante had it 8-6-1 Frazier. Judge Arthur Aidala scored it 9-6 Frazier and Judge Bill Recht had the largest disparity, 11-4 Frazier. Breaking down the scoring, the officials agreed on only seven rounds.

Ali wisecracked, "Joe hit me so hard, it jarred my kinfolk in Africa." He went to a hospital for X-rays on his jaw which were negative and he was uncharacteristically silent until the next day. Frazier declined to meet with reporters and photographers because his jaw was swollen and he had knots on his face. Frazier was the undisputed world heavyweight champion with a record of 27-0, 23 by knockouts. Frazier asked an aide to tell the sportswriters, "I always knew who the champion was." Privately, Joe wanted Ali to "crawl to me." It wasn't to be. Instead, the next day, Ali ridiculed Joe again. Even in victory, Smokin' Joe could not get respect from the man he still called Clay. His violent fifteen rounds with Ali exhausted Frazier. He secretly spent 3 weeks in a Philadelphia hospital and recovered slowly.

Mercante recalls, "Ali gave away a couple rounds with that foolish pitter-patter stuff on the ropes. He could have won that fight, really. The 15th round knockdown was decisive. All in all, it was a night that never will be duplicated. It was simply fantastic. It was the highlight of my career."

It was a memorable night in more ways than one. LIFE Magazine had its pictorial history of the epic fight, including a front cover action photograph, all taken by Sinatra, with text by Norman Mailer working on a two-day deadline. After the fight, Acquafreda escorted Sinatra to his limousine on the Garden's inside ramp. Sinatra was effusive in his gratitude and offered Joe his expensive Patek Philippe wristwatch. Acquafreda took it, said thanks, and added, "Do you think you could have it engraved to me." Sinatra laughed loudly at the naivete and agreed.

The amused Sinatra immediately called him "Joey . . . . Joey Coldwater." He asked Joe if he had ever been to Palm Springs, California. He said no. Sinatra invited him to the southern California desert oasis to vacation for a few days. That's why Joe Acquafreda and his wife, Dawn, spent their next vacation and the rest of their lives in Palm Springs.

As a good will gesture, Joe brought two five-gallon pails of mussels in tomato sauce from his favorite restaurant in the Bronx. Sinatra invited the couple to dinner at his home. Once they became familiar, Sinatra suggested something that changed the Acquafredas' lives. Sinatra had a new neighbor in town, a certain friend who had moved from New Jersey with a desire and the cash to invest in a local business. Since, the singer was sophisticated in worldwide travel, he was appalled by the inadequate security in this town of millionaires. He offered the opinion that times were changing for personal security. Why not combine resources, Joe's expertise in security and his friend's money to partner a new business. So that's how Control Securities was formed and Joe and Dawn moved from the Bronx, along with their 5-year old son Joey and her parents, to the resort town of Palm Springs, southeast of Los Angeles. JoAnn, Joe's daughter by previous marriage, also joined him.

Control Securities prospered. Acquafreda's first big account was the Canyon Hotel. Up till then, an old man and his son patrolled the resort. There was still too much thievery. After Joe was hired and his men secured the sprawling layout, word spread in Palm Springs about his effective work. Control Securities was hired by The Spa Hotel, the Ocatillo Lodge and the Palm Springs Airport. Joe won the contract for the Colgate Dinah Shore Golf Tournament at the Mission Hills Country Club in Rancho Mirage. Nabisco took over sponsorship of the event which became the 4th annual major championship on the Ladies Professional Golf Association tour. Control Securities was hired to secure Nabisco's new corporate headquarters in Palm Springs.

The flashiest restaurant in town was Melvin's at the Ingleside Inn. Mel Haber, a Brooklyn guy with cash and vision, took over the old small resort hotel, favored by the movie stars of the 30's that had languished for years. Haber was smart enough to envision it not as a small hotel but as a setting for a high-end restaurant. He converted the dining room into the "21" of Palm Springs. Haber put a small jewelry store in the lobby and all his wait staff dressed in formal black tie. Haber parked vintage automobiles in the driveway and lit the hacienda style inn with dramatic lighting. Control Securities insured the safety and protection of the tailored rich of the community who dined and danced in Melvin's, the most exclusive club in the desert.

From the start, Joe was involved with the local police and they welcomed his expertise and cooperation. When former President Gerald Ford built a new home, Control Securities was hired to work with the Secret Service to supervise the construction.

The Acquafreda family leased a lobby space in the Canyon Hotel to sell clothing and accessories. They lived in a new condominium with Dawn's parents in their own home only a couple of miles away. Besides suddenly making lots of money, Joe became a significant member in the tight Sinatra entourage, enough to rile Sinatra's right hand guy, Jilly Rizzo. Joe was so trusted and presentable, Sinatra would have him escort his wife, Barbara, to charity events and functions while he was away singing. "Joey Coldwater" called him "Francis" or "The Old Man." The two often rode around the area in Sinatra's low-key station wagon. They were pals and "The Old Man" was first and foremost with Joe.

Life had changed for the better for the Acquafredas from the Bronx. Dawn was a close double for the actress, Suzanne Sommers and she had a business mind, too. Realizing there was no store in Palm Springs for bathroom products, Dawn opened LE JOHN and was an instant success. Joe invested in his own limousine service. He hired male retirees to work security at home parties. The Acquafredas drove expensive cars and socialized among the Palm Springs "A-listers."

Joe Acquafreda in Palm Springs 1972

Daughter JoAnn opened the family mail one day and was stunned to see an invitation to a very exclusive party. Her parents were among the fifteen invited couples. Barbara Sinatra's guest list to benefit her Children's Center included the Firestones, the Jimmy Stewarts, the Gregory Pecks, the Roger Moores, Gene Autry, and leading Palm Springs dignitaries. JoAnn's parents traveled by private jet with the others to Las Vegas for a special Don Rickles show at the Golden Nugget. The Acquafredas joined the Mission Hills Country Club and, ironically, Joe became a social friend with his old boss at Madison Square Garden, Irving Mitchell Felt, the retired CEO who now resided in Palm Springs. TV actor Paul Burke also became a close pal. Joe organized a branch of the national Sons of Italy organization in Palm Springs. He developed a site and plans for social events that could be enjoyed by Italian-Americans living in the area.

Control Securities landed another big account, the Bob Hope Desert Classic which was an annual weeklong event drawing thousands of tourists to the Palm Springs area. Everyday, Joe personally escorted Hope in a golf cart everywhere. On the day before the tournament, the pro-am benefited intercollegiate golf, attracting thousands of people. The Master of Ceremonies at the end of the day, on the 18th green, was Howard Cosell. One year, a heckler was shouting insults at the controversial sportscaster who was addressing the gallery on a public address system. Joe excused himself from Tommy Lasorda, the Los Angeles Dodgers manager and approached the heckler. He whispered something into his ear and walked back. The man kept quiet. A stunned Lasorda asked Joey, "What did you say to him?"

"It wasn't only what I said, it was what I did." Joey answered, "I dug my golf cleats into his foot."

The Palm Springs police asked Joe to help them with a special request. A visitor from Saudi Arabia had telephoned with fears that she was very wealthy and felt unprotected. She was Her Royal Highness Princess Madawi who came to the desert oasis with a girlfriend for extensive plastic surgery. Acquafreda met with her and was hired. Soon after, she felt immensely secure. Armed men from Control Securities protected her in Palm Springs and on shopping trips to Los Angeles. The Princess paid him well and trusted him so much, she took Joe and Dawn with her on a month long trip by private jet, making stops in New York, London, Paris and Rome, staying in luxurious hotel suites all the while. When her son, Saisal, turned 21, the Princess gave Acquafreda a budget of over $100,000 dollars to arrange a three-day weekend party for family and friends in Las Vegas. Princess Madawi was especially pleased with the cake Acquafreda personally designed for the occasion. A real gold coin garnished each slice of the elegant cake.

Almost every morning, Acquafreda had a cup of coffee with Gene Autry in the restaurant of his hotel, The Hacienda, on Palm Canyon Drive. The legendary singing cowboy, who was worth several millions of dollars, lived in a huge home in the back of the property. The Hacienda had a reputation for cleanliness and excellent Mexican food. Control Securities protected all of the property as well as Autry's home. Joe endeared himself to Autry when he discovered, during routine in-house wire-tap conversations, a plan by two of Autry's employees to abduct him for ransom.

"Joey Coldwater," a former high school dropout from a tough neighborhood in New York City, had become a important man in a community that had the largest concentration of millionaires in the United States. During the '70s, Palm Springs became a destination vacation experience because of its perfect weather for golf and tennis during the winter months. The little town's periphery extended further out and it became more populated. What was once a hideaway for the rich and famous was becoming a sprawling metropolis.

On a typical day, Joe and Dawn rode in a Silver Cloud Rolls Royce to the Missions Hills Country Club where his locker was filled with custom-made golf clothes. He and Dawn lunched with the renowned singer, Dinah Shore, who became a very close friend. In the evenings, they dined at the best restaurants and attended glamorous house parties. Every now and then,

Sinatra hosted a dinner party at home for Joe and Dawn and others. His crony and part-time cook, "Jimmy the Hook" whipped up his specialty which was linguine with white clam sauce.

Just as their lives suddenly turned for the better, they were dealt a double lethal blow by fate. Sadly, their happiness came to an abrupt halt. In May of 1986, Dawn was diagnosed with colon cancer. Sinatra flew her by his private jet to New York to consult with doctors at Sloane-Kettering Cancer Center. He was a generous contributor to perhaps the most respected institution of its kind. Dawn heard the worst news, even surgery couldn't help this late stage of her disease. She passed away 17 months later, on October 23rd, 1987. She was 49.

In October of 1986, just five months after Dawn's diagnosis, Joe's doctors confirmed he was suffering from lung cancer caused by his longtime smoking habit. Sinatra flew him to New York for a consultation at Sloane-Kettering. The news was just as ominous as Dawn's. When Joe returned to Palm Springs, he was hospitalized. His daughter Joanne remembers Sinatra visiting his pal everyday, regaling the doctors, nurses and attendants with stories about his show business past. There was much laughter. The visits were like a tonic for Joe who had specially prepared Italian food delivered from Tony Riccio's restaurant for everyone to enjoy. To the end, Joe was taking care of others. The 72-year old Sinatra would wear his favorite New York Yankees black satin jacket and he always brought fresh cut roses from his garden which he wrapped in tin foil. It was a very sweet gesture, one man to another.

Seventeen years after they first met in New York, the night of the first Ali-Frazier fight, "Joey Coldwater" said goodbye to his idol who not only changed his family's life for the better but also became his closest friend.

Four months after Dawn's death, Joe Acquafreda passed away, at the age of 54, on February 11, 1988. Most of their medical costs had been paid by Nabisco. Years earlier, CEO Ross Johnson, who admired Joe so much, had the Acquafredas written into his company's medical coverage.

Joe and Dawn Acquafreda are buried in the Palm Springs Desert Memorial Cemetery, not far from the grave of Frank Sinatra.

HOWARD "THE DING" COSELL

Howard Cosell was a broadcasting phenomenon because his personality was so original and distinctive. He intrigued sports fans despite never being athletic, despite his odd looks, despite his annoying voice and "Nuu Yawk" accent.

When erect, handsome and affable talking heads were the standard in television, lanky Howard was stoop-shouldered with a long nose and whatever was left of his dark hair was shiny and slicked down. He spoke sarcastically in a nasal twang and used multi-syllabic and obscure words. He irritated his audience while maintaining a deep sense of moral consciousness. Howard knew what is right isn't always popular and what is popular isn't always right.

Howard's early defense of Muhammad Ali's refusal of military induction on religious beliefs angered many patriotic Americans. Howard's stance on the controversy proved to be correct when the former heavyweight champion of the world was allowed to return to boxing while his conviction of draft evasion was overturned by the Supreme Court.

Cosell was so provocative and compelling; he was among the rare talent who increased TV ratings. He was Roone Arledge's idea. The head of ABC-Sports broke from network television's Anglo-Saxon ideal of broadcasters and featured a New York Jew on nationally televised sports events.

In 1970, ABC-TV acquired the rights to NFL football and invaded prime time on a weeknight. NFL Monday Night Football captured one-third of the audience and became an institution. Cosell was initially teamed with Don Meredith and Keith Jackson. Frank Gifford replaced Jackson the next year. "Suddenly," as Cosell liked to say, there was "chemistry" in the TV booth and the nation watched at home, at bars and restaurants which profited from the additional business. For 13 years, ABC blitzed the other networks on Monday nights, earning huge profits from eager advertisers.

Cosell eclipsed Gifford and Meredith in popularity. It could be countered that America's whimsy about Gifford and Meredith made three hours of Howard Cosell easier to take.

Howard Cosell—holding two of his favorite things—NYC 1972

Cosell charmed most everyone, while aggravating many, because he had a strong sense of right and wrong. His was a new melody. He was critical of the athletes, brutally honest with a sarcastic wit, delivered with an odd sound. He relished saying "Before me, the TV football analysts said 'the wide receiver ran a great route.' I say, the cornerback missed his assignment."

In an era of "positive-speak," Howard was the first who dared to be negative. After all, sports competition is about mistakes as well as successes. To his credit, Howard could back up his remarks with deep knowledge about the games and the personalities.

Ichabod Crane grew up to become a national television star. In 1975, ABC attempted to earn some more money on his celebrity. The network gave him a Saturday night variety show to host, a blatant rip-off of the departed Ed Sullivan Show that dominated Sunday nights for CBS. The program didn't work and quickly left ABC's lineup.

On November 23, 1970, Cosell slurred his words and became ill during halftime of a Monday Night football game on ABC. He puked on Don Meredith in the booth. The sportswriters, who detested Cosell, as much he loathed them, jumped on the speculation that Howard was drunk. He denied he was affected by martinis sent by the Eagles' owner, Leonard Tose. Cosell claimed he had an inner ear infection, "a virulent virus," that caused him to lose his balance and slur his speech. A few days later in New York, ABC Sports producer-director Joe Aceti asked him, "How did you contact this infection?" Cosell said he didn't know. Aceti wisecracked, "When you drank those martinis, you must have poured one in your ear."

Aceti directed all of the fights Cosell hosted on ABC-TV. He gave Howard the nickname "The Ding" because he invariably instructed Cosell "to go" after the sound of the bell that started a round.

In 1981, Aceti and I were on the same flight as Cosell from Los Angeles to Reno to cover the Sugar Ray Leonard-Bruce Finch fight. Above all else, Howard delighted in minimizing people in his company. This ugly trait was the obvious clue about his lifelong insecurity. His first words to me were, "Funny . . . last night . . . . I didn't spot you in New York at the 'Night of A Hundred Stars'. I just got off the Warner company jet. I rode out from New York with Billy Crystal." It wasn't yet ten in the morning and Cosell was dropping names like nutshells.

When we landed in Reno, we waited for our luggage at the carousel. Along came rock n' roll entertainer Little Richard, with his young son in tow. "HOWARD COSELLl!!!! MY MAIN MAN!!!!" Howard kept sucking on his thick cigar, staring at an exuberant and cheerful black man who had piercing eyes. Sensing some sort of celebrity, Howard turned to Aceti and me and spit a quick "Whoinafuckisdis?."

Aceti and I decided the "new Ed Sullivan" was on his own. Little Richard was all over Howard and he clutched his son to his side. As they conversed about the Leonard-Finch fight, it became obvious Howard didn't know he was talking with the self proclaimed "King of Rock N' Roll," who burst on the national scene as a recording artist as long ago as 1955.

So, Little Richard started to sing a medley of his song hits, right there, at the carousel, in the airport in Reno, Nevada.

"Howard . . . it's me!!!

Little Richard!!! . . . . Remember??? . . . . LUCILLE!!!!!!

Cosell feigned recognition and charmed him with some expertise about Ray Leonard. Howard chucked the boy under the chin and said, "See you at the fight." Still refusing to take the cigar out of his mouth, he waved goodbye and chortled "Good luck . . . . Richie." When they were out of range, he squeezed his cigar with his teeth and huffed to Aceti and me, "Whoinafuckwasdat!."

Cosell preened in his celebrity, especially when women recognized him. One morning at the airport in Atlanta, while Cosell, Aceti and I were waiting for a flight to New York, a beautiful young woman began a conversation with him mentioning that she was an aspiring actress. She said she was flying to West Palm Beach, Florida. Cosell boasted that if she came along with him to New York instead, he would make her a star. She went to the airline counter and changed her flight to New York. Cosell started to stammer and fidget and Aceti took great delight in reminding him that his wife, Emmy, would be picking him up at the airport. Cosell became exasperated and begged the woman to rethink her travel plans and send him her resume and picture, which she did.

I was Cosell's backup for his daily ABC-Radio network radio sportscasts and on boxing for ABC Sports. I learned more from him than any other person I encountered in broadcasting. While I had to type out my entire commentary, spending much time preparing it, Howard's immense ability to communicate extemporaneously was extraordinary. He carefully prepared his content but delivered it without notes. I marveled at his knowledge and story telling, especially on the radio. He was a master communicator. Each morning and evening, "Howard Cosell, Speaking of Sports" was broadcast on the ABC Radio Network. He did those two and a half minute sportscasts from his home. A few minutes before air, producer Peter Beilen would cue the engineer at the ABC control room to open Howard's microphone at home. Cosell would be asked, by Beilen, "Howard, are you ready?" And, the same answer, every morning and every night, came back, ". . . . I'm always ready." Using no script, Howard's two and a half minutes had a beginning, a middle and end, masterfully told to time. Cosell's radio sportscasts were a lesson in originality, content and adlibbing brilliance.

I learned how to call boxing matches at his elbow. Only important punches mattered, as he wove a tale about the contestants. He let the natural ebb and flow of the match-up take its course. He embroidered its natural drama. It was, after all, a fistfight and there is a point when one man imposes his will on the other. It is the blow-by-blow man's job to accurately describe what leads to the ultimate moment of truth in any fight.

Cosell's best advice was about attitude on the air. He said being clear and thorough wasn't enough. He advised me to take positions on issues and offer opinions. This makes the reporter memorable to the audience. He said this was his blueprint for success.

But, here was the rub. Despite his big-titted stardom and bravado, Howard was paper-thin insecure. He was a classic narcissist, grandiose, self-centered, overly-sensitive to criticism and unable to feel empathy for others. Cosell would spoil everyone's day by spewing venom about some "lower case" sports columnist, writing for a minor city newspaper, criticizing him in print that morning. Dick Young of the New York Daily News was his arch-rival. Young vilified Cosell because of the bitter fact that the star print reporter had been eclipsed by the star broadcaster. Young constantly wrote that television and "Howie the Shill" were ruining sports. Howard read everything about him. He had a catchall phrase for his enemies in the press box, "The dogs bark but the caravan continues on!"

Howard had vast mood swings. Colleagues could always tell when his contract option with ABC had been successfully renewed. He was gruff on windy days because of his hairpiece. He would ignore fellow workers, but when he engaged them in conversation, he would tease them about some triviality. Too many times, he bored his colleagues about his weekly card playing with ABC's Chairman of the Board, Leonard Goldenson.

Most of all, Howard relished his celebrity. He preened while filming an interview with famous athletes, insisting to the cameraman that it was framed in a two-shot. Howard lectured me on this subject, saying, "No news reporter can stand next to the President of the United States, but we can be shown next to the biggest stars in sports." Howard attached himself to winners, as if their success made him feel grander and more secure. He constantly sought admiration and it was immensely meaningful for him to engage in a social situation and dominate the conversation.

At an ABC Sports Christmas party, Cosell and his wife, Emmy, were having a cocktail with my wife, Bernadette, and me. At one point, Bernadette countered his strong opinions about sportswriters saying, "Everyone is entitled to their opinion." Like a high school English teacher, Howard admonished her, "My, dear everyone is entitled to 'His' or 'Her' own opinion." Emmy immediately dug an elbow to the ribs, hard enough for him to wince, and chastised him, "Howard, the point isn't about grammar."

Most people he encountered, including athletes, were glad to see him and were pleasant. Of course, there were exemptions, like one night in the crowded Mr. Laffs, Manhattan's meeting place for ballplayers, years before the term "sports bar." A young woman, we knew as a stewardess for American Airlines, who was so beautiful she was featured in her company's television commercials, called out his name. Cosell rose to shake her hand. She said aloud, "Mr. Cosell, I can't believe I'm meeting you. Back home in Ohio, my father, my brothers and I watch you on TV all the time." By now, Howard was beaming. She continued, ". . . . and we think you're the biggest asshole we ever saw." Everyone within earshot laughed riotously. Cosell had been ambushed and he was embarrassed. He couldn't retort in kind. He muttered to me, "Nobody likes a wise ass."

Howard's elephant-sized insecurity fueled his craving to dominate, so he could be contemptible. One early morning, I was waiting at a traffic light, just after pulling away from ABC Radio on Broadway. I had done my early morning network radio sportscast and I was headed back home, to Manhattan's East Side, in my light blue, dented and worn Volkswagen. A black stretch limousine pulled up alongside and the window slipped down. First, cigar smoke appeared. Then, Howard slouched forward and peered out. He was wearing sunglasses, his drooping magpie face marked by his big nose. In the early morning breeze, he fingered his ill-fitting toupee to make sure it was still there and there was spittle on his lower lip. He wisecracked, "Hey, Sal, when you get on Good Morning America, you'll get a chauffeured limo, too."

One mid-afternoon in 1974, Cosell popped into the sports office at WABC-TV Eyewitness News. He asked me a rhetorical question. "What would you do, if we switched bank accounts?" I said, "I assume you're a millionaire?" Howard gave me a knowing nod with raised eyebrows.

I said I would grab my coat, needing nothing in my desk, and I would go see the world. He was astonished, "WHY?"

I said there was so much to see and experience. If money was no longer an issue, then let's go to a life's party. Cosell asked me, "Don't you have things you want to say?" I said, "Sure, but what I say won't change a thing." We sportscasters are mere entertainers, as much minstrels as pro-athletes and the ever-popular 'student-athletes,' we report about."

I asked Howard why, in his 60s, he wasn't retired, "Sitting on a rock, in an exotic place, getting sun like an old turtle?" Howard intoned solemnly "Because I still have things to say." He lived another decade, about half in retirement.

Howard William Cohen, the son of a Polish immigrant and grandson of a rabbi, was born March 25, 1918 in Winston-Salem, North Carolina. Before his third birthday, the Cohen family moved to Brooklyn, New York. A fraternity brother of Howard's at New York University told me that he had the same caustic personality when he was 20 years old and considered the nerd of his fraternity house. Because he wasn't handsome, Howard drew attention to himself with his wit and humor. But, according to his old frat brother, there was a certain meanness.

Most of all, Howard was argumentative. Isn't that the core issue in sports?

Sports fans naturally argue with other sports fans. Until Cosell, sportscasters were "eunuchs or dramatists," devoid of opinion because their networks did not want to alienate any part of the audience or sponsors. Decades after being the fraternity house resident "ball-breaker" at New York University, Howard's bombastic demeanor was kinetic magic on television. His crankiness, his gawky looks and nasal, "New Yorkese" sound were exaggerated, as he clutched an ABC Sports stick microphone in his unsteady left hand. A TV Guide poll found that the audience considered him the most liked sportscaster, and at the same time, the most disliked sportscaster. He was perceived as wearing the white hat and the black hat. In gambling terms, Cosell hit the middle and prospered.

His pet expression was, "I tell it like it is." Legendary sports columnist Jimmy Cannon wrote, "Howard changed his name from Cohen to Cosell and wears a hair piece and he says he tells it like it is."

Beginning in 1976, Cosell hosted ABC's Battle of the Network Stars. The primetime program matched celebrities from the three major TV networks against each other in tugs-of-war, relay races and other picnic sports. The enthusiastic stars were entertaining while plugging their own shows. Cosell wisecracked and leered at actresses like Farrah Fawcett-Majors and Lynda Carter. The program was a ratings success, further enhancing Cosell's recognition factor with the country's TV watchers.

Despite the protestations of the print media, Cosell didn't claim to be bigger than the games he covered. He did claim to be the driving force on any of his telecasts. To the American public, Cosell and sports had become one in the same. Howard had become so well-known, his television network seriously considered him as an anchor for its Evening News and its 20/20 magazine program. But, the crossover was too risky, as was his flirtation with politics, a topic that tempted him. In 1976, this former attorney thought of running for the Senate, as a Democrat. He backed off citing expected undo pressure on his wife and two daughters. The New York seat was won by Patrick Moynihan who held it for a quarter century before Hillary Rodham Clinton.

Privately, Cosell could be unbearable. He had a familiar routine meant to disarm someone. "What are you doing wasting your career for an obscure and uncaring company? Why don't you test yourself in times of adversity? Go back to your superiors and tell them you're not taking their garbage anymore, you're quitting your job. Who cares if you have home mortgage payments to make and education bills to pay? You're too big for this hypocrisy."

When we first worked together, Howard started calling me "Little Sal." I told him to stop referring to me in the diminutive saying "There isn't anything diminutive about me . . . . Howie." He was suddenly respectful of my position and apologized awkwardly. Howard was so insecure he verbally attacked and embarrassed people when they met. For instance, he'd playfully slap a guy on the cheek while shaking his hand. It was his way of reducing the other person, making him or her feel diminutive. I know it wasn't comfortable for at least two men, Nat Asche, a radio executive and Stan Hochman, the renowned Philadelphia sports columnist.

I saw each of them, in return, slap Howard in the face.

Cosell especially detested former athletes who had a free pass to become broadcasters. His exception was O.J. Simpson, the former Heisman Trophy winner from Southern Cal and Hall of Famer with the NFL's Buffalo Bills. Simpson was hired like a car hood ornament by ABC Sports. As Cosell aligned himself with Muhammad Ali, he did the same with Simpson, coining the phrase, "Miami's got the oranges, but Buffalo's got the Juice."

Another favorite target, another reason to use the word "travesty" was what he termed "The deplorable transfer of professional franchises from city to city, an affront to fan loyalty."

Cosell repeatedly exclaimed that the best thing that ever happened in his life was Mary Edith "Emmy" Abrams falling in love with him. Emmy was a lifelong companion. They had two daughters, Jill and Hilary. He took Emmy along on his road trips and once said to me, "She is my life. If she goes first, I will go down the toilet." Emmy was lovely and bright and not reluctant to correct him, challenging him when he would say something especially negative about someone. No one was good enough for Cosell. He liked to say, "Isn't so-and-so pathetic?" Emmy would grimace and tweak him.

The day the Mets announced the trade for Willie Mays in 1973, we were lunching at a charity affair held at Leone's Restaurant. Knicks coach Red Holzman was at our table along with some ABC guys. I received a telephone call about the trade and I informed Howard I was leaving for Shea Stadium. Before everyone at the table, Howard lectured me about the importance of the story, as if I didn't realize the return to New York of the "Say Hey Kid" wasn't huge news. I left without saying anything and covered the developments for ABC. While editing the film for the early news, I telephoned Howard at home. Emmy told me he was showering and they had a dinner date at Duncan's at 7PM. I said I would be waiting at the East 53rd Street restaurant. When they arrived, I asked Emmy to go inside, while I had a private word with my idol.

On the sidewalk, I told Howard how disappointed I was in him. Yes, he was "the man" and I respected his work, but I would not be trampled again by him in public for his gratification. I went on and on and did some yelling. Howard began to tear and then he cried. He apologized and confessed he knew he had a problem. From that time on, Howard was nicer to me and didn't bully me anymore. In Cosell's 1974 memoir "Like It Is," published by Playboy Press, he paid me a compliment regarding an incident that cast false light on him. On January 24, 1974, Cosell taped a conversation with Muhammad Ali and Joe Frazier in ABC's New York studio to be included, two days later, in the first replay of their 1971 bout on home television. The first Ali-Frazier collision had been seen by only a fraction of the population on closed-circuit television. Frazier had to be talked into the taping by his manager Eddie Futch because Joe disliked Ali for demeaning him with public slurs.

During the taping, Ali said that Frazier was "ignorant." Frazier jumped to his feet and shouted at Ali, who grabbed his waist and they wrestled to the floor. After they were separated, Frazier stormed out. Dave Anderson of the New York Times and Will Grimsley of the Associated Press were among a handful of sportswriters who wrote that it was a spontaneous brawl. Other sportswriters, not in attendance, did not, and depicted Cosell as the instigator for a fraudulent TV moment. The next day, the New York State Athletic Commission held a hearing. Jim Dooley, the commission chairman announced that both fighters were fined $5,000. Kenneth Sherwood, one of the commissioners, made a statement, accusing Cosell of agitating the incident even though Sherwood wasn't at the taping and hadn't seen a videotape of it. Sherwood said Cosell always caused trouble for Ali in their interviews.

In "Like It is," Cosell wrote, "Then, Sal Marchiano, a sports reporter for WABC-TV in New York, went after Sherwood with both barrels. He demanded to know how Sherwood could have made the statement about me without seeing the tapes. He demanded to know what Sherwood knew about the relationship between Ali and me, and he pointed out that I had defended Ali against the very action taken by that commission when they stripped Muhammad of his title and his right to fight. All of this happened at noon on Friday January 25th. Sal went on local television that night and excoriated Sherwood with biting commentary."

The studio fight was broadcast the next day, as part of the replay of their first encounter. The following day, Sunday, January 27th at the weigh-in for the second Ali-Frazier bout, Sherwood announced that the fines would stand but, after viewing the videotape, he apologized to Cosell and ABC-TV for portraying the studio encounter erroneously. Sherwood made a public apology on ABC's Wide World of Sports telecast. I received personal telephone calls from Howard and our boss, Roone Arledge, thanking me for challenging Sherwood at the commission hearing.

Howard enraged Frank Gifford for calling him "wooden," not knowing his microphone at home was open and audio tape was recording while Mr. and Mrs. Cosell were having a breakfast conversation. During the day, the tape of Cosell's venom for Gifford was played by ABC Radio engineers for fellow workers. By the end of the day, Cosell heard about it and roared into the control room, threatening firings. But, the harm had been done. Gifford heard the tape, too.

Eventually, Howard lost Gifford's friendship when he drank too much at the 1977 World Series and yelled to a crowded hotel barroom that Frank and Dandy Don avoided him after Monday Night Football games because they wanted to go somewhere and smoke pot. After hearing about this, Gifford ignored Howard. They didn't speak for years. In 1995, when Howard was very ill and still grieving the death of Emmy five years earlier, the Giants' Hall of Famer relented. The classy Gifford paid a last visit to Howard at home. Whatever was discussed has been kept private by no. 16.

In his two books, "The things he had to say" were mostly putdowns of old targets. There was a sour reaction to his bitterness from his colleagues. The most celebrated sportscaster of his time was lonely in his last years. I remember seeing him at sports luncheons and dinners, as a solitary figure, mostly ignored by his peers. Ichabod Crane had come full cycle.

After she died in 1990, Howard became listless without his beloved Emmy. He continually muttered the sad lyrics of Irving Berlin's song "What'll I do." It was his auld lang syne.

"What'll I do? When you . . . are far away . . . and I am blue. What'll I do?"

Howard underwent cancer surgery in 1991 and died of a heart embolism at New York University Hospital for Joint Diseases in 1995, at age 77.

We never thought he would run out of air but broadcasting's biggest mouth was finally silenced.

While Howard was on his death bed, Hall of Fame sportscaster Curt Gowdy telephoned him. "Howard, this is the Cowboy . . . . I'm worried about you . . . how are you doing? Are you gonna get over this?"

After a stage pause, Howard droned, ". . . . Cowboy . . . . isn't . . . . Dan Dierdorf shit on Monday Night Football?"

ALI'S DECLINE

It was high noon in the blasting heat of the Nevada desert and I caught the vibe the moment I walked into the air-conditioned lobby of the Hilton Hotel in Las Vegas. The jingle jangle cacophony of the gambling casino's bells, chimes and gongs was the background noise for an eclectic assemblage of "Life on the Wild Side" on February 15, 1978.

There was extra noise at the gambling tables. "Superflys" were in town with their high-assed bimbos. There were cowboys in boots and buckles, semi-wise guys wearing pinkie rings from back east, young couples in black ties and gowns, and many Asians, Mexicans and Arabs.

That night, Muhammad Ali was defending his world heavyweight championship against 25 year old Leon Spinks, the U.S. Olympic light heavyweight gold medalist who was getting a title shot despite only seven professional fights.

Guys were hawking tickets because it wasn't a sellout. It figured to be easy for Ali and while there was a lack of suspense, the players in Vegas were partying early. The theme of Ali, himself an Olympic gold medalist, beating Spinks, as well as two other gold medalists, Floyd Patterson and George Foreman, had been ignored by the public. But, the common buzz was "Hey, 36 year old Ali is fighting at Hilton and he won't be around much longer."

I was on vacation with my wife and daughter in Palm Springs, California. I took a side trip because I couldn't stay away from the action. That morning, I flew to Las Vegas with my buddy Joe Acquafreda, a former New Yorker who had been the head of security at Madison Square Garden. He applied his skills and knowledge to running a very successful security business in Palm Springs. Because Joe was a familiar figure at the Garden at all the big fights and I reported on the major boxing events, including the first two between Ali and Joe Frazier, we were familiar to the several boxing characters in the lobby and coffee shop. We spent a couple of hours schmoozing with guys who were part of boxing's traveling circus.

Spinks' manager, Butch Lewis, was chirping about Leon, his Philly crew in agreement like a choir. Also, swarthy Lloyd Wells, an Ali aide de camp, laughing at Butch and teasing him, but keeping a wary eye in the lobby for anyone looking to buy a ticket. We encountered wise-cracking Richie Giachetti, Larry Holmes' trainer from Cleveland, enjoying a newfound business relationship with actor Sylvester Stallone who was intrigued with the notion of managing fighters and staging promotions. Gene Kilroy, Ali's business manager, could always be found in continuous coffee shop conversations. Kilroy knew everyone in the Las Vegas gaming industry. He had left a marketing job with Metro-Goldwyn-Mayer to work for Ali. I heard boxing gossip from Ali's savvy public relations guy, Harold Conrad. For this promotion, Conrad was helped by the affable Bobby Goodman who teamed with his father Murray, to handle all press problems. There were opinions from Bundini Brown, Ali's witch doctor/assistant trainer but none from the always silent trainer, Wali Muhammad, who was called "Youngblood." It was always pleasant to speak with Howard Bingham, Ali's personal photographer.

Ali's chief trainer, Angelo Dundee, who wasn't much of an influence before the event but extremely valuable during the fights, seemed to always be kibitzing with a sportswriter or two. Angie said a lot and joked a lot, but revealed little.

Over coffee shop food, the buzz was that Ali's promoter, Bob Arum, was using a defense against Spinks to dodge two of rival Don King's contenders, Larry Holmes and Ken Norton. Spinks was an easy target and not experienced enough to handle the champ who was a 10 to 1 favorite at Las Vegas sports books.

Spinks was nicknamed "Neon Leon" because he preferred the night lights and a wild lifestyle. He was a likeable kid with a wide grin and a warm and unassuming personality. But, he was too inexperienced and naïve to handle the sudden fame, the newfound wealth and the media attention. Years later, Spinks revealed he was doing crazy things, like drugs, because he hadn't sown his oats yet. Leon defiantly slept late, trained late and hit the streets late. He was lucky to survive the nightlife.

Ali didn't take Leon seriously and he didn't train hard enough. He was in his sixteenth year as a pro, coming off the three strenuous bouts with Joe Frazier and the upset of George Foreman in Zaire where he fooled the champion with his rope-a-dope technique that meant absorbing body shots.

Against the younger and eager Leon, Ali's staleness showed. He gave away the first six rounds to the clumsy and awkward Spinks who didn't stop punching despite his idolatry of Ali. The champion mounted a late rally, but his stamina was weak. Spinks was too quick and determined. While Leon couldn't knock out Ali, the champion didn't have the power to hurt Spinks. The bout went the full fifteen rounds. Judge Art Lurie had Ali by a point while his two colleagues voted properly for Spinks.

It was the first and only time; Ali lost his title in the ring. After the shocking outcome, it became apparent that Ali wasn't coming directly to a news conference. At the time, I worked for WABC-TV in New York. I knew the ABC News producer who waited with his crew, along with the others. We had worked together on some New York sports stories. I asked him if I could borrow the cameraman, light man and soundman to attempt to interview Ali in his suite at the Hilton. He knew I had a working experience with Ali, so he agreed.

I knocked on his door and when someone answered, I asked for Pat Patterson, Ali's head of security. The Chicago policeman took time off for Ali fights which I documented in a story about Ali's entourage, only months earlier. Patterson came to the door and without questioning me, allowed all of us to enter. It happened as if it was an automatic for me to interview Ali, in his private quarters, minutes after he was upset by Spinks.

Ali was still wearing his white terrycloth ring robe, boxing trunks and shoes and he was consoling his mother, saying, "Don't worry, it was my mistake. I'll win it back." The sitting room was filled with members of Ali's entourage which included family, friends and oddball characters, like Bundini Brown, his trainer/witchdoctor and his brother Rahman. ("I give Rahman fifty thousand dollars a year, that's not bad for drivin' and jivin'.") Some in the room muttered that Ali was robbed by the judges. He told them to put that notion aside. When Ali spotted me, I asked him for an interview and he motioned to sit beside him on the couch and my guys setup the shoot.

CBS had televised the bout but came up empty afterward. This is the way the exclusive interview played the next morning on ABC's Good Morning America and the next night on World News Tonight.

"I'm sitting in Muhammad Ali's hotel room . . . ."

"Boo, hoo, hoo, I was the champ and now I'm the tramp . . . ." (LAUGHTER)

. . . . minutes after he lost his title to Leon Spinks. Are you gonna come back and regain your title?

"Yes, for the third time. As for tonight, I don't wanna feel bad about it. I'll get another rematch. I'll recuperate, get the swollen eye down, get a little bit of rest, next time be more serious. Doing the rope-a-dope—giving away

4 or 5 rounds—making it hard to pick up. Hoping he'd tire, but he didn't tire. I've got to get back on my toes from beginning to end. Patterson was the first man to win back the title. I was the second man. But, NOBODY HAS COME BACK THREE TIMES. If I could make the best of this loss, take advantage, get in good shape, come back and win my title for a third time.

One more shot, if I can't do it, then I have to get out and really retire."

"So, you're not paying attention to those people who say maybe you should retire."

"No, it was close. I took no real punishment. We both fought good but he's better than I thought."

"Did you see something in him tonight that you saw of yourself years ago when you upset Liston?"

"Yeah, I felt like Liston probably felt. My reflexes weren't what they should be. Age is getting to me. I'm 11 or 12 years older than him. I could feel his youth and stamina in the later rounds. Next time, from the beginning, I just have to win the early rounds and just keep moving and don't play with him no more. Don't do the rope-a-dope."

"You don't feel sad tonight?"

"No, you lose. What's to be sad about? Some people lose their mothers, lose their fathers, lose their children, lose an arm, and lose a leg. You've got to live with defeat. This is a good test for me. I just lost. Other people lose. Naturally, I feel bad I lost. But, I don't have a give-up attitude. I got to keep going."

"That's a nice thing for you to say."

"Yeah, You may lose your job someday." (LAUGHTER)

"With Muhammad Ali, the FORMER world heavyweight champion, this is Sal Marchiano reporting from Las Vegas." "FORMER champ . . . . damn!"

Seven months later, September 15, 1978 in their rematch at the New Orleans Superdome Ali's prophecy came true. Neon Leon's party-time reign as world heavyweight champion was brief. Ali, as promised, was back in shape. He scored a 15-round unanimous decision, recapturing his crown a third time. It would be Ali's last victory.

Muhammad retired on June 27, 1979. Regrettably, he returned for a dismal encore in Las Vegas on October 2, 1980, losing badly to the younger and hard-hitting Holmes for the vacant world title. Ali wouldn't go down and Holmes, who idolized him, yelled for the mismatch to be stopped. Ali couldn't answer the bell for the 11th round, his only technical knockout defeat in 61 pro fights. For Holmes it was his 8th successful title defense.

Ali's boxing odyssey began in Louisville, Kentucky, and was spring boarded in Rome where he won a gold medal at the Olympics. For two decades, he was a blockbuster-at-the-box office, one-man road show, in exotic locales and venues, in Europe, the Far East and Africa. This pied piper's charisma drew big crowds and huge television audiences.

Ali's resolve in the ring was remarkable. For instance, the way he cleverly defeated George Foreman to regain his world heavyweight title. It was "The Rumble in the Jungle," October 30, 1974, in Kinshasa, Zaire. Foreman pounded Ali in the early rounds. Muhammad covered up and took many blows. It became known as his "Rope-A-Dope Trick." Foreman told me that in the fourth round, he unleashed the hardest right hand he ever landed. He caught Ali flush on the jaw. Foreman said Ali hooked his arms and drew George to the ropes to get a moment of rest. Foreman vividly remembers the clinch. "He sagged on the ropes, holding on, and I was looking over his left shoulder and whose face do I see at ringside? Joe Frazier! And Ali's shouting in my ear, 'yeah, you got me good, but you're not gonna knock me out.' This infuriated me."

Foreman let go with a barrage of punches, absorbed mostly by Ali's arms and shoulders as he protected his face with his gloves. Ali strength was tested to the maximum. Foreman became arm weary and a revived Ali scored a technical knockout in the 8th round to recapture his championship, yelling "That's all you got, George!"

With Muhammad Ali at Deer Lake PA 1975

Privately, Muhammad was puzzling because he could be sweet and sensitive to those around him, then cold and arrogant. He was always accommodating to the press. Once, at his training camp in Deer Lake, Pennsylvania, we had a debate about our respective religions. He was proud to be a practicing member of the Nation of Muslim. I maintained it was a Chicago-based storefront religion that borrowed some basic laws and traditions from Islam. When I said I was a devout Catholic, he questioned my logic about the Immaculate Conception. I said it was a matter of faith. He said it was the same for him with his beliefs, one of which was monogamy. I called him a hypocrite because many times he whispered to me, "Do you have any white girls for me in New York?"

Ali's farewell fight was in a squalid sandlot baseball stadium, with decaying wooden bleachers, in Nassau, the Bahamas, on December 11, 1981. His opponent was a rugged heavyweight named Trevor Berbick, a Jamaican who lived in Halifax, Nova Scotia. Ali fought his last ring battle in the Caribbean because he couldn't get licensed anywhere in the United States. I was there for ESPN and in a pre-fight essay; I described Ali as "A ghost ship, adrift." The promotion, "The Drama in the Bahamas," lost money and the feature bout was under-whelming.

Weighing a bloated 236 and a quarter lbs., Ali had no firepower and little stamina. It was like a pillow fight because Berbick couldn't hurt him either. The dull ten-rounder went to the 28-year old Berbick by unanimous decision. Ali's glorious, and often tumultuous, ring career was over. No longer stinging like a bee, he was the butterfly.

Three times he owned the most-prized championship in all of sports, winning 37 of his 61 fights by knockout, 19 by decision, losing four by decision. He was stopped by one opponent, Larry Holmes. Along the way, he shook up the American consciousness about the Vietnam conflict and it cost him three years of his prime in the ring. The sporting press labeled him a loudmouth trouble maker and most of white America considered him a black racist and draft dodger. But, he revived boxing, as arguably the most popular fighter ever.

His popularity transcended the ring. It was true: "They know me in the jungles." Muhammad Ali became one of our most popular athletes like Babe Ruth, Jack Dempsey, Joe Louis and Joe DiMaggio.

In the glory that was Rome, victorious warriors returned home in triumph, parading, while thousands cheered. Ali's curtain call was ignominious. The last bell that tolled for boxing's "greatest of all time" was a cowbell. That last sad night in the Bahamas, with inexorable time more of an opponent than

Berbick, no one had thought of getting a boxing bell for the event. There was no glory, no shouting, only a tiny "ding" to mark the end of a legend's fantastic journey.

Afterwards, in his dressing room, his hands sore, his face swollen and bruised, but not disfigured despite 21 years of professional fighting, the three-time champion who defeated the best fighters of his day, sighed and said to me, "Ain't I bad for 40?"

When Ali collaborated with Thomas Hauser on his autobiography, in 1991, the sportswriters and broadcasters he was familiar with were invited on a one day outing to his old training camp at Deer Lake. On the bus, Muhammad sat among us and dodged questions about his boxing days. He spoke humbly about his good works for humanity and his worldwide travels preaching the Muslim faith. Parkinson's Syndrome had taken hold of him, so his speech and movements were slow. But, Ali still had his wit. He told jokes softly and slowly snuck up on guys talking and snapped his fingers in their ears, still delighted to be the prankster. At the sprawling, mountain top camp, Ali posed for pictures alongside big boulders that bore his opponents' names like the "Liston Rock" and the "Patterson Rock." Some of his old entourage was there, including his trainer Wali Muhammad. It was a sentimental day.

On the way back to New York, I asked to be let off the bus after we passed through the Lincoln Tunnel so I could get a taxi to WNBC and air the videotape on the evening news. When the driver pulled the bus over to the curb for me, I passed Muhammad at the front window. Thirty years after he won a gold medal at the Rome Olympics and a little over a decade after his last fight, he remained one of the most recognizable men on earth. He was wearing eyeglasses and we embraced. I whispered in his ear, "You're still the greatest" and he softly slurred, "I used to be."

MARTY GLICKMAN'S REGRET

The last time I saw Marty Glickman was in August of 2000. He was days short of his 83rd birthday, grudgingly using a cane and taking my arm as we slowly walked across Second Avenue in Manhattan. The one-time "fastest schoolboy in America" and Olympic sprinter was ravaged by back pain. He said the motion he used out of the sprinter's crouch, all those years, had affected his spine. Three surgeries didn't lessen or remove the constant ache in his lower back. The deep pain didn't diminish his love of tennis, skiing and sailing, aboard his beloved "Frigate." Now, in his 80s, this former world class sprinter was shuffling his feet.

Over the second half of the century, when sports and broadcasting merged into a national mania, Marty was the distinctive voice of New York sports. At the beach in Brooklyn, in Bronx apartments, on Manhattan streets and in Staten Island homes or under the covers in Queens, the youth of New York grew up listening to him on the radio, describing Knicks and Giants games, later the Jets, harness racing and his first love, public high school sports.

At 5 feet, 9 inches and 160 lbs., Marty had been a standout athlete in football and track at James Madison High school in Brooklyn. He was the same at Syracuse University and became the first successful jock to become a broadcaster. His reputation was that of a confident but humble man, hard working and above all, honest. He was the guy on the radio who didn't pull any punches. Unlike the velvet-toned, eunuch-announcers of the time who avoided controversy, Marty sounded like one of us because he was one of us, from Flatbush. He played street games as a kid and married his high school sweetheart, Marjorie. They raised their family in New Rochelle. Calling games, hosting nightly sportscasts, and calling the harness races at Yonkers Raceway, he was always a man in a hurry.

On Thanksgiving holidays, he did the play-by-play of the Public Schools Athletic League football championship game. He was New York to the bone.

When I was a teenager in the '50s, I was a radio rat, hanging out at various stations like WNEW, WMGM, WINS and WBAI-FM. Marty caught my ear, before and after Dodgers broadcasts on WMGM, 1050 AM. Ward Wilson, Marty Glickman and Bert Lee hosted "Warm-up-Time" and "Sports Extra."

Ward Wilson, Marty Glickman and Bert Lee 1954

They were a "must listen" for sports fans. Wilson, Glickman and Lee were an argumentative trio, 40 years before all-sports-talk radio became a sensation. Wilson would yell "I'm wichya kid, I'm wichya" every time Carl Erskine ("Oiskin") pitched for the Dodgers. Marty was more knowledgeable than Ward and Lee and challenged their opinions. Their free form and lively broadcasts had a profound effect on my career choice. In the '50s, theirs was a new melody and it was orchestrated by Glickman. They didn't use listener telephone calls to lean on. Marty once told me that angry listeners would wait outside the WMGM offices and studio on Fifth Avenue to wait and argue on the sidewalk with Wilson, Glickman and Lee about sports issues.

While a sophomore at Fordham University, I was hired as a production assistant at WMGM. I worked nights, commuting between home to Rose Hill in the Bronx and the mid-Manhattan studios, managing to keep my grades up. When I felt too hectic, I only had to look at Marty, scurrying in and out on his way to another assignment. Yet, he found time to listen to audio tapes of my broadcasts on WFUV-FM, the Fordham radio station. In his no nonsense manner, Marty offered constructive criticism and guidance.

"Remember," he used to say, "You must be energetic and enthusiastic. You are the 'eyes' of the radio audience. Tell them what you see and feel." Marty was my mentor and a positive role model. I later found out, he did this for dozens of others.

Marty's protégé, Marv Albert, followed him on Knicks broadcasts and also became a Hall of Fame basketball play-by-play man. Marty's generous advice and teaching also helped the careers of Bob Costas, Dick Stockton, Spencer Ross, Bob Pappa, Mike Breen, Bruce Beck, Ian Eagle, and former athletes John Andariese, Dave Jennings and Bill Walton.

Marty was the most successful sportscaster in New York but he was overlooked for national assignments. For white bread Anglo-Saxon television executives, he was "too Jewish and too New York."

"The reason why I didn't change my name was because I could never look my father in the eyes again. Our name was Glickman not some phony name so I could get ahead." Marty's father, Harry, and his mother Molly had immigrated from Romania.

Sportscasters all over the country studied and copied his basketball broadcast techniques. He diligently described the swift moving action, as well as the lulls in games, with vibrant verbs and colorful adjectives. He was the first to document the "geography" of the basketball court so that the radio listener could imagine what was happening. While others were content to say who had the basketball, he said where the player was on the court, for example, "at the top of the key, along the baseline or cutting across the foul lane."

"My approach was to do the game, as I played the game. My inflections were the result of the way I felt as an athlete. For instance, you don't describe a guard walking and dribbling the basketball up-court in an excited way. This should be delivered in a calm cadence. When the ball is directed toward the basket, in an effort to score, that's when the voice is raised and excited."

Marty was calling Knicks and Giants games at age 32. His common sense approach figured out that athletes, like himself, were not robots or stick figures. They were individuals with different bodies, movements and attitudes. He painted word pictures about them.

"Remember, the game is the most important thing. Only your mother tunes in to listen to you. You are the spectator for the listening audience. You must paint word pictures using descriptive words like a high-arcing, one-handed shot in basketball, or a stumbling run in football."

His stamp is forever more on the method of calling a basketball game. He knew the game, he dedicated himself to accuracy and the broadcast wasn't about him. He invented terminology and phraseology. We grew familiar with "swish," his word for nothing-but-net and "Good . . . . like Nedicks." (And, didn't we all meet at Nedick's in front of the old Madison Square Garden before a game to have a hotdog and orange drink?) This was his radio call of a football field goal, ". . . the snap . . . placed down . . . kicked . . . . it's HIGH enough . . . . it's DEEP enough . . . . IT'S GOOD."

In the '60s, when the Giants telecasts were blacked out and the Giants played in three straight NFL championship games, Marty's radio play-by-play was the link for most fans. All over the city and the tri-state area, we heard Marty's precise and passionate voice, ". . . Giants break the huddle . . . . 1st and 10 at their own 37 'yaaard' line . . . . Ray Wietecha over the ball . . . . Del Shofner splits right and Aaron Thomas left . . . . Hugh McElhenny and Phil King are the setbacks . . . . tight end Joe Walton on the right side . . . Y.A. Tittle calling signals . . . . the snap . . . the handoff to King . . . . HE BUSTS OFF RIGHT TACKLE . . . . HIT AT THE LINE OF SCRIMMAGE . . . . KING KEEPS DRIVING!!!!!! . . . FOUR . . . FIVE . . . SIX 'YAAARDS . . . . BEFORE HE'S DRAGGED DOWN FROM BEHIND . . . . IT'LL BE SECOND AND FOUR AT THE GIANTS 43."

As good as Marty was doing football games, this man for all seasons wrote the textbook on how to call a basketball game. So, what happened in 1952 was astounding. The televised NBA game of the Week switched from the Dumont Network to NBC but Marty did not continue as the play-by-play anchor, despite his obvious outstanding broadcast abilities. Lindsay Nelson was hired and Marty was devastated because continued network television would have validated him as the voice of basketball. It took him years to find out why.

According to Marty, executive producer Perry Smith, an assistant to Tom Gallery, the head of NBC Sports, told him of the pivotal meeting held by NBA commissioner Maurice Podoloff. Smith heard Podoloff's reason for hiring someone other than Marty. The first NBA commissioner noted he himself was Jewish and so was his NBA Director of Publicity, Haskell Cohen. Smith told Marty that Podoloff said, "I don't want three Jews running the show." Fifty years later, many Jewish sportscasters work on national television. Back in 1952, the young man out of Brooklyn, by way of Syracuse University, didn't make an issue of his anti-Semitic rejection. He had experienced this before, on a world stage.

In the 1930s, Marty had been a standout New York City schoolboy athlete in track and football. But, there were no scholarships available to him. He needed a Jewish Fraternity, Sigma Alpha Mu, to sponsor him into Syracuse University. He majored in political science. Marty developed into a world-class sprinter and at 18, was a member of the 1936 U.S. Olympic team. It was no coincidence, he and another Jewish teammate, Sam Stoller, were excluded from the 400-meter final a day before the event at the Berlin Olympics. U.S. Olympic officials were influenced by host Adolph Hitler, whose belief in Aryan supremacy soiled those summer games. He refused to invite any non-German gold medal winner to his box for congratulations, including Jesse Owens who was the first American Olympian to win four gold medals in one day.

German Jews were already under oppression. The Berlin Games were two years before "The Night of Broken Glass," when the Nazis attacked Jews and confiscated their property. In three years, World War II would break out. During the opening ceremonies for Summer Games in Berlin, when the American contingent passed Hitler's stadium box, the American flag was not dipped as is traditional to the leader of the host country. Within days, Marty's Olympic experience was shattered by politics.

As we sat at lunch in a New York restaurant, 64 years later, Marty's eyes moistened while he quietly recalled the historic race in Berlin in 1936. The 18-year old Glickman had to watch from the stadium stands, among 120,000 others, knowing he wasn't competing because the U.S. Olympic Committee, headed by German sympathizer Avery Brundage, did not want to embarrass the Nazis.

"The U.S. relay team included Jesse Owens, who personally had won three gold medals, in the 100-meters, 200-meters and broad jump. Owens was the starter. He endeared himself to me forever when he pleaded with the coaches to start me instead because he had already won his gold medals. They refused. In the final, Owens led by three yards when he passed the baton to Ralph Metcalfe. When Foy Draper took the baton, he had a 10 yard lead. Frank Wykoff extended the lead and the U.S. won the event in 39.8 seconds, a world record that stood for 20 years. Holland was second but disqualified, followed by Italy and Germany at 41.2."

"I wasn't as fast as Owens or Metcalfe, but I could beat the others. I vowed I'd be an Olympic competitor in 1940. But, World War II got in the way. When the Olympics resumed in 1948, I was married with two children and not in proper shape. For the rest of our lives, Stoller and I had to accept the bitter fact that we qualified for the U.S. Olympic team and trained for the Summer Games in Berlin but were the only American athletes not allowed to compete by our own coaches. We were blatant victims of anti-Semitism."

In 1937, Marty scored two touchdowns in a Syracuse upset of Cornell.

A local haberdasher, "Jack Lord," was impressed by the story in the New York Times about Marty returning a punt for a touchdown. He hired Marty, the new local "celebrity," to host a weekly 15-minute radio program for $15.

"I stuttered and I stammered, so I took speech courses. I slowed down my speech. I walked the streets, talking to myself, describing everything I saw. I listened to Bill Stern and Ted Husing closely and studied their voices and speech patterns."

Marty graduated from Syracuse in 1939. The outstanding halfback played a season with the Jersey City Giants for $50 a game and led the American Association of Pro Football Teams in rushing. "Marge convinced me not to return for a second season, playing pro football, to fully commit myself to what I had started in broadcasting."

However, like many other American men, he had to take a timeout from his budding career. Marty saw action in the Pacific's Marshall Islands during World War II, as a Marine lieutenant.

Marty came home to call Knicks games for 21 years, the Giants for 23 seasons and the Jets for another 11. He also did college basketball play-by-play, hosted track meets and called harness races at Yonkers Raceway for 12 years. He especially liked broadcasting high school football and basketball games. Accuracy and emotion were his broadcasting hallmarks. He had been a successful athlete because he was intense. His passion for sports and reportorial integrity enabled him to be an outstanding radio broadcaster.

Giants' head coach Allie Sherman was a close friend of Marty. During Sherman's first training camp, Marty spent some days on the field getting familiar with the players. "After one practice," Sherman recalled, "Marty had three of my running backs down in sprinters' stances. He raced them over 40 yards and beat them. He must have been 45 or 46 at the time. I told him, 'if you do that again, I'll ban you. You're demoralizing my running backs.' He loved that."

Marty teamed with former player Al DeRogatis on Giants broadcasts. Coach Sherman allowed them to have knowledge of the Giants playbook and access at practice, so that they could understand his coaching philosophy and enhance their broadcasts. At key moments in games, when the Giants were on offense, Glickman and DeRogatis made several "anticipatory calls" that stunned listeners and caused exciting radio.

As Marty aged, he didn't lose his desire to compete athletically. Agent Peter Beilen remembers watching an intense tennis match at Kutsher's resort in the Catskill Mountains, in upstate New York in the '50s. Marty and the Boston Celtics' legendary coach Red Auerbach in yet another rowdy, insult-filled, match-up. Marty's language was just as salty as Red's, but he always called Auerbach "Arnold." It didn't matter who won that day. At the end, sweating and exhausted, they laughed and hugged each other.

Marty lived with the disappointment that despite his success in New York, he would not get national assignments. Ironically, years later, he was hired by HBO, NBC, MSG Network and Sportschannel to coach their young talent. In his '70s, at Syracuse University and Fordham University, Marty lectured and counseled students who wanted to become sportscasters. "It was a labor of love. I love the business. It was good to me. It gave me an opportunity to disseminate my experience of sports. If I didn't, my experience will have been lost. I can remember my first experience as a broadcaster. It was a night game up in Syracuse. I'll never forget it. It was 9:15. My first words ever spoken on the mike were 'good morning, ladies and gentlemen.' I know what it's like."

In the category "what goes around, comes around," like me 40 years ago, Marty coached my daughter Sam in the basic rudiments of sportscasting when she was beginning her on-the-air career. True to his high standards, Marty said to her, "I'm gonna tell you some things about your work your father won't."

With my daughter Sam and Marty Glickman NYC 1997

For 55 years, New York sports fans grew familiar with his enthusiastic staccato voice, his word pictures, his reportorial skills and honest personality. He was a broadcasting standard of excellence until his retirement in 1991. He was inducted into the Basketball Hall of Fame, the Sportscasters Hall of Fame and the New York Sports Hall of Fame. Marge and Marty were married for 61 years. They had four children, 2 girls and 2 boys. Marty and Marge enjoyed 10 grandchildren and 6 great-grandchildren.

In 1985, he returned to Berlin for a celebration of Owens. His visit to Olympic Stadium rekindled his anger about his exclusion from the 1936 Games. In 1998, the U.S. Olympic Committee presented Marty with a plaque in lieu of the gold medal he didn't help win in 1936.

After our last lunch, in 2000, as we stood in the lobby of his apartment building, my mentor since I was 17 years old said with a feeling of finality, "The Jewish thing was with me all my life." He said that with sadness and resignation that no matter what he accomplished publicly and privately the rest of his life, he couldn't change the fact that he was denied a chance at a gold medal in Berlin in 1936 because he was Jewish.

He passed away six months later, at age 83, on January 3, 2001. He didn't win his gold medal but he became one of the greatest sportscasters of all-time. Many of those he coached became successful behind the microphone. His legacy is evident on the airwaves. Marty Glickman was loved and admired by those who knew him. Such a mensch couldn't change his name.

VITAS AND JOHNNY MAC

It was close to midnight on Sunday night, September 9, 1979. I was driving across Central Park on the 65th Street transverse toward the East Side of Manhattan and I had to stop for a red light at Fifth Avenue. After a few moments, a canary yellow Rolls Royce pulled up alongside me. The license plate read "VITAS G." It was the familiar luxury car belonging to Vitas Gerulaitis and he was driving with John McEnroe alongside him in the front seat.

"What are you guys doing?" I shouted. Vitas, with a big grin, yelled back "We're bar-hopping."

I had to laugh in amazement. Earlier in the day, they were the two finalists in the men's final of the U.S. Open and hours later they're socializing at midnight. That spoke of their friendship and history. Two New Yorkers in the championship match had never happened before. It was also the first all-American men's final since 1953. Years later, McEnroe said to me, "It probably won't happen again, two kids from New York City in the championship match of the U.S. Open."

In the '70s, tennis enjoyed increased popularity and it became a booming business. Linked with sporting apparel and playing equipment, tennis revenue was at an all time high and the leading players earned record amounts of money. Champions became household names on the men's side, Bjorn Borg, Jimmy Connors, John McEnroe, and among the women, Billie Jean King, Chris Evert, and Martina Navratilova.

In the late summer of 1979, the two weeks of competition at the U.S. Open had come down to this: buddies faced each other across the net for the men's national championship. McEnroe was 20 years old and on the rise. Gerulaitis was 25 years old and ranked fourth in the world.

Both enjoyed competing in the spotlight, relying heavily on movement and strategy. Both were brash and talked tough. They reflected the attitude of the boisterous city and its tennis fans. Gerulaitis was slight but extremely quick afoot. His shoulder length, curly blond hair gave him the predatory look of a young lion. Vitas' tennis whites were skimpy and tight. The lean McEnroe was a deft shot-maker with 20-15 vision. He was a raucous tennis assassin who pecked at his scalp hair when he wasn't wearing an unlikely bandana on his head.

The match took place on the asphalt-based court at the National Tennis Center before a sellout crowd of 18,288, near the competitors' origins in the borough of Queens. The day before they had advanced passed their semifinal opponents in different ways to setup this unique final. The third-seeded McEnroe, a scrambling net-charger and shot-maker, had beaten defending champion Connors 6-3, 6-3 and 7-5. The year before, the moody McEnroe had lost to Connors in straight sets, so he was euphoric. It was Johnny Mac's third win over Connors that year and it was marked by his accurate first serves and dizzying volleys. Every year at the Open, the New York crowd adopted the feisty Connors as its favorite. What a switch! The homeboy McEnroe took the crowd out of the match, never giving Connors an opening. Jimbo's sore back didn't help as he committed 56 unforced errors, including 34 on his backhand.

In the other semifinal, Gerulaitis struggled against the hard-serving Roscoe Tanner. Behind two sets to love and a break in the third, Vitas rallied to overtake Tanner by winning the third set tiebreaker and the next two sets. The fifth-seeded Tanner was characteristically hitting bullets on his first serve. After futile attempts at muscling service returns, Gerulaitis was successful chipping low returns that made Tanner's first volleys awkward. For Vitas, it was a glorious rush to victory, 3-6, 2-6, 7-6 (7-5), 6-3, and 6-3. Vitas said the 3-hour marathon was "The most satisfying moment of my tennis career." He gushed, "Tomorrow is the biggest title I've ever had a chance to play for."

Vitas grew up in Brooklyn and Howard Beach, Queens, so he was speculating about the national championship along with hometown bragging rights. McEnroe grew up in Douglaston, Queens. Both had been schooled at the Port Washington Tennis Academy on Long Island by Harry Hopman, the legendary coach who trained the top Australian players in the '50s and '60s.

Hopman said of Vitas, "He's got as much natural ability as anybody." Gerulaitis' high school was Archbishop Malloy in Queens. McEnroe went to the Trinity School on the Upper West Side of Manhattan. Both were quick and relied on finesse and they were brash and quick-tongued. Vitas and John were far from shy, chiding court officials and providing the press with colorful quotes. At the time, Vitas had two pelts, his only Grand Slam singles title, the Australian Open in 1977, and the Italian Open the same year.

At the U.S. Open, Gerulaitis caught a break in the quarter-finals when Tanner stunned the world's current no. one, Borg, who Vitas simply could not match. They were extremely close friends and the Swede practiced on Vitas' court at his luxurious home in Kings Point, Long Island. I was back at WCBS-TV for my second tour of duty, and that week Vitas allowed me to come to his home with a videotape crew for exclusive interviews with him and Borg. They let me tape them practicing on Vitas' private court beside his sumptuous home overlooking Long Island Sound. For laughs, Vitas had a tee box built and he slammed golf ball after golf ball into the water. He'd say "Bjorn is a great guy, my great friend." Vitas was so friendly, he couldn't get an edge by "hating" an opponent. Most tournament weeks, Borg was his practice partner, but Gerulaitis couldn't understand why Bjorn would disappear during the second week at Wimbledon, for instance. It was the Swede's way of stating, "This is serious time." To that date, Borg had won all 13 of their matches.

Vitas wasn't successful either against McEnroe, losing their previous two matches that year and winning only once in four career matches. A couple of years earlier, when McEnroe was 18, he moved into Manhattan and tagged along with Vitas at night to the discos and clubs. I was a close friend of Richard Weisman and went to many of his fabulous parties in his U-N Plaza duplex apartment. That's where I met Vitas and we became pals. Weisman spoke for my loyalty and confidentiality and Vitas trusted me. He allowed me into his inner circle. Vitas was a big sports fan and rooted especially for the Yankees and Knicks. I was never as close with McEnroe because he was a shy kid whose only interest was to shadow Vitas.

I remember seeing John in mid-winter, during those boogie nights at the back of Vitas' entourage, wearing a long overcoat and black combat boots. He was quiet, sober and polite. The older and more street-smart and gregarious Vitas never had a problem attracting women and being the center of attention. It didn't take long for McEnroe to gain social confidence. Soon enough, John was hounded by photographers and gossiped about in newspaper columns. "Suddenly, I was viewed differently. I didn't expect the scrutiny. It seemed everyone was trying to invade my privacy." He shunned notoriety and he didn't automatically warm up to strangers the way Vitas did. McEnroe was extremely loyal to his former "midnight mentor."

The first prize for the U.S. Open's men's title was $39,000. Hardly an afterthought, but Gerulaitis and McEnroe were two street guys from New York competing for more than money. Because of my connection with WCBS-TV, I was able to get two seats in the CBS-Sports tower for myself and my daughter, Susan who was 12 years old. When the finalists were finished with their warm-ups and the crowd settled in, there was a feeling of heightened anticipation. The sport of tennis was enjoying a boom in public interest and participation. The national championship was at stake and it was a neighborhood scrap because the big guys, Borg and Connors, were out of it.

Gerulaitis' strength was his foot speed. He was crafty and imaginative but McEnroe's attack from the baseline and at the net was too powerful and he was superior in anticipating their volleys. Vitas managed only one break. There were no surprises and no major skirmishes with officials as McEnroe carved out a 7-5, 6-3, 6-3, convincing victory, making him the youngest men's champion in 31 years. After only 2-hours and 4-minutes, at match point, McEnroe flipped his wooden racquet. He had won his first major championship. In a nearby box reserved for family and friends of the finalists, John McEnroe Sr. hugged his wife, Kay and both were immediately congratulated by Vitas Gerulaitis Sr. Both families knew each other for years and it had been an emotional afternoon.

John Sr. was a Depression-born, first-generation New York Irishman who married Kay Tresham, a Long Island nurse, in 1947. Mr. McEnroe had done an overseas stint in the U.S. Air Force (John was the first-born in West Germany) and worked various jobs to put himself through Fordham Law School. He became a partner in a major New York law firm. John and Kay had three sons, John, Mark and Patrick. They were a middle class family on the edge of Long Island suburbia but very much urbane in their interests.

Vitas Sr. had taught his son the game with a certain expertise. He was a native of Lithuania and the champion of the Baltic States from 1936 to 1939. Because Lithuania was invaded by the Russians, he fled to a refugee camp in Germany and immigrated to the United States in 1949. He taught Vitas and his sister Ruta on the city's public courts. As a teenager, Vitas worked for the grounds crew on the tennis courts of Forest Hills.

Vitas was extremely disappointed when his first U.S. Open final ended rather quietly and convincingly. He always put a great pressure on himself when he played in New York. But, he wasn't sullen. From city playgrounds to debuting at Madison Square Garden, in an exhibition as a 14-year-old, to Grand Slam events, Vitas rose to no. 3 in the world. He won a fair share of championships, 27 in singles and 9 in doubles, including his only Grand Slam title, the Australian Open in 1977 and the Italian Open the same year. He earned millions in prize money and endorsements and proudly provided for his family rather well.

McEnroe replaced Borg as the world's no. 1 in 1981, 1983 and 1984.

Despite his reluctance to train and practice more, McEnroe was almost technically perfect. His backswing was short but accurate. His first serve was confident and he was a swordsman at the net. No one disguised the lob better and his drop shot was deadly. He understood that tennis is a game of pace and angles, always the angles. McEnroe was the catalyst on Stanford University's national championship team, winning the U.S. National Intercollegiate singles title as a freshman. He immediately turned professional in 1978. His aggressive serve and volley style put many people in the seats.

At 18, McEnroe became the youngest male semifinalist ever at Wimbledon and his life changed forever more. The Rolling Stones wanted to hang out with HIM backstage at their Wembley Stadium concert. The London tabloids were full of gossip about his personal life, nicknaming him "Superbrat." Successful musicians, actors and fashion models related to his solitary striving and wanted to be in his company. McEnroe was a pro athlete who yearned to be a rock star and, without really trying, he crossed over from sports to entertainment.

He had memorable rivalries with Connors, Ivan Lendl, Mats Wilander and Borg. In a three-year span from 1978 to 1981, he and Borg battled 14 times, splitting their matches. Their 1980 Wimbledon final was a classic, perhaps the greatest match ever played. In the fourth set tiebreak, McEnroe saved five match points and won it 18-16. McEnroe says, "It was the greatest moment of my tennis career." The stoic Swede rallied and took the 5th and deciding set 8-6. A year later, McEnroe stopped Borg's 5 year reign at Wimbledon. Though they were rivals at the highest level, there was deep mutual respect.

In a spectacular playing career that ended at age 33 and continued on the Seniors circuit, John won 77 singles titles, (third all-time behind Connors and Lendl), including 3 Wimbledon titles and 4 U.S. Open championships, along with 77 doubles titles. In Davis Cup competition, he was a passionate participant and helped the United States win 5 of them. Playing for patriotism and expenses, he helped capture a record 59 wins in singles and doubles.

McEnroe said, "It's an honor and responsibility to play Davis Cup. I don't understand anybody who won't do it."

McEnroe was inducted into the International Tennis Hall of Fame in Newport, Rhode Island, and was named captain of the Davis Cup team. McEnroe's early immaturity, while playing, obscured his sense of righteousness. Yes, he was obnoxious and insensitive with a tennis match in the balance. "My bad part overpowered me."

In 1981, he bellowed "You're the pits of the world" at a Wimbledon umpire. In 1983, in Paris, while losing a quarterfinal to Mats Wilander in the French Open, he screamed "I hate this country." But, while raging and dark, McEnroe hacked his way to his lofty and rightful place in tennis history, master of the touch, the spin and the lob, and always, always, the angles.

As time goes by, the bold tabloid headlines that vilified him as "Superbrat," "McEnrowdy," and "McNasty," become more vague, along with the reams of psychoanalytical inquiries as to why John didn't smile on the court and was a cry baby. There was more to him than a loudmouth brat who intimidated opponents and match officials and earned a lot of money. McEnroe was arguably the best combined singles and doubles competitor ever.

When he left the tennis tour, he was reportedly worth $150 million. McEnroe was curious about art and became seriously involved after Vitas suggested they visit the art galleries in Soho, in lower Manhattan. McEnroe soon invested more and more in art and eventually opened his own gallery. Vitas' passion for rock guitar also influenced McEnroe who had started playing guitar when he was 20. His idol was another left-handed player, Jimy Hendrix. McEnroe formed his own band and wrote music and lyrics.

John made an easy transition as a tennis commentator on television. He overcame the preconceived notion that his broadcasting style would reflect his tennis style, that is, loud and brash. On the contrary, McEnroe's analysis is delivered in a controlled, evenhanded and conversational manner. He is always interesting and doesn't let his "celebrity" interfere with his tennis reporting. He allows his hidden sense of humor to go public. For all his tantrums on the court against umpires and lines people, McEnroe evolved into a likeable personality. He, indeed, enjoyed a second life after tennis. He fathered three children with his first wife, actress Tatum O'Neal and two more children with his second wife, pop singer Patty Smyth.

After Vitas retired from big-time competition in 1983, he traveled the same path as McEnroe, dabbling in rock music and art while making strides as a tennis commentator for CBS and the USA network. His sister Ruta recalls that Vitas had loved music since childhood and fantasized "A second life as a rock star" Good friend Richard Weisman says Vitas became so proficient on the guitar, Eddie Van Halen remarked, "Vitas can play." Throughout his tennis playing career, he was close friends with Mick Jagger, David Bowie, Elton John, Mick Jones, the groups Foreigner and Pink Floyd, as well as Mark Chambers, the drummer for the Pretenders.

To trace Vitas' progress with the guitar, Weisman remembers an anecdote concerning their birthdays. Both were born on July 26th. When Vitas was still competing on the tennis tour, Weisman decided to give him a quality guitar for his birthday. Weisman telephoned Jagger. The most famous of the Rolling Stones said he would arrange everything at Manny's, the famed Manhattan musical instrument store. Weisman said Jagger arranged for the purchase of a Les Paul model. When Vitas unwrapped his birthday gift, his eyes bulged and he asked, "How did you know about this one? There's no way you know about this." Weisman said Jagger helped out.

Vitas was upset, saying, "You told Jagger I play guitar? I can hardly play a note." Vitas subsequently not only learned how to play but his technique and music were praised by some of the leading rock guitarists.

He traveled the world, playing top-flight tennis while partying with friends from Milan to Hong Kong. Vitas was an international sports star and hometown Manhattan was his special playpen. He was one of the few athletes who mixed with the rich and famous at Le Club, Regine's and Studio 54. In a room full of tycoons, politicians and A-list celebrities, the sports darlings were Vitas and Pele, the world-renowned soccer player.

Vitas and Glynna Fowler at Studio 54 1978

Vitas wasn't in the fast lane, he was in the supersonic lane. He was a VIP at Studio 54, on West 54th Street between Broadway and 8th Avenues. He was one of the famous faces of the time who helped "decorate" the world's most notorious disco. Vitas loved the exclusivity and the attention. In his familiar white polo shirt, jeans and sneakers, he seemed to be always grinning.

The Kid from Queens, ranked in tennis polls as high as third in the world, relished the glittering nights at "Studio" like New Years' Eve, Valentines' Day and owner Steve Rubell's birthday. Arriving in his canary yellow Rolls Royce which he parked in the adjacent public garage, Vitas sliced through the hundreds of hopefuls on the street, and swept past the red velvet rope diligently protected by Mark Benecke. The West 54th Street converted opera house/theater/TV studio was decorated differently for each party, stretching the limits of avant garde chic. There were always fresh flowers, ice statuary, and cages filled with exotic birds and semi-dressed young women. The lighting was theatrical and enhanced the look of the clothes, the makeup, the jewelry, the feathers and the sequins. A long and wide hallway led to the theater. The seats downstairs had been pulled out. A huge round bar was surrounded by an 11,000 square foot, strobe-lit dance floor with an 85-foot ceiling. There was a mezzanine area for lounges and rest rooms and the balcony seats were still intact. The legal capacity was for 2,000 customers.

The pounding disco music filled Vitas' ears as his eyes gazed on the long legged females in outrageous attire. He preferred to squire faces from fashion magazine covers whose slinky bodies in disco fashions almost took his breath away.

He once said to me, "If I could be as successful on the tennis court as I am off it, I would be number one."

"Disco-mania" was at its height and Vitas was among the rich and famous who partied at the greatest club of all time. On those sweaty boogie nights at "Studio," Vitas' long blonde hair became matted with shiny spangles that cascaded from the ceiling as he danced opposite the supermodel of the moment. The high overhead whirling lights illuminated the "fashionistas," the young turks from Wall Street, ingénues from the suburbs wrapped in skin tight spandex, scruffy downtown artists, the rock legends, the movie stars, the Euro trash and decadent foreign nobility, the Park Avenue elite, South American desperados, and the dancing gays who sniffed "poppers," also known as "Amy," (amyl-nitrite) to get higher and higher.

The parties at Studio 54 were synonymous with cocaine use. At that time, it was the drug of choice, shared in the dark balcony seats and in the coed toilets on the mezzanine. Vitas partied in the VIP basement rooms, as a prime guest, among Studio 54 owner Steve Rubell's inner circle. Vitas was at ease with writer Truman Capote, pop artist Andy Warhol, singer Liza Minelli, the Rolling Stones, Mick Jagger's wife, Bianca, Rod Stewart, Peter Frampton, Diana Ross, socialite Cornelia Guest, beer heiress Catherine Guinness, designers Diane Von Furstenberg, Calvin Klein and Halston, fashion illustrator Joe Eula and fashion photographer Francesco Scavullo. The party didn't begin till after midnight and the express train to nowhere continued till the break of dawn.

After Borg retired prematurely at age 25, one of his major endorsement deals was with the Bank of Sweden. He was contracted to play lucrative exhibitions for the bank all over the world. Vitas was invariably his opponent. It was a great way to mix business and pleasure. Sometimes, they couldn't control the latter. For instance, Borg had an exhibition with Gerulaitis scheduled for a Monday in Los Angeles. Vitas hosted a party, the previous Friday night at his Manhattan apartment on East End Avenue. When I left after midnight, it was getting wilder. Later on, I heard the party lasted non-stop through Saturday and Sunday. Bjorn and Vitas kept changing flight reservations to L.A., until they missed the last one on Sunday night. Borg had to rent a private jet plane to take them overnight to Los Angeles to keep the date. The cost was in the thousands.

Add that to the cost of drugs, hookers and fulltime limousines and it was a blockbuster of a dirty weekend.

I knew Vitas to be disappointed in himself for his transgressions but he conquered his addiction to cocaine, while others died or disappeared. Weisman recalls Vitas saying, "Richard you know what? I have a new addiction . . . . golf. I'm awake at 6 a.m. and I play three rounds a day. My handicap is 18 and I'm gonna get it down to 2."

Vitas never married but had a couple of serious relationships. Ruta says the supermodel Cheryl Tiegs and Vitas made a pact. They were very close and decided if neither married by age 40, they would unite and produce "a beautiful baby."

Vitas was one of the first professional athletes to form a foundation to benefit charities. In his case, it was New York City's underprivileged children. This was especially dear to his heart because he and Ruta had learned tennis on public courts and he wanted to give something back. With much passion, the kind and generous Vitas supervised clinics given by McEnroe, Borg, Chris Evert, Connors and Navratilova. Thousands of youngsters received free lessons and free racquets. Vitas hosted a glittering fundraiser every year. Warhol donated four portraits to raise money.

The last time I saw Vitas was at a Knicks playoff game in the spring of 1994. We sat together and he boasted about his good health and joked that the Knicks City Dancers probably thought he was too old for them.

Vitas' sense of charity led to his accidental death at age 40 in September of 1994. Sportscaster Jack Whitaker hosted a benefit dinner for the Long Island Cancer Society and Vitas had committed to a free clinic in the morning. The night before, Vitas was in Seattle and he played in an extremely competitive doubles exhibition that included Connors. Vitas flew all night from Seattle and when he arrived at home, he remarked to Ruta what great fun he had because the level of play in Seattle "was like the old days." Vitas was in much discomfort because of his chronic back pain, but he would not disappoint Jack by not showing up. Ruta gave her brother a muscle relaxer and a pillow for his lower back, as he drove to the eastern end of Long Island. Vitas gave the free clinic and was thankful he had time for a nap before the glamorous dinner.

He went to the Southampton home of friend Marty Raynes, a Manhattan real estate executive. He used the pool house bedroom. Because the weather that weekend was unusually cold and damp for late summer, Vitas did not open any windows and fell asleep. He never woke up. A subsequent investigation revealed that the gas heater for the pool, in the basement below the bedroom, had been installed incorrectly. The plastic pipe that was installed to vent the heater was too short to reach the outside of the small building. Instead, the deadly carbon monoxide reached Vitas through an air-conditioning vent.

The gas heater had been incorrectly installed five months earlier, in April. But, a Suffolk County jury found the 34-year-old pool mechanic, Bartholomew G. Torpey of Sag Harbor, who had never installed a gas-fueled heater before, not guilty of negligent homicide in the death of the tennis star. The Gerulaitis family has continued litigation against everyone concerned and to this date, it is not resolved.

The funeral in Oyster Bay, Long Island, was attended by more than 500 mourners, including McEnroe, Borg, Connors, as well as Billie Jean King, Tony Trabert, Jack Kramer and Bill Talbert. There were famous friends and boyhood buddies because Vitas had collected people for most of his forty years. Shocked and saddened, they shared their happy memories.

During our friendship, Vitas endeared himself to me on a March night in the mid-80s. I was staying with him in Florida, during a baseball spring training assignment. He had remembered my birthday and surprised me with a dinner party. His thoughtfulness will stay with me forever. I will also never forget his charity to a female friend of his who was newly pregnant, but seeking drugs at a Ft. Lauderdale disco. With a reminder about responsibility, he drove her home, stopping at a convenience store and buying her a bag full of groceries. I was in the car and witnessed his kindness.

At St. Dominic's Church in Oyster Bay, teary Ruta bravely gave the eulogy and revealed she put her brother's favorite five-iron golf club in his coffin. Throughout the grieving there was the common phrase, "everyone loved Vitas." In tennis, his greatness was unfulfilled, but in his shortened life, he had touched many people in loving ways. Ultimately, that was his greatest success.

The words of good friend, Chris Evert, haunt us to this day, "Poor Vitas . . . he never went into his second life."

McEnroe told Sports Illustrated he wrote a ballad in tribute to Gerulaitis: "I remember you when I was just a kid. I looked up to you and the things you did. You showed me places I'd never ever seen. The world took notice of two kids from Queens."

STEW ZOO

STEW ZOO

It was a chance meeting for Phil Linz, who played shortstop for the New York Yankees in 1964, when he stumbled onto a "sorority house" that could satisfy most men on Manhattan's Upper East Side. He met a flashy looking stewardess named Judy in the St. Moritz Hotel lobby while waiting for Mickey Mantle to come down from his suite. The Yankees were leaving for a road trip and Linz asked for her telephone number. She gave it to him and mentioned she lived at 435 East 65th Street. When Linz returned to New York, he dated Judy for the first time. She complained that her high rise apartment house didn't have enough men. Linz was astounded that 435 East 65th Street contained about 350 single women and only about 50 men. The building was nicknamed "Stew Zoo."

"I was rooming with Tracey Stallard who pitched for the Mets in a hotel on the West Side. I told Tracey, we're moving. A week later, we rented a furnished two-bedroom, two-bath apartment in 435 East 65th Street. With daily maid service, it was only $287 a month. (The Yankees paid Linz $14,500 a season) And, the switchboard, connecting every apartment, was a bonus. We'd tell the switchboard operator that there was a party in 7-A and a half-hour later our apartment was packed with women. We were having at least two parties a week and apartment 7-A in "Stew Zoo," was like a nightclub in a sorority house."

Because of a major shift in the real estate business in the mid-'60s, mid-Manhattan's Upper East Side from the 30s to the 90s changed because of the influx young women who rented apartments. Women were demanding equality at work and in the bedroom and that caused a sociological shift in the New York culture. "The Swinging Sixties" known for drugs, sex and rock n' roll gained momentum, "full-tilt boogie," and in the social swirl and in the piles of horny hogs and heffers were some pretty big name athletes.

The families of the immigrants, mostly Irish, were leaving as tenements were torn down and the avenues near the East River re-gentrified. The new high-rise apartment buildings were affordable for secretaries, school teachers, nurses, models and the legions of airlines stewardesses who worked out of the area's three main airports, LaGuardia and JFK in Queens and Newark Airport in New Jersey.

To become an airline attendant, a woman had to be younger than 32, fit and pretty. She had to be single and childless, weigh no more than 130 lbs. and stand no less than five feet, two inches. Her facial makeup had to be subdued, reflecting the classy elegance of the airline. She was a glorified waitress in a costume that was a tease for the traveling salesmen, but not threatening to female customers of all sizes who envied the look. The typical airlines uniform was a white blouse and skirt suit with high heels, stockings, a girdle underneath, and white gloves. Hair had to be cut above the shoulder. The ideal was a close-cropped hairdo, on which a company cap or pill box could be pinned. The girls may have been walking advertisements, but they felt a certain prestige. Many a prom queen and local Miss "something-or-other" settled for being a "skygirl," topped with a corporate tiara. Airlines were like modeling agencies and used their stewardesses in television commercials and print advertisements.

The women shared rentals to save expenses, as many as five and six to an apartment. They socialized together because they were, invariably, from other parts of the country and lonely in the country's biggest city. They were earning about $125 a week and split the rent, so they had disposable income. Free from the shackles of Mom and Pop back home, happily lost in the anonymity of New York and its endless possibilities, the younger sisters of "Holly Golightly" were searching for Truman Capote's "cocktails and laughter" version of New York. They wanted to party.

Linz recalls, "Some women in our building told Tracey and me that their favorite bar was one block away on First Avenue, Sullivan's between 66th and 67th Street. Until then, unescorted women weren't welcome to drink alone at the bar of a New York establishment unless they were prostitutes. But, owner Barney Sullivan changed that for his neighborhood female clientele. At Sullivan's, unescorted women were welcome and so many females made it their hangout, word spread and the guys showed up and every night was like December 31st."

The women were young and wholesome, away from home and family restrictions and they were sexually aggressive like guys. The whole area was filled with young single people who had come to New York from all over the country and the world. They enjoyed themselves to the hilt and there was no longer a taboo about a one-night stand.

In the postwar years, there had been a gradual metamorphosis for American women, from the aproned housewives of their mothers' generation to independent career-minded and sexually emancipated singles. Many had read Betty Friedan's best selling 1963 book "The Feminine Mystique." The seminal study of feminine frustrations had feuled the women's liberation movement causing so much social change in American life that it was considered feminism's second wave following the suffrage campaigns at the turn of the century. Marriage and motherhood and all the daily menial tasks, could wait while these young women celebrated their femininity with several male partners and no legal commitments.

Because of the sexual revolution, relationships between women and men changed more than ever before and one of the first signs occurred in the bars of New York's East Side. The scientific development of the birth control pill and its approval by the Federal Food and Drug Administration emancipated young women from their fears of pre-marital pregnancy and that begat promiscuity. Young American women wanted more rights and more sexual partners. There had to be mating grounds and the phenomenon of singles bars began in New York and spread to other major urban centers across the country and soon enough everywhere. The so-called "Baby Boomers," children born after World War II, were now legally free to drink alcohol, free to "rock on." The arrival of the Beatles' lyrical and memorable music, followed by the rhythm and blues decadency of the Rolling Stones, changed popular music for more cultural impact. Their lyrics contributed to the notion of an alternate lifestyle. Arm-in-arm or "touch dancing" became a thing of the past. Now, men and women stood opposite each other and shook their torsos. There were no formal dance steps or routines and the stationary shaking was called the "boogaloo."

The psychedelic decade of the '60s was a time for experimenting with mind altering drugs and for relatively safe sex. The drug of choice was marijuana and the AIDS virus didn't exist, at least not in the United States. Professional athletes weren't millionaires yet and weren't targets of litigation. The "paparazzi," photographers and gossip columnists, weren't waiting outside the bars and taverns that dotted First, Second, Third and Lexington avenues. The guys followed the gals as the juke boxes blared the Rolling Stones lyric, ". . . let's spend the night together. Now, I need you more than ever." The comedy motion picture about wife-swapping, titled "Bob and Carol, Ted and Alice," was the rage. The June-Moon-Spoon notion of romance at the soda fountain was over. Single women, as well as single men, could hang out in a bar. Not-so-coincidentally, their hemlines rose from below-the-knee to mid-knee to miniskirts to higher mid-thigh "maxies." Men and women wore their hair longer and shaped full and the style was called "the shag." Both sexes dressed flamboyantly in blue jeans, leather and beads. Guys let their sideburns grow larger to Brillo pad size called "muttonchops."

While the subject of race relations in America was a tinderbox, the collapse of American innocence was also evidenced by the antiwar movement. The protesters to the war in Vietnam and Cambodia reminded the rest of us that America was stuck in the quagmire of a losing conflict and the only solution was withdrawal. We were divided, either "Peaceniks" or "Hawks." Although the conflict on the other side of the world was not threatening to our shores, the Vietnam conflict was a military and political disaster. There were massive demonstrations in the United States to protest Vietnam War policies and troop withdrawls began. Young people, who were born after the Depression and after World War II, wanted to be distracted from the American and enemy body counts on the evening TV newscasts.

The popular songs of the time, "The Age of Aquarius," "Good Morning, Starshine," and "Let the Sun Shine In," were from the musical score of "Hair," the first rock n' roll musical on Broadway. It opened in 1968, focusing on the loves and antics of a tribe of "hippies" on the night before one of them is to be inducted into the Army and shipped to Vietnam. "Hair" reflected growing concerns about the unpopular war and the show ran 1, 750 performances. Young people who opposed what America represented wanted to be distracted and they partied amongst themselves.

The conservative law abiding age of "Ike" in the '50s became a distant memory when Dwight David Eisenhower, the victorious American general and beloved 34th president of the United States passed away in 1969 at age 79.

MR. LAFFS

Phil Linz's nickname in the major leagues was "Supersub" and he enjoyed New York notoriety. Certainly not for his 11 career home runs over 7 years with the Yankees, Mets and Phillies. It was about "The Harmonica Incident." In 1962, Linz became the Yankees backup shortstop to Tom Tresh while Tony Kubek was on military duty. In 1964, after a loss in Chicago that worsened the Yankees slump, first-year manager Yogi Berra didn't appreciate Linz giving himself a harmonica lesson on the back of the team bus heading for the airport. Yogi yelled to knock it off. Linz asked Mickey Mantle, "What did he say?" Mantle answered, "He said to play it louder" which Linz did. Berra was so incensed, the normally affable legendary catcher got up, stormed to the back of the bus and swiped the harmonica out of Linz' mouth in front of the team's beat reporters. For weeks, the tabloids blared about Berra's rare temper tantrum and Linz became a household Yankee name. The team played better and by the end of the schedule they were the American League champions and played the St. Louis Cardinals in the 1964 World Series. Linz hit two home runs, the second in the 7th game loss. The popular Berra was fired and replaced by Johnny Keane. Linz said, "Yogi never held it against me, but part of that season was defined by the "Harmonica Incident."

To cash in on the new wave of women on Manhattan's East Side, Linz decided to open a bar of his own. His partners were Bob Anderson, a former running back with the Giants and an All-American at West Point, and Sid Freedman, the superintendent at 435 East 65th Street, who knew about leases and licenses. They found a store for rent at 1189 First Avenue between 64th and 65th Street, on the West Side of the Street next door to the York Theater, a block south of Sullivan's.

Linz remembers, "Sid found the location, negotiated the lease and did the paper work. We got a 10-year lease for $800 a month with no cost of living increases. It was a bargain. We called it Mr. Laffs. We opened early December of 1965. Because of advance publicity, we were a hit from opening night. Dick Young, the Daily News sports columnist, wrote about our venture and Bill Gallo illustrated a cartoon. Howard Cosell came in with a film crew and interviewed me on a typical busy night. Bob and I invited a lot of athletes who, in turn, attracted the women. Tucker Fredrickson of the Giants lived across the street and he came in, so did Rod Gilbert and Bob Nevin of the Rangers who lived above Mr. Laffs, in the Buxley, at 360 East 65th Street. The Sporting News published a full-page article about Mr. Laffs. Visiting athletes, as well as the local guys, came in to say hello to Bob and me, but they were really there for the girls. We had a legal capacity of 180 people but most nights we had about 300 in there at the same time. We didn't have any off-nights. We got away with that as long as we put a hundred dollars in the Fire Inspector's hat when he came around. It was understood if we didn't bribe him, fire engines would pull up Friday night and we would be ordered to evacuate."

Mr. Laffs opened at 5pm everyday of the week and closed at 4 am. Entering, there was a large square room with the bar on the left. Three quarters down the space, a low wrought-iron fence separated the standing drinkers from people at a dozen tables covered in red and white checkered linen. There were framed drawings of clowns on the crimson walls and it was dimly lit. There were no waitresses, only male waiters and bartenders, most of them Scots, led by manager Duncan MacCallum. Little John Henderson was an impish, wisecracking waiter with a gambling problem. His partner, "Bobby Lightning," earned his nickname because he was so slow. They had to empty a lot of ash trays. It seemed everyone smoked cigarettes, becoming addicted and toxic and kidding themselves with filter tips.

Larry McTague worked the front door with a couple of beefy bouncers. He was a stern looking, but affable Irishman, whose real job was as account executive at the financial brokerage firm Bear Stearns. So, he had a lot of contacts in the financial district of Wall Street. Larry boasts, "I had telephone numbers for at least 1,500 stewardesses. I knew their scheduling chiefs at the airports. We handed out special cards with a picture of an airplane. Whoever possessed these cards didn't have to wait on line outside and they paid only half price for drinks. Rockettes, who danced at Radio City Music Hall, also didn't have to wait on line. They mixed with the local professional athletes and the visiting teams that used to socialize together. A dozen guys from the same pro team would come to Mr. Laffs and party. Many people came in to stare at the athletes and the pretty women."

McTague continues, "I didn't let in drunks. We had few fights because we were quick to stop arguments and we threw the guys out. The girls felt safe. To keep out the riff raff, we insisted on suits or sportsjackets for the men. Many women brought in their visiting parents and we would buy them champagne and assure their parents their daughters were safe at Mr. Laffs. On the holidays of Thanksgiving and Christmas, we had parties for our steady customers. Many were away from home and they found the family atmosphere those nights comforting."

After games, visiting players made Mr. Laffs their destination. McTague says, "Teams back then had curfews, generally and hour and a half or two hours after night games. The baseball players, basketball players and hockey players would come in and leave to make bed check back at the hotel. Then, they would sneak out and return to Mr. Laffs and stay till closing at 4 AM. They could do this because they could sleep late. So, could the stewardesses who weren't scheduled and the Rockettes who didn't have to dance till one in the afternoon, unless it was during the pre-Christmas period when they had morning shows at Radio City Music Hall."

A liquor drink at Mr. Laffs cost $1, but only fifty cents to women. Draft beer was 75 cents. A hamburger with French fries was a $1.25. The most expensive item on the menu was shell steak for $4.50. Checking a coat was only 25 cents. Linz claims Mr. Laffs sold scotch 10 times to one over vodka. Wine wasn't overly popular yet because the young generation considered it their parent's drink of choice. The ratio was 80% liquor to 20% food. Mr. Laffs in its heyday was grossing $15,000 a week, amazing for such a small space.

In 1966, Warner Leroy purchased the York Theater, on the Northwest corner of First Avenue and 64th Street and built a jewel of a restaurant and bar named Maxwell's Plum. Instead of hurting Mr. Laffs next door, the spillover from the popular Maxwell's Plum went to Mr. Laffs. Tittle Tattle, adjacent to Mr. Laffs on the North side, did a booming business. A block south, the original Friday's, was prospering. A block north of Mr. Laffs, Sullivan's was still roaring. The three block area on First Avenue, at night, looked like the French Quarter in New Orleans during Mardi Gras with crowded sidewalks and customers packing bars and restaurants.

Friday's, on the corner of First Avenue and East 63rd Street was originally The Good Tavern, a dingy beer joint. Alan Stillman, an unmarried perfume salesman, bought it with $5,000 borrowed from his mother, figuring it would be an easy way to meet the stewardesses in the neighborhood. With an eye toward attracting young career people, he renamed it TGIF, Thank God It's Friday. He spent $15,000 converting the bar, adding bright red-and-white striped awnings, red-and-white checkered table cloths, Tiffany-style lamps and nostalgic, old-fashioned saloon décor. The menu was simple featuring huge hamburgers and roasted chicken. He hired young attractive waitresses and they wore red and white shirts with tight black skirts. Only young and handsome bartenders need apply and they wore white shirts with a black tie and tight jeans. Steve Hanson, who later became a New York restaurant mogul, started at TGIF. So did Sharon Pearson who later became an owner of a national restaurant chain.

The cheery background at TGIF was conducive to breezy socializing while having a hamburger and a beer. Plain corner bars paled in comparison to Friday's, as it became known. Within days of opening, police barricades were needed to handle the crowded sidewalk. Stillman claimed his Friday's earned a million dollars in its first year of operation. In the ensuing years, Stillman franchised that red-and-white concept into a chain of about 500 restaurants, nationally and overseas, including Russia. In 1972, he sold the business. By 1997, the worldwide chain of Friday's reached one billion dollars in sales.

Yankees at Mr. Laffs with newly signed contracts, January, 1966. Top left to right : Horace Clark and Joe Pepitone. Bottom row left to right: Jim Bouton, Jack Cullen, Al Downing, and Phil Linz.

Linz remembers about Mr. Laffs, "Bob Anderson and I made sure to remember everyone's name. It was big thrill to be part of it. I was living like Rick in the movie Casablanca. It was a fantasy world, one big party. I moved to the Buxley upstairs and my apartment was known as 'Club 21-C'. If a ballplayer friend of mine met a girl and they wanted some privacy, I let them use 21-C. They could slip through the backdoor of Mr. Laffs into the service hallway of the Buxley and take the elevator without anyone seeing them. 21-C was also our after-hours club. Any given time, there would be 15 to 30 people drinking and dancing, or whatever, until the sun came up. I don't ever recall a complaint from our neighbors in the building because we were on the next to top floor, so the noise wasn't much. People were more tolerant then."

At the height of Mr. Laffs run, within 17 months, 3 first-time world championships were won by New York teams. In January of 1969, the Jets upset the Baltimore Colts in Super Bowl III. The following October, the Mets stunned the Baltimore Orioles in the World Series. In May of 1970, the Knicks shocked the Los Angeles Lakers for their first NBA crown. New Yorkers were abuzz with sports. Athletic heroes emerged and, unlike now, they were highly visible in restaurants and bars. Add the two world heavyweight championship fights between Muhammad Ali and Joe Frazier at Madison Square Garden and New York was the sports capital of the nation.

I was a sportscaster for WCBS-TV and I hung out at Mr. Laffs and met many athletes. After socializing with them the night before, I didn't have to introduce myself around the batting cage or at the arena the next day. Making lasting friendships, I developed some news scoops at Mr. Laffs, the original sports bar in New York. It became little Cooperstown, the Hall of Fame of Jocks and a destination for the jock sniffers who loved them. The bigtime sportscasters who made pit stops at Mr. Laffs included Frank Gifford, Kyle Rote, Pat Summerall, Howard Cosell, Jack Whitaker and Don Criqui.

Mr. Laffs Regulars: Top Row Left to Right: Tom O'Neill, Don Criqui, Lynn Bradley, Jack Dolph, Middle Row: Bill Mathis, Greg Herbert, Bob Stenner, Lance Rentzel. Bottom Row: Me and Fred Dryer

For those of us who were married before the sexual revolution of the mid to late '60s, frequency at Mr. Laffs posed a problem. Sexually, the culture changed the deck on us because emancipated women were simply easier to bed. At least I had a semi-excuse for business reasons to hang out at Mr. Laffs. But, there were too many women, too pretty for the room and married guys tested their own self-discipline. Any young woman who got involved with a married man was playing the fool. Many a mistress was told at the end of a baseball or football season, "I told you I would go home to my wife."

Former Cowboys quarterback Don Meredith had become a television personality on ABC's Monday Night Football. When breaking up was a hard thing to do, he was a victim of a prankster. Successful sports entrepreneur Ken George was a Mr. Laffs regular and very funny at the expense of others.

Meredith was separated from his wife Susan and traveled to New York for distraction. George thumbed through his little black book of female telephone numbers and arranged for three blind dates for Dandy Don, on the same day, one for lunch, one for late afternoon cocktails and one for dinner. All three were named Susan.

O'NEILL AND HIS BOYS AND GIRLS

Linz hired Tommy O'Neill to manage Mr. Laffs two nights a week from 1968 to 1970. Called O'Neill by everyone, he was an associate producer at CBS Sports and also lived upstairs in the Buxley. He was a blue-eyed, very handsome Irishman from the New Jersey shore who smiled more than anyone I knew. His hiring was a brilliant idea because O'Neill knew athletes, coaches, managers, team owners, publicity men, horse owners, jockeys, race car drivers, tennis champs, legendary golfers, TV executives, heiresses, beauty queens, crooners of tunes, card-sharks, crapshooters, scamps, vamps and various harlots, vagabonds,gypsies and spinners one meets on the road. Wherever O'Neill traveled for CBS Sports and whomever he encountered, including stewardesses from all airlines, he suggested they drop by Mr. Laffs when they traveled to New York.

O'Neill drew women like bees to honey and they accepted his flirting along with his generosity. Although he was polite and endearing to all, he was allowed a quirk. When O'Neill drank too much vodka, he liked to drop his pants in public and moon everyone. Fifteen years before actor Tom Cruise danced in his underwear in "Risky Business," O'Neill jumped atop the bar at Mr. Laffs and danced in his athletic supporter. At a crowded Memorial Day party in his hometown of Deal, New Jersey, he streaked around the outside of a house in the nude. At a Halloween Costume party, he appeared at the door nude, wearing a bowtie and a ribbon tied around his love stick.

O'Neill had personal telephone numbers for dozens of athletes. He recalls, "Phil and Bob were supportive and they looked the other way when I picked up tabs for big name athletes and especially pretty girls. Our male clientele included not only pro athletes, from all over the country, but everyone involved in their sport. Not only did the bachelor athletes live on the East Side, but many married—guys, who didn't want to move their families to New York, shared apartments. It was common to see Tug McGraw, Art Shamsky. Tommie

Agee, Gary Gentry, Don Cardwell and Kenny Boswell of the Mets in Mr. Laffs along with Yankees like Mickey Mantle, Billy Martin, Joe Pepitone, Gene Michael, Bobby Murcer, Thurman Munson, Stan Bahnsen, Mel Stottlemyre and Sparky Lyle. Also, Tucker Fredrickson, Fred Dryer, Bill Swain, Ernie Koy and Bobby Duhon of the Giants, and Jets John Dockery, Billy Mathis, Gerry Philbin, Pete Lammons and Joe Namath before he opened his own bar, Bachelor's III. Dave DeBusschere. Phil Jackson and Bill Bradley of the Knicks were regulars and their teammate, the flamboyantly dressed Walt Frazier, made Mr. Laffs a stop on his nightly rounds, double-parking his Rolls Royce on First Avenue."

"If the Chicago Bears were in town, Mike Ditka and Dick Butkus showed up. Paul Hornung of the Packers and Craig Morton of the Dallas Cowboys were regular visitors. Others included Johnny Unitas, Tom Matte, Alex Hawkins and general manager Don Klosterman of the Colts, Sonny Jurgensen and Billy Kilmer of the Redskins, Fran Tarkenton and general manager Jim Finks of the Vikings, Rusty Staub of the Houston Astros, Jim Fregosi of the Angels, Denny McLain of the Tigers, Richie Allen of the Phillies, Bob Allison of the Twins, Phil Niekro of the Braves, Don Drysdale of the Dodgers, Tony Conigliaro and Carl Yazstremski of the Red Sox, Ken Harrelson of the White Sox, Jim Palmer and Brooks Robinson of the Orioles, and golfers Tom Weiskopf and Raymond Floyd. When the Celtics visited New York, Bob Cousy and Tommy Heinsohn came in. So did Wilt Chamberlain, Oscar Robertson, Elgin Baylor, Rick Barry, Pete Maravich and Kevin Loughery."

Former Miss America Phyllis George got her broadcasting break in Mr. Laffs. She dated Tucker Fredrickson, who was dating about eight or nine other women. Bob Stenner, a producer at CBS Sports, noticed her natural charm and likeability and introduced her to Bob Wussler at CBS. She had her audition at the Sun Bowl interviewing fans in the stands. She took to the camera so easily, the following year Phyllis was included on the pre-game program, the NFL Today, with Brent Musberger, Jimmy the Greek Synder and Irv Cross. Broadcasting history was made because Phyllis George was the first female sportscaster on national television.

The athletes who frequented Mr Laffs were glamorous personalities to their fans who yearned to be like them because they were professional athletes who were adored and admired by millions. Pro athletes lived a charmed life, making a living at sports only part of the year but socializing all the time. The other anonymous guys at Mr. Laffs, who had to work 9-to-5 to pay the bills, were transported from their humdrum lives by just being in the same bar as the athletes who were having so much fun. The athletes were irrepressible because they were young and athletically talented, undeniably sexy and well-paid. The Jets, Mets and Knicks were winning championships and because of more attention paid to them by the media, professional athletes were the new celebrities. Everyone wanted to stay up late like them, drinking and laughing and dancing "till the break of dawn" The so-called "civilians," many of whom picked up the bar tabs, enjoyed instant recognition and attention as well from the females on the prowl.

Tom O'Neill, Bill Brendle, and Bob Stenner NYC 1971

Vito the Tailor was a typical outer-borough married guy drawn to the singles bars of Manhattan for secret affairs and there many guys like him who were customers night after night. Vito the Tailor became so involved with a stewardess, he invented reasons to get away from his wife. One Saturday night at a black tie wedding reception in Queens, he kept refilling his wife's wine glass and put a lot of licorice liquor in her expresso coffee. She fell asleep during the car ride home and he carried her to bed, undressed her and gently put a blanket on her. Vito the Tailor easily made his date sometime after one in the morning in Manhattan at Stew Zoo.

Sometime after seven in the morning, Vito the Tailor was back in his bedroom, his wife still asleep as he carefully took off his tuxedo shirt and then his shoes which he carefully placed on the floor. Suddenly, she opened her eyes. "Vito, what are you doing?" He fumbled with his tuxedo trousers and ad-libbed, "I'm going out for the bread rolls and the Sunday paper."

"In your tuxedo, Vito?."

"It was layin' here, so I put it on again."

"Oh, Vito, you're so crazy."

So that's why Vito the Tailor had to walk into Sorrento's Bakery in Queens that Sunday morning in his tuxedo to get the bread rolls and the newspapers.

There was a group of women who would fornicate with almost any big name athlete or well-heeled guy who came into Mr. Laffs. The players had their picks and they exchanged telephone numbers and kinky notes. The athlete "wannabees" took the scraps.

The happiest stew was Katie from California. An American Airlines cutie, based in New York, ricocheted from O'Neill to Tucker Fredrickson to real estate tycoon Larry Fisher. They married and lived happily ever after in the Billionaire Triangle, that is, from the penthouse in Manhattan to the mansion with the ocean view in Palm Beach to the sprawling ranch in Colorado and back again aboard the fastest private jet this side of the military.

The saddest woman at Mr. Laffs was a dark-haired and homely temptress named Wanda "The Witch," who held the unofficial record for bedding the most athletes even though she was the least-pretty regular. Wanda was always available and better looking late, after the guys had several scotch and sodas. Linz recalled Wanda leaving with Baltimore Orioles pitcher Jim Palmer, who was so handsome and fit he was the model for Jockey underwear.

Trolling Mr. Laffs and spending the night in a sexually aggressive woman's apartment could lead to exotic surprises. A pair of twins from Long Island named Becky and Emily, who were show-business make-up artists insisted on changing their visitors' faces into disguises for fun. There was Jo-Ann, "The Tent Lady." Visitors to her apartment discovered a tent in the living room and she acted out the role of an Arabian sex slave, complete with an Oriental rug and burning incense. There was "B.J.," a workout freak with a killer body, who loved to change into her blue and red Superwoman costume. A Radio City Music Hall Rockette named Sonya had a mostly pink apartment adorned with dozens of female dolls. Stern and brooding Madeline preferred older men and kept a suitcase of sex toys and accessories under her bed.

Other Mr. Laffs regulars included Big Carol who was based in Dallas and flew for American Airlines and could match brews with the best of them. She assumed the missionary position for some selected few who played in the NFL, the Major Leagues or the NBA. Black brothers need not apply. It had everything to do with her upbringing back in Tyler, Texas. Big Carol was most definitely not interested in pro golfers or tennis players who she considered too self absorbed. She had nothing in common with hockey players. Not so for Susie the Rink Rat. She wanted to marry and have babies with a hunk from the National Hockey League and she sport fucked her way through the rosters looking for one. She got teary eyed when she heard her national anthem "Oh, Canada." It reminded her of those radio broadcasts on Saturday nights during her youth back in Banff, when she sat on her dad's knee and listened to "Hockey Night in Canada." Three road groupies serviced NHL players and they were Chicago Shirley, Detroit Judy and heavyset Omaha Donna who preferred goalies.

Then, there was Vickie who developed and ran her own polling company that was hired by prominent advertising agencies. At Mr. Laffs, this closet bisexual brought her own luscious babe to make sure she ended up in a threesome. Another serial lover was a blue-eyed blonde, big-breasted cowgirl named Rita who billed herself as the former "Miss Tight Jeans of Beaumont, Texas." She couldn't miss with any ballplayer who spoke with a twang. Tina Tits was a men's magazine model whose hourglass figure framing her "Guns of Navarone" made men nervous like German Shepherds in heat.

O'Neill adds a strong point, "There were no hookers in Mr. Laffs because the female customers were giving themselves away for free."

In the Kingdom of the Cute and Kinky that was Mr. Laffs, the fairest of them all was a trim, brown-eyed, ash blonde so perfectly beautiful and sweet-natured, her nickname was Ugly Mary. She was a classic self-assured stunner, cut from the same silky cloth as Grace Kelly, a heartbreaker in a tan camel hair coat, glamorous in a black cocktail dress with a necklace of pearls and voluptuous in just a cashmere sweater and jeans. This debutante-looking blonde possessed understated elegance, as if she emerged from the old money breeding of Palm Beach high society or Main Line Philadelphia aristocracy or Newport, Rhode Island blueblood hierarchy. In reality, she grew up in Bucks County, Pennsylvania, in a working class family.

Like legions of women before her, Ugly Mary's ambition and beauty took her to New York. She was an aspiring model who worked as a waitress at Peartree. Bartender Marvin Cohen introduced her to customers as "The most beautiful woman ever created by God." Ugly Mary used a minimum of facial makeup and eschewed hairspray. Guys stared at her, over-tipped her, offered her free clothing and vacation trips. Some tried to lure her with rent money. They sent flowers, candy and chauffeur driven limousines for her use. Some Peartree male customers become so obsessive with her, they would sit only at tables in her work area. Ugly Mary had her pick of men. The Fair Miss Frigidaire was their wet dream. But, sexually she was almost untouchable. She always wore a Crucifix, and was a devout Catholic.

Peartree was at the Northeast corner of 49th Street and First Avenue, on the street level of the Beekman Towers Hotel. The attractive bar and restaurant was owned by Buzzy O'Keefe and a favorite hangout of insiders from the NFL, Major League Baseball, thoroughbred racing and television. Peartree regulars included thoroughbred racing fanatics like Paul Hornung of the Green Bay Packers and sports columnist Pete Axhelm. At the bar one Sunday night, after their network broadcast, Brent Musberger and Jimmy The Greek Snyder of CBS Sports had a brief fight that was publicized.

Hank Goldberg, now a correspondent for ESPN, hosts a daily sports talk program in Miami. He was an eyewitness at Peartree's that night. Goldberg recalls, "The Greek showed up that Sunday morning with the scoop that Gerry Faust was going to be hired by Notre Dame as its next head football coach. On the air, instead of teeing it up for the Greek, Musberger said, 'What's this about Gerry Faust and Notre Dame?' That night at Peartree, Jimmy yelled at Brent for faking like he had the inside story. Brent wisecracked, 'so what, I can knock you off the show anytime I want.' The Greek slapped Brent in the face and all hell broke loose. Frank Ross, a CBS production guy who was nicknamed "Skylab," pulled the Greek off Musberger and out of the bar." The tussle was reported lustily by the tabloid newspapers, which was embarrassing to CBS.

O'Keefe hired the prettiest waitresses for Peartree. Most were part-timers who were trying to crack into the fashion and entertainment industries as models and actresses. Competition was keen because the best looking women invariably came to New York to seek fame and fortune. Bills had to be paid, so serving cocktails and food in bars and restaurants was a lucrative side job. O'Keefe's motto was "I can make a beautiful woman into a decent waitress. I can't make a ordinary looking waitress into a beautiful woman."

O'Keefe added, "One outstanding looking waitress is worth more in business than a dozen bland types."

Starting in the 1970's, Buzzy elevated his game, owning and operating two of New York's destination and landmark restaurants, The River Café and The Water Club, which are continuing successes.

Ugly Mary bounced from a heavy romance with Joe Namath to a tumultuous relationship and marriage with Mets outfielder Dave Marshall. Lesser looking women snared rich husbands and wealthy boyfriends while Ugly Mary eventually bailed out of New York, as beautiful as ever, back to the anonymity she came from. Years later, we heard she was hanging out with a guy in Connecticut.

BRENDLE AND DOLPH

Every night at Mr. Laffs, there was an eclectic mixture of fascinating people, and not just athletes. Young Wall Street predators picked up the scent and so did advertising and television executives. In this busy corral of the rowdy and wild, affable and chain smoking Bill McPhail, the head of CBS Sports, sipped his scotch almost every night with his two aides and devils of delight, Jack Dolph and Bill Brendle at his side. During the business day, their midtown clubhouses were Rose's, Toots Shor's and Mike Manuche's, but at night their excursions for cocktails, riotous laughter and good times began on the East Side at P.J. Clarke's then uptown at Mr. Laffs and to Clarke's late. Their table was always a party, attracting a who's-who in sports. As Director of Sports at CBS-TV, Dolph was McPhail's right-hand man. Their best friend was former Giants kicker and CBS football analyst Pat Summerall who was also a regular on the drinking circuit. Brendle was CBS Sports' Director of Public Relations and known to all as "Catfish." Dolph later became the commissioner of the American Basketball Association. One morning, O'Neill had to unlock Mr. Laffs and look for Dolph's briefcase, which he found under a table. Dolph needed it immediately. It contained the contract of a player the ABA had signed and there was a noon news conference. Every night, Mr. Laffs was Dolph's last stop. The regulars had a ritual when Dolph's head sank to the tabletop. We'd take his necktie and put it around his head, raise it and cheer "Lets hear it for the commissioner of the ABA, hip, hip hooray." One night, Teddy Drucker, a local cop, waited till Dolph passed out and he tied Jack's shoelaces. Jack was always ready to fight anyone. Drucker threw a roll at his head and woke him up and cursed him. Dolph jumped up and went to punch Drucker and his feet locked and he went flying over a table. After each night of carousing and boozing, Dolph's limousine driver took him home to Old Greenwich, Connecticut. Dolph's colorful life inspired Mr. Laffs regular Dan Jenkins to write "Limo," one of his many successful novels. Jenkins held forth with sportscaster Jack Whitaker, newscaster Jim Jensen, TV directors Frank Chirkinian, Mac Hemion and Tony Verna and advertising executive Bob Drum who once survived crashing through a plate glass window at Duncan's, another watering hole. Their group nickname was "The 5:42 Club" because one day after work they decided they needed a nickname and one of them checked his wristwatch and said . . . "it's 5:42."

The buddies, cronies and pals at CBS Sports enjoyed liberal use of company expenses, like renting a railroad car, complete with bar and small band, for the annual party trip to the Preakness Stakes at Pimlico in Baltimore. That had some validity because CBS televised the Triple Crown. But, not hiring a driver and bus to take at least 35 of the guys and some stewardesses to a Willie Nelson concert on Long Island, followed by an all-night party back in Stew Zoo on East 65th Street.

O'Neill recalls, "In the summer, Brendle's family stayed at the New Jersey shore, at Spring Lake, while he worked all week and he would join them for the weekend. One Friday night about 8pm, as the sun was still up, Brendle was blitzed and staggered to a taxi cab to take him to his parked car in a lot near the George Washington Bridge. Bill passed out for the 15 minutes or so, it took to get uptown. When the cab lurched to a stop, Brendle woke up and saw the sun slanting on the Hudson River. He thought he was up all night, and it was just after sunrise instead and he panicked. He ran to a public telephone, and remember it's 8:30 in the evening, and he called his wife, in Spring Lake. After she said hello, Brendl blurted, 'Frances listen, don't worry about me. I just had a few drinks too many and I passed out in O'Neill's apartment and I'll arrive by mid-morning.' Frances (who was known as 'St. Frances') said 'It's alright darling, don't worry about it because it's only 8:30 and it's Friday night.'"

Brendle leaned on his CBS Sports expense account so much, he used to tell bartenders and waiters, "Bill me with tomorrow's date because I spent today, yesterday."

At Super Bowl-IV in New Orleans, I saw Brendle slap his forehead in astonishment the night before the game at Al Hirt's jazz club, yelling "I forgot to do the one thing I had to do" and he scurried to a pay telephone. NBC televised the game between the Kanas City Chiefs and the Minnesota Vikings. The public relations head for NBC Sports "hired" his opposite at CBS who was Brendle for the week. When CBS televised the Super Bowl, Brendle would do the same for his opposite at NBC. So, Brendle enjoyed an all expenses paid week in the Big Easy but forgot to arrange for the telephone call from President Nixon to the winning coach. Of course, he couldn't get through to the White House that Saturday night, but he arranged it the next morning.

Tragically all the good times were wiped away when Brendle and Dolph drank themselves to death in their early '50s.

BIG RED

Martha Haines was a twenty-something, red-headed, shapely flight attendant from Georgia who was knockdown gorgeous. Her nickname was "Big Red." Haines flew for Eastern Airlines and shared a one-bedroom apartment on East 52nd Street with four other stewardesses. Because of their flying schedules they were never there at the same time. There was a feeling of sorority. "The pay wasn't great," says Martha, "and we were on tight budgets. We did a lot of things together. We'd go to Mr. Laffs, Tittle Tattle, Duncan's, Play Street . . . all on the East Side . . . sometimes in our airlines uniforms right from the airport, if it was at night. We didn't have to pay for our drinks or what we ate. Basically, we had our choice of most any man. Those places were filled with big name athletes and I knew quite a few of them intimately. But, it was never serious. We didn't have to worry about getting pregnant because we were on the pill. It was all about fun. Speaking for myself, I wasn't looking to get married. If I had an affair with a married athlete, it certainly wasn't serious because I believe if you play on your wife, you play on your girlfriend."

Roommate Liz Goldberg's favorite story was an apartment's mistaken identity. One late night, all the women were out and Martha was alone waiting up for Bob Uecker. The big league catcher and humorist was familiar with the fact that her apartment door on the 9th floor was always unlocked. He didn't know such was the case at the apartment next door where George Burke, a bachelor, lived. This particular night, Uecker went to the 9th floor and opened an apartment door. It was dark. He took off his clothes and went to the bedroom and slipped under the covers. Burke bolted awake and shouted "Who are you?" Uecker yelled, "Who are you and where is Martha?" With great embarrassment they figured out the blunder. Burke was a very sociable guy and a gourmet cook. He offered Uecker a drink and some freshly cooked pasta. The guys sat around drinking and eating while Martha waited in her apartment. A couple of hours later, Uecker went to Martha.

Haines eventually opened her own singles bar, partnering with other flight attendants. It was called McMasters, after one of the partners, Dory McMaster. It opened on 58th Street and First Avenue and moved to 74th Street between First and York avenues. "All the baseball players came in, along with the basketball, football and hockey guys. On Thanksgiving Day, some of the Jets and Giants joined us for dinner and we actually said a prayer. We were away from home, but felt like a family. Sometimes, a group of us would have a picnic on my apartment floor. The girls would pull pranks. Dory once invited some of the Red Sox over to her apartment for dinner. She put some laxative in their cooked food and, the next day, they had diarrhea and couldn't play against our pals, the Yankees. Hey, we also pulled pranks on the Yankees, like sending their luggage to San Juan instead of Oakland."

"Sure guys stayed over and, if they were married, the wives didn't know about us. Remember, in those days, most pro athletes couldn't afford to have their families living in New York during their seasons. If a wife was in town visiting, we had a saying . . . 'so and so is dead'. Onetime, we sent a fake coffin to Yankee Stadium by taxi, addressed to our friend, pitcher Fritz Peterson whose wife was visiting. We put flowers in the box with a condolence card about Fritz's death."

A night at a singles bar could lead to a new relationship or break an old one. Martha recalls the most over-used, get-acquainted lines from men, like "You have beautiful eyes . . . . I think I know you from someplace before . . . . didn't I see you at the airport? . . . and . . . . I was on one of your flights, I know that."

(Leon Horne, who ran a very successful printing business, used a unique approach for stewardesses. On flights, he handed them his personal card and said, "This is the key to the city of New York." Leon ended up in and out of five marriages.)

One of Martha's many roommates, Nancy Stephenson, met Dick Howser of the Yankees one night on the East Side and they eventually married. Two others, Melanie and Carol, met their future husbands in the bars. "Otherwise," says Big Red, "they were mostly fun relationships. No matter how hot the affair, you never gave up your job or your apartment. There was no moving in."

Martha Haines admits to a 25-year relationship with Mickey Mantle. "We loved being with each other, we were always best friends."

A mutual friend of Martha and Mickey was Alex Hawkins. When he wasn't catching passes for the Baltimore Colts and the Atlanta Falcons, he was a carouser and didn't let his marriage stand in the way. Hawkins was known for his line, "That's my story and I'm sticking to it." He first uttered that phrase to his wife at sunrise. It seems Hawkins staggered home from an all-nighter and she was waiting in the kitchen. When asked where he was all night, Alex said he slept off his drinking stupor in the hammock in the yard. Mrs. Hawkins reminded him that the hammock had been taken down two weeks earlier. Alex couldn't come up with anything except "That's my story and I'm sticking to it."

The regulars at Mr. Laffs had their own chaplain. Father Joe Dispenza, who grew up on Manhattan's Lower East Side, was a priest in his original parish. But, in the evenings, he didn't wear his cleric color uptown at Mr. Laffs where many good friends sought out his advice about their moral conduct. I don't know how many souls Father Joe saved, but he was very good company and a caring person.

As for off-beat tales, there were a couple. Mr. Laffs regular Bob Devine and a buddy were picked up one night by a woman, who invited them back to her apartment. When they got there, she fixed them a couple of drinks and said she wanted to change clothes. When she emerged from her bedroom she wore a dominatrix outfit, and held a white wedding gown in her right hand. She said "One of you has to wear this." Devine's buddy refused, and started to leave. Bob said to him "Before you go, do you mind zipping me up?"

ABC Sports producer Geoff Mason and his close buddy, ABC Sports Vice president John Martin, were at Mr. Laffs early on a Thursday night when two women and a man sat at the bar. They said this was their first visit to Mr. Laffs. The better looking of the two women told Geoff she was with her sister and brother. Mason suggested he hire a chauffeured limousine and they go bar-hopping. They said they were never in a limo before. Mason put the sister and brother in the limo and told the driver to take them around for a while and then take them home.

That's all Mason remembered until he awoke the next morning, obviously in a hotel room, but he had no idea where he was and there were no clues in the room. He heard the woman singing while taking a shower and he didn't know her name. He grabbed the telephone and dialed Martin's number in New York and read him the number on the room telephone. He asked Martin to call back and introduce himself to the woman, so Mason could find out her name. Neither recognized the area code. Martin called back less than a minute later and said, "How in the hell did you get to the bridal suite at the Racquet Club in Puerto Rico? I left you late and you were fine." Mason said he had no recollection but he and his new friend had taken the late flight to San Juan. Martin faked a conversation with her and Mason heard her say her name. "We had a delightful weekend, poolside at the San Juan Racquet Club and met some pilots who were deadheading a Falcon jet back to LaGuardia Airport on Sunday night. They asked us to join them and we flew back, enjoying champagne and sandwiches. I dropped her off at her apartment and never talked to her again the rest of my life."

In 72 hours, "Old what's her name" went from the bar at Mr. Laffs to San Juan and back. Mason said, "I didn't know till a couple of weeks later, when I got the limo bill that the sister and brother lived in Philadelphia."

The TV sports guys worked weekends and played during the week. Mason recalled, "Don Ohlmeyer and I were married with families in Scarsdale, in Westchester County. We thought we were so cute, bolting to Grand Central Terminal, to catch the last train at 1:15 AM, having been totally wrecked for the previous five or six hours, with God knows whom. We'd call our respective wives in Scarsdale and say we were held over editing videotape. All the while, we're standing in Charlie O's, shouting above the background sounds of clinking glasses and laughing people. We're thinking we're pulling it off. Our wives weren't thrilled."

Mason recalls, "Those were wonderful but tragic times for a lot of us because of alcoholism."

THE BUSHES AND MR. FEBRUARY

There were 5 American Airlines stewardesses, who shared an apartment at 511 East 80th Street, nicknamed the "Bushes." Maureen was from Michigan, Barbara and Maryanne from California, Ginger from Boston, and Sandy from San Antonio. They had met at flight school in Dallas in 1968. Since they were assigned to be based in New York, they lived together. They were good-looking and had a tremendous sense of humor and they were confident because of their beauty. They were also loyal to each other and had no problems getting dates. Guys loved hanging out with them in public because they knew so many other airline stewardesses. Dating one of the "Bushes" was a big deal among the athletes. Barbara, nicknamed "Bozo," was a steady with Linz. At times, Sandy hung out with Rod Gilbert of the Rangers, Maryann with Art Shamsky of the Mets and Maureen dated Lou Piniella. Ginger had a crush on Rangers' Captain Bob Nevin. The Bushes made Mr. Laffs their sole hangout and all of them went upstairs to Linz' apartment for after-hours parties. Phil rented a summer house in Hampton Bays on the Atlantic Ocean and the Bushes were always welcome.

I flew to Los Angeles and back several times without paying because of the Bush Bunch. Friends of the Bush Bunch scheduled flights when they were working because there was no security at the airline terminals. If you knew the Bush Bunch, you simply handed one of them an empty envelope while boarding the jetliner. The added bonus of flying with the Bush Bunch was the free champagne.

Teddy Drucker and Harry Sakin were a pair of handsome New York City motorcycle patrolmen who bedded dozens of stewardesses they met at Mr. Laffs. Drucker eventually married a flight attendant, who was a former Miss Pennsylvania. After closing time one night, Drucker and Sakin took target practice with their service revolvers on a napkin pinned to the wall. After a few shots, the men's room door swung open and a Mr. Laffs waiter named "Lightning" bolted out, screaming curses. "Lightning" was sitting on the toilet when the gunshots whizzed about him.

Another night, Teddy went to a rowdy party at Joe Namath's apartment on East 76th Street that lasted till the wee hours. The next morning, Drucker woke up abruptly on the floor of Ray Abruzzese's bedroom. Namath's roommate was in bed with a woman and their sleep was interrupted by the shrill voice of Howard Cosell, coming from the living room television. Abruzzese cursed, got out of bed and went to the living room and was startled. He found Cosell about to film an interview with the Jets quarterback. Abruzzese shouted, "I was coming in here to turn off the TV."

There were four Eastern Airlines stewardesses from Boston who shared an East Side townhouse apartment and lived rather well. Their three bedroom duplex was furnished tastefully and they entertained either with small dinner parties or jammed packed beer parties. They had a garden area in the back and they barbecued in the summer. The quartet worked the new Eastern Airlines shuttle flights to and from Boston and Washington D.C. that departed and arrived every hour. They averaged four flights a day, sometimes six, and they were diligent about their schedules. They rarely called in sick. Their appearance away from home was neat and clean and they were very courteous. They appeared to be the model flight attendants.

Part of the new convenience for shuttle commuters was no check-in counter. One could simply walk aboard without a ticket. In flight, the attendants took either cash or credit cards for the airfare. Not only was there little security at the area airports, at the time, the Eastern Airlines shuttle flights had few supervisory personnel. Since there was no head count, the four flight attendants skimmed cash. This went undetected, for quite awhile, until the airline stopped being so sloppy and realized it had partners. One of the stews was supporting her husband through medical school back in Boston.

Many stewardesses also enhanced their earnings carrying illegal drugs, mostly marijuana, back to New York from Miami and the West Coast. A pound at a time, when there was no scrutiny at the air terminals, was rather easy to hide in their carry-on baggage. Security was so lax, Liz Goldberg remembers stewardesses wearing the spare uniforms of girlfriends and flying with them to other cities without paying so they could hook up with ballplayers.

Apartment 12-E in the Buxley, atop Mr. Laffs, at 360 E. 65th Street, was a 2-bedroom, two-bath shared at various times by Rod Gilbert and

Bob Nevin of the Rangers and by Tommy O'Neill and J.J. Cunningham, an American Airlines pilot. It was the meeting place for shortstops, tight ends, point guards, pro golfers, goalies and faces from the covers of Vogue. One May night, I went to 12-E because Rod hosted a party for the celebrity athletes who were in New York to take stock broker courses and become licensed. After their final examinations, Rod gave them a "getaway party." Washington Redskins linebacker Marlin McKeever had too much liquor in him and took umbrage when someone bumped my elbow and my glass of vodka splashed him. McKeever lifted me up by my armpits and snarled "Pretty boy, I'm gonna mess you up." McKeever had an IQ of 150 and graded better than the other guys in the eight-year history of the tests and finished the written test in half the time than the others, but he couldn't hold his liquor. Dallas Cowboys tight end Mike Ditka headlocked McKeever and muscled him to the floor, yelling "These are nice people, don't get stupid." Ditka was a lion of a man. He easily tamed McKeever like a cub and I avoided a beating.

In that very same apartment there was an odd incident. Nevin's girlfriend was a 21-year old redheaded model named Debbie. She enraged him by showing up at Rangers games in Madison Square Garden, dressed in tight skirts and blouses cut down to her navel. Before games, while Bobby was warming up on the ice, he would hear the hoots and whistles and he'd be fuming before they dropped the puck. They had a stormy relationship and fought often. To begin with, Nevin was angry over his trade from a Stanley Cup winner, the Toronto Maple Leafs, to the mediocre Rangers and his wife wouldn't move with him to New York.

One day, Debbie surprised him with a 9-month old Siamese cat. Nevin was allergic to cats and he started to sneeze and his eyes became watery. An argument ensued and he threw the cat out the window from their 12th floor apartment. Debbie freaked and started screaming hysterically. Nevin went into the bedroom. A few minutes later, the doorbell rang and when the sobbing Debbie opened the door, their next door neighbor, Stanley Moss, handed her the cat. It had landed on the front canopy and bounced onto the shoulder of Eddie-the-doorman, without injury. Moss said the cat knocked the cap off the doorman's head but he was unharmed. Eddie knew it was Debbie's cat, so he gave it to Stanley to return it. The cat survived a 12-story free fall. She was grateful and embraced the cat like a baby. But, when Nevin came out of the bedroom, the cat hissed at him, and exposed its claws in an attack mode. Debbie was told to get rid of the cat or pack her clothes.

Rod called himself "Mr. February," the month between the football season and the baseball season. "The rest of the time, I had to compete for women with the Jets and Giants, the Mets and Yankees. A lot of us lived in apartments in the same area, so we socialized together and, in a competitive way, boasted of our conquests with the women we all knew."

Rod Gilbert—"Mr. February"

Rodrique Gabriel Gilbert was a French Canadian from a Montreal suburb. No. 7 in the New York Rangers red, white and blue was a stick-handling rightwing, with a slap shot like a cannon blast. He was the Rangers' high scorer off the ice as well. He was good-looking and usually the star of the game. He attracted all kinds of women. One night, after a game, Gilbert ended up in the apartment of twin sisters. They were gorgeous and theatrical makeup artists. During their threesome, they made up Rod's face like an old man. In the wee hours, Gilbert thought he had removed most of the makeup when he went to his apartment to sleep. His girlfriend came home from a road trip the next day and awoke Rod, asking what he was doing with half a mustache on his upper lip. Rod went to the bathroom mirror, and flushed it in the toilet, saying "Honey, it was a feather from the pillow."

Rod remembers, "The biggest problem with the stewardesses was dating a couple of roommates. They were very competitive with their boyfriends. You had to be sure the other was traveling. Sometimes, I would see the same dress and realize, it was borrowed from the other roommate."

On Rangers road trips, Rod met groupies like "Chicago Shirley," "Detroit Susie" and "Omaha Donna." After games, there was a team curfew, but many times, Rod and his teammates returned to their hotel at six or seven in the morning, just in time to shower and pack their bags for the trip home. On the team bus to the airport, Coach Emile Francis sat in the front seat, with his players behind him. You could tell who was out all night, because they wore sunglasses and were napping at nine in the morning.

Gilbert had many relatives and friends in his hometown of Montreal and had a financial interest in a nightclub called "Une, Deux, Trois." It was a hotspot for French Canadian girls and they dressed very fashionably. Their look was European. It was at "I-2-3" that I saw the latest rage from Paris for the first time "Hot Pants."

One night after a game, Francis called Rod into his office for a private meeting and said, "I need to know how you do it. You scored 3 goals with 2 assists . . . five points . . . and we win 7-5 and you're the first star. Somebody called me this morning and said he was with you at four a.m. with two girls and you were drunk. How do you do it? From now on, Rod, I am not taking those phone calls. I think he was bullshitting me." Rod laughed and said, "Why are you bothering with these people, they're telling you fibs."

Gilbert was the Rangers' star and 27 years old when he went to Toots Shor's bar for some beer with the guys, after practice, one late afternoon. The legendary saloonkeeper was a bouncer in the speakeasy days of the "Roaring '20s" in New York. Even in his 70s, Toots liked to playfully poke customers on the jaw. He always called Rod "foreigner" because he was from Quebec. The previous Memorial Day, at the New Jersey shore in Deal, Shor hosted Gilbert at his home and they played golf. So, they were pals. But, this particular afternoon, while the guys were sitting around drinking, Toots sucker-punched Rod with a short right hand that caught him flush on the jaw and knocked him unconscious onto the floor. When he regained consciousness, Rod was embarrassed by the laughter and walked out, never to return to Toot Shor's. He said, "I got paid to get hit on the ice. I didn't need more of that. If he was a younger man I would have knocked him on his ass."

Rod and his buddies pulled a prank on the retired Toots at a bachelor party for Giants running back Bobby Duhon. The elderly Toots sat at one end of the living room of Burt Schultz's apartment watching us make fools of ourselves. Rod rigged the lottery for a hooker so that Toots' name was drawn. Toots was embarrassed and refused and after he was ridiculed, Schultz took his place.

TITTLE TATTLE

New York in 1969 was bursting with sports pride. The Jets were the Super Bowl champions, the Mets were climbing from last to first and the Knicks were driving toward their first NBA crown.

Jerry Koosman of the New York Mets, the winning pitcher in the World Series victory over the Baltimore Orioles—Oct. 1969

There was increased joy nationally because in July, we witnessed on television the amazing accomplishment of Apollo-11 astronauts Neil Armstrong and Buzz Aldrin who walked on the moon. In August, a million young people experienced a spontaneous communal expression of freedom at the long weekend rock concert in the upstate New York town of Bethel, called "Woodstock." There were four days of drugs, sex, rock n roll and rain. Meanwhile, the unpopular Vietnam conflict was winding down as the first U.S. military units were withdrawn.

The counter-culture films, "Midnight Cowboy" and "Easy Rider" were the most popular. We danced to the Beatles and the Rolling Stones and sang along with the counter-culture's poet; Bob Dylan who wrote "Everybody must get stoned . . ." Marijuana became more important than scotch, gin and rye. Since it was illegal to toke on a joint in public, the obvious option was in private, in those apartments packed with stewardesses, models and secretaries. Dylan proclaimed "The times, they are a changing." "Weed" was the drug of choice for pro athletes, as well as our next door neighbors. All had to be discreet and Dylan warned, "You don't need a weatherman to know which way the wind blows."

In October, there was bedlam at Mr. Laffs the night the Mets upset the Baltimore Orioles in five games to win the 1969 World Series. It was a weekday afternoon clinch and, in the champagne celebration in the Mets locker room, I interviewed Kenny Boswell among others. The second baseman said, "See you all at Mr. Laffs tonight." That aired on our early evening and 11 p.m. sportscasts on WCBS-TV, channel-2. By the time I got there about midnight, vehicular traffic in front of Mr. Laffs on First Avenue was stopped because a couple of thousand people crowded the street. O'Neill called the 19th precinct and police were dispatched. Traffic began easing up First Avenue in one lane instead of four. The Mr. Laffs regulars entered by using the rear entrance through the Buxley apartment house lobby, around the corner. At least 200 people squeezed inside Mr. Laffs for a party that lasted all night. Many of the Champion Mets were there, including Tommie Agree, Cleon Jones, Don Cardwell, Wayne Garrett, Jerry Grote, Art Shamsky, and Ken Boswell. Lots of champagne was consumed, as we danced and sang. There was dancing on the bar and some clothes came off. It was the mother of all parties. Many moved in and out of the back door, up the elevators, into many of the apartments in the Buxley. When the sun came up, Phil Linz cooked bacon and eggs for breakfast, for those who were still awake.

O'Neill remembers, "One night in 1969 after a Knicks game at the Garden, Jacqueline Kennedy came in with her young son John John for hamburgers. She was delightful as Secret Service guys stood close by.

Mr. Laffs' successful run lasted from 1965 to 1972. Because they differed on so many aspects on how to run the place, Linz and Anderson stopped speaking to each other and lost interest in the business.

Tittle Tattle, next door, was managed by Timmy Secour who was friendly with many professional athletes and hundreds of airlines flight attendants. When it opened in 1969, Secour handed out Tittle Tattle pink cards to stewardesses he described as "The women of choice."

Secour remembers "It was the golden age of jocks and girls. The pink cards meant half price. That cost incentive and the possibility of meeting athletes, attracted gorgeous women from all over the United States. They didn't want to meet 'civilians' . . . ya know, executives, lawyers and accountants . . . . anyone who wasn't a jock. They wanted a hunk, a stud and, many a girl suffered a broken heart because a player was cut from a team, sent the minor leagues or traded. Sometimes, the guys went back to their wives."

After closing time at Tittle Tattle, many an early morning, the party moved upstairs in the Buxley, to Secour's apartment. He says, "After all the hard drinking and dancing, the men and women were restless. The perfect ending to the mating dance was obvious."

Later, the new management of Tittle Tattle hired a big-boobed woman to pose on the sidewalk, trying to lure customers inside, like it was a B-girl joint in the Times Square district. Unlike Mr. Laffs, next door, Tittle Tattle welcomed prostitutes and gamblers. The new Major League Baseball Commissioner, Bowie Kuhn, ruled Tittle Tattle off-limits for anyone in the game.

In those days, just after the merger of the AFL and NFL there was little fraternization between New York's two pro football teams. Jets running back Billy Mathis and Giants running backs Tucker Frederickson and Bobby Duhon were the exceptions. They were a very close trio and remained that way for decades.

One August night in 1969, some Jets and Giants had a fistfight in Tittle Tattle after their first-ever game and it has remained a secret till now. Seven months after the Jets upset the Baltimore Colts in Super Bowl III, the Jets and Giants pre-season game felt like a playoff game. It was played in the sweltering heat at the Yale Bowl in New Haven and the Jets dominated 37-14. Giants owner Wellington Mara, usually a mild mannered gentleman, hurled a tray of soda bottles at a wall in the locker room. Head coach Allie Sherman was fired a month later.

There was an electric moment in the grudge match. Jets kick-return specialist Mike Battle returned a punt 86 yards for a touchdown and along the way hurdled Dave Lewis of the Giants. That night, several players went to Tittle Tattle because the television replay of the game began at midnight. Fred Dryer was one of them and the Giants defensive end recalls how intently the players watched the replay of the game. "When Battle's play was on the bar

TV, he reacted enthusiastically to his spectacular touchdown. Battle jumped up from his table and hurdled other tables. Some Giants argued with him and a fistfight broke out. There were no major injuries, the police weren't summoned and the incident went unnoticed. Amazingly, no one leaked it to the tabloid newspapers."

Battle played recklessly and when he had a few drinks in him he used to win bets eating martini glasses. Somehow he digested the crunched glass. Secour saw him do that, so did Tommy O'Neill.

When Tittle Tattle closed down, O'Neill noticed the demolition workers wore extra large gloves and asked why. They said "There are rats in that basement as big as dogs . . . . scariest job we ever had."

Business dwindled at Mr. Laffs and Tittle Tattle as the women and the athletes found newer places. The sporting crowd drifted to Duncan's on East 55th Street. Tommy O'Neill and Tucker Frederickson of the Giants reconverted a pub on First Avenue and 59th and called it T.J. Tucker's. On 52nd Street and Second Avenue, Runyon's was opened by Joe Healey, another Mr. Laffs alumnus. Copycat singles bars opened up all over Manhattan as women moved elsewhere, renting in buildings in the 70s and 80s as well as Manhattan's West Side.

Linz tried to resurrect interest in Mr. Laffs but there were fewer customers and the business languished. Like a tattered and stained curtain in a tenement window, the once-busy First Avenue bar was a grim reminder of what used to be, but still there, looking lonelier with each passing night.

The lusty "Stew Zoo" era at 1189 First Avenue ended one evening in 1972 with one guy drinking at the empty bar of Mr. Laffs. It was the upstairs neighbor, Rod Gilbert, the bon vivant Mr. February who raised one last glass of beer in memory of all those rollicking good-times at Stew Zoo.

REFLECTIONS

THE THRILLA IN MANILA

"Champions aren't made in the gyms. Champions are made from something they have deep inside them—a desire, a dream, a vision. They have to have last minute stamina, they have to be a little faster, they have to have the skill and the will. But, the will must be stronger than the skill."

Muhammad Ali

The first familiar face in the heat and humidity of Manila was Harold Conrad's. Before saying hello, he wisecracked from the side of his mouth, his thin black mustache askew, "The first thing I had to do when I got here, was get them handguns and pot." Muhammad Ali's public relations man was talking about Ali's entourage of about 30 assorted family, friends and court jesters who traveled with him to the Philippines.

It was a week before the third fight in Ali's bombastic and financially-successful trilogy with Joe Frazier, scheduled for October 1, 1975. ABC Sports assigned me to host a segment live from Manila the next Saturday on "Wide World of Sports." After they had the official weigh-in on the telecast, Ali and Frazier had agreed to interviews.

A week earlier, after a production meeting at ABC's headquarters in New York, I was waiting for an elevator to leave but didn't get away in time. Howard Cosell moved down the hallway and shouted, for all to hear, "DON'T FUCK UP IN MANILA."

I had the assignment because Cosell detested traveling internationally, especially to the other side of the world to spend a week in a country whose democracy was fragile, at best. Three years earlier, in 1972, President Ferdinand E. Marcos imposed martial law throughout the country. Since the Philippines won independence from the United States in 1946, Communist rebels in hidden mountain bases were a constant threat. There was a midnight curfew for all citizens in Manila and soldiers were under orders to shoot any offenders. But, this particular week, because of the presence of the world's press, conditions were relaxed. Curfew offenders were stopped and questioned rather than shot on the spot.

For the past 400 years the Philippines served under many masters with the Spanish, Americans and Japanese as rulers. The Philippines total 7,100 islands and islets with an area of 115, 600 square miles. Manila is part of the largest island, Luzon. After the Japanese invaded the Philippines and conquered Manila on January 2, 1942, the defending force of Americans and Filipinos withdrew to Bataan, a province and peninsula on the island of Luzon across the bay west of Manila. U.S. Commanding General Douglas Mac Arthur was ordered to Australia and issued one of the most famous war-time quotes, "I shall return," before leaving the Philippines. True to his word, Mac Arthur returned in October of 1944, liberating the Philippines from the enemy. Thousands of American and Filipino men died together in the infamous "Death March." During World War II, Manila shared the dishonor with Warsaw, Poland, as the most battered city. However, Manila regenerated into the political, business and intellectual center of the Philippines, even though its northeastern suburb, Quezon City, is the national capital.

Three decades later, the locals were very friendly and festive about a world sports event happening and being televised around the world from Manila. The downtown streets were decorated with flowers and signs of self-congratulation. Manila was a sprawling metropolis of four-and-a half million people. Four major languages were spoken, English, a Malayan dialect called "Tagalog," Spanish and Chinese. Most were Roman Catholic. They liked to wear the American look of T-shirts and jeans. They drank a lot of American flavored soda and listened to American rock 'n roll. Every evening, on television, the favorite program was a continuing beauty contest with an eventual winner. The women were a beautiful mixture of Asian, American and European bloodlines. The people traveled in colorful jitneys, elaborately painted jeeps which were relics from World War II. Passengers paid 30 centavos, the equivalent of an American nickel. Spoiling the tropical climate and the colorful flowers was a constant acrid smell because there were no restrictions on fuel emissions.

There was high excitement, but not far from the gaiety of downtown Manila, there were mud alleys where the poor endured in squalid conditions. President Marcos staged this world event to further the notion to his citizens that all was well. Nine years later, in 1986, Marcos' martial law regime crumbled, driving him into exile to Hawaii.

The third Ali-Frazier fight was so big it was co-promoted by arch-rivals Bob Arum and Don King. The world's sports reporters were invited to get there early. Each night of the week, leading up to the fight, there was a party hosted by locals for the visiting world press. The hosts were Manila's affluent society who lived in a walled community called Forbes Park. They lived in air-conditioned homes, surrounded by manicured lawns and majestic palm trees, employing dozens of laborers and housemaids while most people outside the walls struggled to subsist. One of that week's events was laughable. A wealthy Filipino family, wishing to debut their beautiful young daughter, hosted a party at the swank Manila Polo Club, "honoring" ABC Sports, which consisted of Vice-President John Martin, director Joe Aceti and me. The father of the debutant was the president of the national airline and he had fancy and exotic food flown in from Hong Kong. A 15-piece orchestra played in a huge mahogany-paneled dining room, dotted with large tropical plants and flowers. Through the portals, we overlooked the Bay of Manila, twinkling in the moonlight.

The grand entrances by the locals looked like the theatrical arrivals at the Academy Awards. Most of the sportswriters were there along with the Ali and Frazier camps. The promoters Don King and Bob Arum were smiling broadly and schmoozing the local gentry. The ambitious Butch Lewis, Frazier's friend from Philadelphia, was there with his posse, softly chanting . . . "JOOOE FRRRAAZZZRRRR."

Aceti was the size of a sumo wrestler and fearless. He shouted "He ain't nothin!" Butch and his guys moved forward. There was a moment of tension, as they exchanged taunts with a very large white man with blazing blue eyes and the arms and hands of a gorilla. Soon enough, smiles broke out instead of fights and a New York-Philly alliance was made and new-found friendships were formed.

For the better part of 40 years, Aceti would direct sports events of all types for all four major networks. He would be at the seminal sports events of the last half of the century. The Thrilla in Manila was one of the major 80 boxing matches to his credit. Aceti directed ABC's Wide World of Sports for 10 years and directed every Olympics telecast on the network. He was amiable and artistic in his work and went out of his way not to yell in the control room. He abhorred the cliché of the screaming tyrant director. (In 2006, The Directors Guild of America awarded Joseph R. Aceti its Lifetime Achievement in Sports Direction Award, as its 9th recipient.)

One of Butch Lewis' buddies was Willie "The Worm" Monroe, a talented black middleweight from Philadelphia, who escorted a wealthy and married

Filipino woman who clung to him. We heard there was a lot of adultery in Filipino high society because the predominant religion was Catholic, forbidding divorce. That week, several guys in the boxing community were servicing some of Manila's rebellious married women who had rented hideaway apartments in upscale high rise buildings. I told Willie that the boys back on the street corner in Philly would never believe this affair. He said, "They will, I got witnesses."

Aceti and I left the Manila Polo Club early because the parties had frankly become routine. We had an appointment downtown for massages (later, one of the Filipino girls asked me to sneak her out of the country, moaning she had no future under President Marco's dictatorial rule). Only the favored rich could leave the Philippines. I was told many shopped in New York, London and Rome, while the poor could not emigrate.

Another evening, a cocktail party for the visiting media was hosted by a filthy rich British lawyer in his Forbes Park home. His basketball court-sized living room was filled with the stuffed exotic animals he had killed, their eyes fixed in eternal stares. This enraged Aceti who I knew as a lover of animals, so much so, he had swinging little doors on the back of his Monsey, New York home, enabling small animals to feed on food he left on his porch. Aceti, Norman Mailer and his girlfriend and future wife, Norris Church, and I, ended up in the bedroom of the host, smoking hemp. After getting high, Aceti admonished the host for killing so many animals and Mailer chimed in with so much high artillery vocabulary, the insulted host began crying.

Five days before the fight, President Marcos and his wife, Imelda, hosted a reception for Ali and Frazier, inviting the visiting credentialed press as well to the presidential palace in Manila. Ali took his parents, his trainer, Angelo Dundee, and his girlfriend Veronica Porsche. Ali didn't realize that when a president of a country has you over for a drink, it's not a cocktail party, it's a state function and rather formal. After nine years, the marriage of Belinda and Muhammad, which had produced four children, was on the rocks. Belinda had endured other infidelities and knew about the constant presence of Veronica who was one of four beauty contest winners in Los Angeles. They were brought to Zaire to be poster girls at the fight. They were considered diversions for Ali and George Foreman during their month long stay in Kinshasha. Veronica was intended for Foreman, but Ali was captivated by her. King asked George if that would be a problem. He wisecracked that it would fine with him if Veronica kept Muhammad in rapture and busy for the month. But, Ali got the girl and his title back.

A month before Manila, I spotted Belinda and Veronica on the grounds at the same time, while Ali trained at Deer Lake, Pennsylvania. I was there for a pre-fight feature and while the sportswriters didn't write about her, it was obvious Veronica was in love. In her brightly colored Muslim dresses, she gawked at Ali during his workouts, never removing her stare even while she licked ice cream cones. Awestruck and proud of her beauty, I heard him say a mean thing at the expense of another. Pointing to Veronica in the distance, he kidded an old sparring partner who was paid to take a beating everyday. "When you get to be heavyweight champion, you'll get yourself a piece of ass like that, too."

Ali had grown so comfortable with the sportswriters looking the other way; he figured having Veronica on his arm in Manila was no big deal.

At the palace reception, President Marcos noticed the shapely woman with the striking face and mocha-colored skin next to Ali and said, "You have a beautiful wife." Ali didn't correct the presumption and answered "So do you," nodding toward Mrs. Imelda Marcos. Wire service reporters duly noted "Mrs. Ali" and within days there was a tidal wave of controversy that Ali never anticipated. Newsweek's Pete Bonventre broke the story about Ali's contradiction of being adulterous while claiming devout faith to the Muslim faith. At a subsequent news conference, Ali brought up the subject and defended himself expressing his loyalty to his wife. However, his infidelity was contrary to his devotion to his Muslim faith.

Three days before the fight, I had an appointment for an interview with Ali for ABC Sports, in his suite at the Hilton. NBC's Dick Schaap was also scheduled to meet with Ali. Suddenly, the regal Belinda arrived in ill humor, after flying about 13,000 miles from Chicago to vent her anger toward her philandering husband. Of course, we listened from the hallway as the mother of his four children scolded Muhammad for embarrassing her. After an hour-long tirade, Belinda refused a ride back to the airport and continued her 26,000 mile U-turn. Quickly, the American Muslim princess, a direct descendant of the founding father, Elijah Muhammad, filed for divorce ending their nine year marriage. The divorce settlement cost Ali $2 million and 2 homes and forced him to continue fighting 5 years beyond his prime. The punishment he took to his head in those last fights may have caused his numbing Parkinson Syndrome.

(Ali and I were the same age, 35. A few months after Manila, before I hosted an Ali boxing exhibition in Miami on ABC's Wide World of Sports, Ali asked me, in private, if I still played any sports and, if so, did I notice any difference? I said my reactions in tennis were slower. I was getting later and later to the ball. Ali candidly replied that he was having trouble getting out of the way of punches, he ordinarily avoided. I said, "At 35, it's obvious. You're staying too long in the wrong business." He answered, "I have to." Ali's inability to dodge punches worsened in the next five years of more fighting.)

In the pre-fight hoopla back in the United States, Ali insulted Joe at a news conference in New York, holding a miniature doll of a gorilla in his left hand and poking it with his right hand, saying:

> *"It will be a killer*
> *And a chiller*
> *And a thriller*
> *When I get the gorilla*
> *In Manila"*

The film clip became very familiar in the coming weeks on American television, setting the tone for revenge. But, the ridicule of Frazier had gone too far.

Frazier was a good, God-fearing, family man who was regarded by anyone who knew him as decent. He was born in 1944. His family, in Beaufort, South Carolina, had lineage back to slave stock. By age 20, he was a burly slaughter house worker in Philadelphia. Amateur boxing was his passion and the Philadelphia Golden Gloves champion went to Japan in 1964 with the U.S. Olympic team and won the gold medal for heavyweights. No one in boxing smiled quicker than Joe. His children seemed to be always around him. Ali's portrayal of him as an ignorant animal to sell the promotion was unfair. Ali resented Joe for calling him "Clay." Joe loved rhythm and blues music and sang in front of a touring group he organized called "The Knockouts." Ali's review was biting, "Joe fights just like he sings, bad," Cassius Marcellus Clay was born in 1942, in Louisville, Kentucky. In his 20s, Clay embraced the Muslim faith and Muhammad Ali evolved. In 1960, Clay won the light-heavyweight gold medal at the Olympic Games in Rome. He became a sensation in professional boxing because of his boastful remarks to the press, calling himself "the greatest of all-time."

On Saturday, two days before the fight, the countdown was on and Ali realized he had a major distraction. He wasn't in a good mood and reticent to speak about Veronica in our interview. Framed against the Bay of Manila in noontime sunshine, we spoke on videotape to be aired by satellite later in the day on ABC's Wide World of Sports.

Ali didn't smile and was tense and clipped in his speech and he made no rhymes or jokes. After he promised victory over and over again, I tried to have him put Frazier in proper perspective.

Marchiano: "Considering how close the first two fights were, considering how he put you down in that first one, don't you have any more respect than that, for Joe Frazier?"

Ali: "I'm glad the fight is coming off, so you can see that not only will I degrade him verbally but physically. I'm gonna destroy Joe Frazier."

An hour later, Frazier sat beside the pool at the Hyatt-Regency. It was oppressively hot and humid, but we wanted an outdoor tropical look as a background for the interview. Joe wore a red jumpsuit. I wore my bright yellow ABC Sports blazer with shirt and tie, despite the conditions. Both of us were sweating, just sitting there. Affable Joe gave me a light and breezy interview. This was a portion of our chat.

Joe Frazier—Manila Sept 28, 1975

Marchiano: "You said you might have some surprises for Muhammad. Like what?"

Frazier: "We're gonna have to wait for that particular time when we're gonna show a whole lot of things. You're gonna see a new Joe Frazier, I think."

When, it was over, we shook hands and the perspiring Frazier got up, turned right and jumped into the pool to cool off. Joe thought he was at the shallow end, but stout-hearted Joe Frazier couldn't swim and he sank to the bottom.

With one-half of the multi-million dollar gate attraction under water, Frazier's shocked handlers jumped into the pool and saved him from drowning, giving all the sports columnists a fresh angle for their Sunday sports sections.

Within minutes, Aceti began his edit session on the interviews for our live broadcast, a couple of hours away. The technician hired from the pay-per-view crew arrived with too much beer in him. The tech from New York was also a staunch and haughty union guy. When he clumsily made his first edit and cut into the master, Aceti grabbed him by the neck and dragged him out of the editing room and threw him against the wall in the hallway. Aceti was in a rage, screaming "There's no tech union in Manila and I'm the fucking boss." Joe returned and did the editing himself.

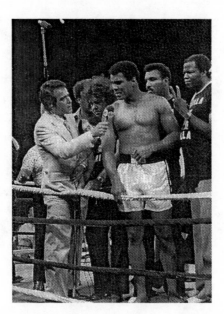

Muhammad Ali at the Thriller in Manila—weigh-in Sept 28, 1975.

The "Wide World of Sports" broadcast from the ring with the principals, went off without a hitch. Ali and Frazier were quiet during the ritual of the weights and calmly confident in their brief remarks. After their last responsibilities to the media were over, they left without clamor into seclusion. The bell for The Thrilla in Manila was only a day and a half away and there was a quiet interlude, the soft tropical winds sweeping the stately palm trees of Manila.

The day of the fight was hazy, hot and humid. It felt like a national holiday in Manila. The local start time was 10:45 am to satisfy primetime evening television back in the United States. The Philippine Coliseum was about the size of Madison Square Garden. Everyone was searched at the gates for weapons. Security personnel examined women's purses. The standing-room-only crowd was estimated at 25,000.

President Marcos sat in the third row with his wife, surrounded by a few hundred armed guards. He sat in a red velvet chair with a high gold back. With the temperature outside about 100 degrees and so many people inside for so long, the air conditioning failed. The arena was a sauna and yet these two great heavyweights would brawl for 14 rounds or nearly an hour.

Quietly and without incident, Drew "Bundini" Brown worked the crowd, picking pockets. Ali's court jester and corner-man complained he wasn't getting any U.S. money, "only pesos." Bundini was a key member of Ali's entourage. This cunning survivor of the streets was spiritually uplifting to Ali, who he called "Shorty." Bundini lived on his wits most of his life. He had a drinking problem and could be whacky. (When the Ali entourage flew back home, the flight was detained at Honolulu so stolen goods from the Manila Hilton like television sets, lamps and linens, could be removed. Bundini was fortunate to avoid prosecution.)

I had asked Ali's man in charge, Gene Kilroy, if I could be allowed inside Ali's dressing room to experience the vibe. About an hour before the fight, Kilroy escorted me past Ali's security men, the Fruits of Islam, into a dressing room. Ali's entourage included trainer Angelo Dundee, his brother Rahman, assistant trainer Wali Muhammad, head of security Pat Patterson, publicity man Bob Goodman and the chanting Bundini. Ali's quarters were a series of connected rooms. There were a couple dozen uneasy and impatient friends and relatives separately wishing him good luck and leaving. Soon, Gene and I were the only white guys in the rooms as voices grew louder and the language more profane.

Ali was silent, as he prowled room to room, wearing no shirt, slowly flexing his arms and aiming phantom punches in slow motion. Not once did I hear him respond to the level of anger that became frightening. The menacing moment is strongly etched in my memory. Unbridled hate was easy for these men who didn't have to face Frazier. It was a reminder that boxing doesn't have anything to do with sports. It's primal and violent, one man trying to impose his will over another. Gene suggested we get back to ringside.

My responsibilities were over with the weigh-in telecast but we were ready to do post-fight interviews in the event of an oddity. Otherwise, Cosell was to interview the fighters later in the week, in New York. Although my work was done, I had a prime ringside seat on the apron thanks to my ABC credential. All I had to do was watch and take notes. Aceti was to supervise the natural-sound version of the fight on videotape and mix in Cosell's call later in the week for a taped telecast of the entire fight the following Saturday on Wide World of Sports. I was seated to the immediate right of Ali's corner. On my left was the actor Hugh O'Brian, who was the star of the TV cowboy series "Wyatt Earp." He was Ali's good luck charm at fights and a special guest because Ali grew up as a faithful fan of the TV series. O'Brian and comedian Flip Wilson were part of the broadcast team and friendships could be the only reason.

Frazier preceded Ali into the ring and he was perspiring freely. Although conditions were stifling and hot, Ali arrived bone-dry. Once inside the ring, he came over to the ropes over us and motioned with his right glove to O'Brian and said, "This is gonna be easy . . . easy." Ali was whistling past the cemetery. Afterward, he would say that Frazier was so brutally tough; the experience was the closest thing to death he had experienced.

After the three Checkmates, friends of Frazier, sang the National Anthem, a four-foot high trophy was brought to the center of the ring. President Marcos had provided it for the winner. Ali walked to it, picked it up and brandished it high as he took it back to his corner. The crowd laughed, but it wasn't funny to the grim Smokin' Joe who couldn't wait for the ring to clear. The ring was larger than usual standards. It was 21-feet by 21-feet.

The introductions were made. Ali, at age 33, was 224 ½ lbs., wearing white trunks with a black waistband and black stripes. Frazier at 31 was 214 ½ lbs., wearing blue trunks with white stripes. Both were in white boxing shoes and white athletic socks. Soon enough, the only man separating the world's best heavyweights was referee Carlos Padilla. Ali was the 6 to 5 favorite among bettors in Manila and back home in the United States he was favored 9 to 5.

The opening bell rang and what ensued turned out to be a thriller and a chiller in three acts. The flat-footed Ali rushed the pace in the opening rounds, out-boxing and out-scoring Frazier, feeling so confident at the beginning of the third round, he bowed in the direction of President and Mrs. Marcos, blowing kisses to them. Ali was using his height and reach advantage. He was convinced Joe couldn't absorb so many shots to the head. But, the determined man who called him "Clay" (for Cassius Clay), didn't stop moving forward, bobbing up and down while shaking off the blows.

Frazier pounded Ali in round 5, gaining momentum through the 11th. He was the same old Joe, rushing forward, punishing the body, always trying to unleash his heavy left hook to the head. He was the same old Joe, who knocked down Ali four years earlier in their 1st encounter in New York's Madison Square Garden, when he won by unanimous decision. He was the same old Joe, who hurt Ali while losing their second battle by a 12-round unanimous decision in January of 1974, also in New York.

The Thrilla in Manila changed in the middle rounds and both fighters were straining in the heat and humidity. The backtracking Ali couldn't stop Frazier's relentless attack. When Ali took refuge on the ropes, Frazier hooked to his body and arms. Ali grimaced in pain and clinched. Smokin' Joe was making Muhammad pay for calling him a gorilla, for calling him dumb and for calling him ugly. A left hook to Ali's head staggered him in the 10th and his legs became weak. Joe was enjoying his assault and his momentum. Ali's look was grim and this was no time for clowning. That close to the action, I felt I was watching a man take another man down a dark alley for a beating. Angelo Dundee, his trainer, kept yelling from the corner, "Get out of the corners!"

Champions never give up. Champions do what must be done. Champions endure. Somewhere in his immense resolve, Ali found the energy to stage his comeback. From the 12th round on, Ali's punches starting taking ugly effect on Frazier's face. Joe was walking into lead right hands that landed with a louder "THWOCK" sound. Late in the 13th round, Frazier's lips were bloodied and his left eye was closing when he took a straight right hand to the chin . . . . "THWOCK." The mouthpiece flew out of his jaw and he stood flat-footed and unsteady. Frazier looked like a drunk waiting for a bus and he couldn't figure in which direction it was coming. The 14th round was a torture chamber for Frazier. Joe was the best man Ali ever fought. Joe brought out the best in Ali. Frazier was taking a pounding and paying the price. His left eye had closed to a slit. His right eye was swollen. In desperation, Joe unleashed a wild left hook, missed badly and spun with his back to Ali.

Joe didn't quit and Ali didn't knock him down. When the bell ended the 14th, Padilla had to point Frazier to his corner and led him there. Frazier's trainer, Eddie Futch, heard Joe say "I can't see, I can't see." Futch made the merciful decision not to allow Joe off the stool for the 15th and final round. Later, when the 64-year old Futch was second-guessed for not letting Frazier battle in the last three minutes, he said, "I'm not a timekeeper; I'm a handler of fighters. I don't want him to wind up a vegetable and not see his kids grow up."

Eddie's compassion was immense, given that moment in time and the callous nature of prize fighting. Joe was arguably ahead on points, but, three more minutes could have cost Frazier his sight and perhaps his senses. Frazier lost the fight, not the respect of his formidable opponent. When Ali saw Padilla's signal that the fight was over, he lifted himself slowly off his stool, raised his right hand in victory and sagged back to his stool. The fatigued Ali was still the heavyweight champion of the world. The handlers rushed to the aid of their fighters. I helped the elderly Don Dunphy scale the steep ringside steps. Dunphy had called the blow-by-blow on pay per view television to millions who cheered around the world. The Hall of Fame announcer tried in vain to interview the fighters who were dehydrated and barely able to speak. These extraordinary fighters were exhausted and we spectators were limp just from watching the action.

Using the 5-point must-system, the referee and the two judges had Ali ahead on their cards. Referee Carlos Padilla Jr had Ali ahead 66-60. Judge Larry Nadayag marked his card 66-62 and Judge Alfredo Quiazon had the champ in front 67-62. On a rounds basis, Quiazon had Ali ahead 8-3 with three even. The others each had it 8-4-2. Since the bell hadn't rung for the last round, it was recorded as a 14th round knockout. Ali's record was 49 victories and 2 defeats with 34 knockouts. He had lost only to Frazier and to Ken Norton, another defeat he reversed. Frazier went to 32 and 3, losing to Ali twice and being dethroned as champion by George Foreman in 1973.

The fighters were rushed to their dressing rooms through hallways of bedlam. The Fruits of Islam protected Ali's door and refused entrance to the press. I saw Dick Young of the Daily News try to push his way into the dressing room. One of the Islamic guards picked him up by his armpits and tossed him against the hall wall.

We were told both Ali and Frazier were being iced down and wouldn't be talking for awhile. In plain terms, they kicked the crap out of each other and enough damage was done to dim both of their boxing careers.

The next day, Frazier and Ali complimented each other. Smokin' Joe said, "Man, I hit him with punches that'd bring down the walls of a city. Lawdy, lawdy, he's a great champion." Ali apologized for insulting Joe before the fight, saying "Joe Frazier, I'll tell the world right now, brings out the best in me. I'm gonna tell ya, that's one helluva man, and God bless him."

Nine months later, Frazier was knocked out again by George Foreman. Joe tried a comeback in 1981 and retired after a 10 round decision over the mediocre Jumbo Cummings. Ali hung on 5 more years, benefiting from 2 favorable decisions against Jimmy Young and Ken Norton, losing his title to Olympian gold medalist Leon Spinks in his 8th professional fight, winning it back 7 months later, taking a beating from Larry Holmes, before losing miserably to the ordinary Trevor Berbick.

Over four years through 41 rounds, Ali and Frazier proved to be classic rivals, a perfect pairing who took so much from each other, neither were the same again in a boxing ring. Their solace was in the bank. Their trilogy set a new standard for combatants because each earned nearly $9 million in purses. On the street, that is the very definition of the brutal art of fighting.

Money slipped through Ali's fingers like water. He had no sense about saving it or investing it. Despite his Muslim beliefs, he was a philanderer.

Frazier had come a long way from earning $75 a week butchering cattle in a Philadelphia slaughter house. He liked to drink alcohol and dance, but his family was his first priority.

In numerous interviews with Frazier, running with him in the early morning, a couple of times in Philadelphia, I found him to be a straight shooter who was committed to training and winning and didn't need adulation. Money was what it was about, but "Smokin' Joe" wanted respect and he gave that in abundance to everyone he encountered. Joe was taken advantage of by the easily quotable Ali who promoted their fights in rather ugly ways. Muhammad's denigration of such a fine man was needless. Their fighting reputations should have been enough to sell their bouts.

Within an hour after the Thrilla in Manila, Aceti lugged the two huge videotape reels of the fight to our waiting car in the alley. We had checked out of the hotel that morning and our bags were packed for a late afternoon flight. Aceti held onto those tapes throughout our marathon journey from Manila to Guam with connections to Honolulu, San Francisco and New York. The return trip back across the Pacific Ocean and the United States took 21 hours.

During the first leg, a 14-hour flight from Guam to Hawaii, the pilot told us about a typhoon far to our left. From a distance, the giant thunderheads, outlined by distant sunlight, were menacingly awesome.

We had just left a tumultuous event and a physical phenomenon of another sort in Manila. In 40 years of covering sports, I can't think of another instance of drama, intensity and true courage. The Thrilla in Manila had fulfilled its promise. It was a thriller. One hundred years from now, when all the current star athletes are forgotten, Muhammad Ali will be remembered as "the" sports personality of our time. Manila was his last shining moment in the ring. Joe Frazier will be remembered for his relentless pursuit and courage, truly one of the greatest champions of all-time. Smokin' Joe pushed Ali to a victory that was "gladiatorial." It was simply the greatest heavyweight fight of all time.

Two nights later in an ABC TV edit session, in the basement of the network's West 66th Street complex in New York; Cosell viewed the videotape of the entire fight and then added his voice to the track. The result would be played on ABC's "Wide World of Sports" the next Saturday.

With heavy sarcasm, everyone in the control room agreed, the replay of the Thrilla in Manila was one of Cosell's better calls.

SPRING TRAINING

Mickey Mantle gave me his best stare. That arctic blast of a gaze that meant "who-the-hell-are-you-and-what do you want?"

I repeated my "Good morning" and said I was Frank Gifford's reporter for his WCBS-TV sportscasts back in New York and he sent me to the Yankees spring training camp in Fort Lauderdale "to interview you about your switch to first base." The Yankees legendary slugger and center fielder said matter-of-factly, "Where-in-the-hell is Frank?" I told him MY BOSS couldn't leave New York, so he sent me down to Florida. Mantle muttered "I'm only talking to Frank" and he turned his back to me and walked toward the batting cage this, otherwise, beautiful March morning in 1967.

I could hear the crack of the bat and the muffled noises from the fans in the small ballpark. I could see the Yankees in their trademark white uniforms with the black pinstripes and black caps and the white interlocking NY. But, it seemed my blood was rushing to my head. I was in a panic. This was my first out-of-town reporting assignment, in the first month of my employment and I'm 0-for-1. The Mick won't talk to me.

About an hour later, I'm in the lavatory of the Yankees' clubhouse, urinating in front of an open stall. Someone flicks my behind with a towel. I turn and it's Mantle. "Hey, I was just kidding you. I'll be back out there in about 10 minutes. Gotta change my shirt."

The first day on the job in spring training. It's supposed to be a piece of cake assignment, but I'm already on a reporter's roller coaster ride.

A similar incident happened to me two springs later, in 1969, when Boston Red Sox Hall of Famer Ted Williams made his debut as manager of the Washington Senators, in Pompano Beach, Florida. The last man to hit .400 was on everyone's list to interview. I was told by the Senators public relations man that Williams would talk to the beat reporters and me at the end of the day, after the intra-squad game. As instructed, my film crew shadowed

Williams on the field and in the dugout. Whether he was just watching or actually instructing a player, we had it on film. Williams' conversation with the writers lasted until late afternoon, while I waited outside the Senators barracks-style clubhouse. The sun was sinking below the horizon. We were losing light and the "we" was me, my cameraman, my soundman and my light man, all poised to work. The screen door suddenly opened and there he was, Ted Williams. He looked like John Wayne in a red, white and blue Senators' uniform, wearing a Senators' red satin windbreaker. His hands were on his hips and he bellowed to no one in particular, "Where's the man from CBS?" I raised my hand and he said, "You. They sent you? Where-in-the-fuck is Walter Cronkite?" He turned and opened the screen door, entered his clubhouse, slamming the door behind him. I was stunned. What will I tell my boss at CBS News back in New York? I'll never get another assignment. Do I go in there and beg him? Suddenly, the screen door swung open again. This time, Williams was laughing. "Relax, son, just having some fun. Let's get this over with. What's your name?" I was shaking and mumbling and I needed a couple of minutes to calm down before I could begin to talk with the Splendid Splinter who, in retrospect, was the only athlete I was ever in awe of when I interviewed him. Not only was Williams the last .400 hitter, he left major league baseball twice to serve in the military in World War II and the Korean Conflict. The second time, Williams didn't have to be a combat pilot. "The Splendid Splinter" was a hero outside of the foul lines and one of the most fascinating characters of the 20th century. He and the best of his generation saved the world.

Covering spring training is a delight whether as a baseball writer or broadcaster and a boyhood dream come true if you're lucky enough to be assigned to it. We grew up as baseball fans, jolted by a flush of excitement on frosty February mornings when we opened the sports pages and gazed at the first photographs of the our favorite team flexing their muscles in Florida and Arizona.

Now, as reporters we can hear optimism as high as an elephant's eye from star ballplayers, rookies and, of course, the managers. Casey Stengel was the easiest interview. Just ask a question and he talked "Metsies" till the film ran out. Billy Martin was the most intense manager at the ballpark. No one took defeat harder than him, but he was a charmer at the hotel bar. Martin, who never knew his father, idolized Stengel, taking on many of his mannerisms and demeanor. One late night, in Fort Lauderdale, Billy said to me, "Don't take me seriously at the ballpark, I'm the old man there, ya know, Casey." In that regard, Bobby Valentine is a lot like Billy Martin, all business in uniform, yet pleasant in social situations.

Ralph Houk was approachable but said nothing. Walter Alston was cold and matter of fact, but Gil Hodges was gracious and offered insights. He understood the interviewer is primarily the conduit between the team and the fans. Meeting and interviewing Tommy Lasorda was a pleasure because he's "old school," a very prideful man who owes his life to baseball. Off-the-record and away from microphones, Lasorda's verbal riffs aren't politically correct, but very funny.

Loveable Yogi Berra had to work hard at answering questions on camera. He was never comfortable about speaking extemporaneously. On the other hand, the slickest is Joe Torre. He understands the media's needs and doesn't meander in conversation, Joe gets to the point and is a delight to work with.

Yankee Don Mattingly and my WNBC-TV crew at Spring Training, Ft Lauderdale, FL 1985.

Spring training is an American ritual. A sign that the earth's rotation is warming and the long winter will soon be over. For everyone in the baseball community and the media, it's time to get back to work. The sportswriters have to cover the teams in depth. The TV guys hit the high points the first week.

Time spent at the ballpark was only half the day. There was golf and fishing in the late afternoon and our evenings were free. I learned quickly that what went on outside the lines may be great gossip but not for publication. However, in the late '60s when I began as a TV sports reporter things were changing. There was a new breed of sportswriters, evolving first in New York, nicknamed the "Chipmunks" by nationally syndicated sports columnist Jimmy Cannon. Young guys like Phil Pepe, Larry Merchant, Stan Isaacs, and Leonard Schecter were shaking the establishment's cage with candid stories about athletes. Their new style of reporting was evident on a greater scale throughout entertainment and the popular culture. Soon enough, scandal and police blotter stories became very much a part of the sports pages. The broadcast media followed suit. There were more of us broadcast types, much to the consternation of the ruling print media who had relationships with teams and their personalities for decades. I experienced some sportswriters shouting curses while a player was answering a question in a mass interview in front of his locker so the sound bite couldn't be used. I also met several outstanding sportswriters who weren't so insecure and were courteous and helpful. My favorites were Milt Richmond, Milton Gross, Dave Anderson, Jerry Izenberg, Arthur Daley, Phil Pepe, Lenny Lewin, Stan Isaacs and Maury Allen.

Because of the switch from film to videotape in the '70s and increasing live satellite transmissions in the '80s, we broadcast reporters became more immediate. So, goodbye to the late afternoons of leisure and those lengthy dinners at night. Instead of working only mornings, our work day was extended into the afternoons when we edited our videotape in new-fangled transmission trucks outside the ballparks. On the 5 to 7 p.m. newscasts, we did "live" on-camera reports. After a break for dinner, more editing and another live report on the 11pm newscast. Spring training became a very long day and hardly the vacation others thought. Although the classic and now overdone cliché is the local sportscaster beside the hotel pool, framed by under-lit palm trees, wearing a flowery summer shirt and teasing everyone, freezing back home, about how comfortably tropical and glamorous it is in "F-L-A."

Major league regular players really don't need six weeks to get ready for the new season. It's really for the pitchers. Most years the daily workouts and exhibition games become routine and it feels like a sleepy village.

Every once in a while, a bombshell drops like in 1987 at Port St. Lucie when the Mets assembled for a team photograph and an argument erupted between Darryl Strawberry and Keith Hernandez. Strawberry and Hernandez exchanged pushes and punches before being restrained. Someone wisecracked that it was the first time Strawberry hit the cutoff man. Yes, my WNBC cameraman was rolling. Later in the day, you would think we were the center of the universe. The executives back in New York arranged live satellite connections and LIVE AT FIVE was a "Metsfest" with video tape of the brawl and reactions from Strawberry and Hernandez and others.

In the '80s, I had to report on two police-blotter-type stories out of the Mets training camp and both involved Mets pitcher Dwight Gooden. First, it was disclosed that Gooden tested positive for cocaine and he left the team for rehabilitation. The other scandal involving Doc was an alleged rape of a woman by him and two other Mets in Port St. Lucie, the year before during spring training. An informed source linked me to the woman's father and I identified the three Mets in a live broadcast at spring training before the Port St. Lucie police interviewed them. Charges were never brought but it smeared the image of the Mets. The married and embarrassed Gooden told Mets public relations Jay Horowitz that it would be sometime before Doc gave me an interview. I told Jay to tell Gooden, "How about the rest of our lives." Later on, to Dwight's credit, he called the "calling-off" off.

My two all-time jerks in jocks were Ricky Henderson and Vince Coleman who came to New York teams with arrogance and ignorance, along with their bats and spikes. The day Henderson reported to the Yankees' spring training complex in Ft. Lauderdale, I introduced myself and requested an interview at his leisure. Ricky stared off to the horizon and pronounced, "Ricky don't need no press."

When Coleman reported to the Mets' spring training complex in Port St. Lucie, I introduced myself and requested an interview at his leisure. Coleman blurted "I'm not interested and I'm gonna forget your name anyway." Mets coach Willie Randolph was within earshot and after he stopped laughing, he advised Coleman to be more accommodating to the media. Coleman was too angry to comply. Henderson was too self absorbed in the third person plural. They played with a lack of goodwill and soon left, leaving little evidence of their stay in New York.

In the always fascinating and competitive world of sports reporting that was tame stuff compared to what happened when the Yankees began spring training in 1973. On March 5th, newspapers disclosed that a pair of Yankees starting pitchers swapped wives. Lefthanders Fritz Peterson and Mike Kekich walked into the Yankees camp in Fort Lauderdale and admitted their family lifestyles had changed. Switching wives was a phenomenon in a culture that popularized the sexy motion picture, "Bob and Carol and Ted and Alice." The previous season, the Yankees relied on both pitchers. Peterson won 17 games and lost 15. Kekich was 10 and 13.

It was a Monday night in St. Petersburg. My crew and I had worked our first day at the Mets and I was telephoned by my boss at WABC-TV and told to check out and drive across Florida to Fort Lauderdale. Jim Bouton, our 11PM sportscaster, had been a teammate and was a personal friend of Peterson and he had arranged for an exclusive interview at Fritz's rented house the next morning. All we had to do was get there on time. That night, to save time and a chance for some sleep later, we raced down "Alligator Alley," a very dangerous two-lane road. As huge trucks roared past us, I remarked to my cameraman that a head-on collision and fiery death would be especially tragic since we shouldn't be in this situation, chasing a story about four oversexed people.

We arrived safely, managed two hours of sleep, and were at Peterson's house at 7. Fritz was waiting on his front lawn and he delayed the interview until he heard Paul Harvey's ABC radio network newscast on his portable radio. Fritz was delighted when he heard Harvey shock America's Heartland with the startling revelation that a pair of lefthanded major league pitchers were trading wives. The Petersons and the Kekiches were in everyone's ears that sunny morning. Peterson and his wife, Marilyn, were from Illinois and he was a big fan of Harvey, the Chicago-based dean of American newscasters. Inside the house, Mrs. Susanne Kekich was serving breakfast to her two daughters, Kristen, aged 4, and Reagan who was 2.

These days, tabloid television techniques would demand the camera in the kitchen, with close-ups of the adulterous mother and her children. Fritz agreed to be interviewed alone on the lawn.

Peterson said both couples knew each other for 4 years and their feelings weren't "smutty." Off-season, they lived just 8 miles apart in New Jersey. The previous summer when their new relationships evolved, they had been married at least seven years and all were in their late 20s. It began as "a goof" but deeper feelings set in. Fritz talked about affection and compatibility. He said when they switched partners in their Franklin Lakes, New Jersey, homes during mid-season last year, there was a feeling of bliss shared by all four. To make sure of their decisions, they spent Thanksgiving week with their original partners. In December, their original exchanges were resumed. They decided to go public at the start of spring training. Peterson said double divorces and double marriages were planned, along with an exchange of the family dogs. He admitted guilt about how his sons, Gregg, aged 5, and Eric, aged 2, would be affected, but he was confident of their mother, Marilyn, and his new relationship with Susanne. Peterson was almost casual in his defense of going home and eventually marrying a teammate's wife. He said it wasn't "a wife swap, it was a life swap."

Back in New York, the entire front page of the Daily News was a photograph of the two couples posing on the deck of a yacht during a Yankees outing the summer before, hosted by sponsor Ballantine Beer. Framed against the schooner and sea, they switched partners as an inside joke. Now, the full, front-page photograph fueled the scandal. It was visual proof of WIFE SWAPPING!!! That night during his 11pm sportscast, Bouton alerted the audience that Eyewitness News would have an exclusive report on the 6 p.m. broadcast, the next evening, on Tuesday. Susanne refused to be interviewed, but Fritz was very accommodating. After we finished with them, I easily shipped the film on a 10 a.m. flight to New York.

That night, at six, the familiar "Eyewitness News" logo-and-music opening rolled on channel-7 to more viewers than usual all over the tri-state area. Because of the most unique trade in baseball history, WABC-TV Eyewitness News quadrupled its ratings. The interview with Fritz and the accompanying exclusive footage of his new life style with Susanne and her two daughters was a stone-cold, "leave-the-opposition-with-their-tongues-hanging-out," exclusive. The TV audience couldn't get enough. We repeated the report at 11PM and used more of the interview the next night.

Baseball Commissioner Bowie Kuhn was "appalled" but the pitchers' sex lives were out of his jurisdiction. Across morning cups of coffee, Americans from coast to coast, harrumphed: "Imagine, a couple of Yankees swapping wives. My, oh, my, what's happening to this country?" And, the many of those same people probably paid to see "Bob and Carol and Ted and Alice," a hit motion picture about two married couples switching mates.

Kekich and Peterson were the first big-name jocks to switch wives and cross the entertainment arc into gossip and scandal, the culture's new national pastime. Since 1973 till now, the evolution of syndicated TV trashy embarrassments, like the Jerry Springer Show, haven't been much of a stretch.

When I returned to the WABC-TV office a week later, News Director Al Primo called me into his office and greeted me warmly, his smile wrapped around an unlit pipe. Primo had transformed a bad third in local TV news ratings into a runaway hit. Now he was very pleased with the record ratings for Eyewitness News" thanks to the Kekich-Peterson story. Al wasn't a sports fan and didn't know a balk from a fungo but said, "I love spring training."

PS . . . . Mike and Marilyn had been along for the ride. After public disclosure, their combination lasted only months. Kekich moved to the Southwest and Marilyn to the Midwest. Fritz and Susanne married and had 4 children of their own. They live near Chicago. Fritz became a casino-boat dealer in Elgin, Illinois.

RAY ARCEL'S RAG

The TWA airliner was in the air only 20 minutes, streaking northeast out of Las Vegas heading for JFK airport in New York. It was the morning of June 12, 1982, after Larry Holmes defeated Gerry Cooney to retain his world heavyweight championship. Many people on the flight had something to do with the fight or were boxing fans. Actor Ryan O'Neal and his wife, actress Farah Fawcett, were seated in front of me. O'Neal was a big boxing fan and he was still excited about what happened the night before in the desert heat which reached 99 degrees in the parking lot stadium of Caesar's Palace.

Holmes versus Cooney was a $40 million promotion and each fighter earned over $8 million. Regrettably, the promoters played the race card, that is, the black champion against the white hope. Cooney's camp was especially vile in its racist attitude. National news magazines fostered the hate for expediency. Holmes was openly critical of Time and Sports Illustrated for their front cover photographs of the challenger instead of him. To date, the 32-year-old Holmes had successfully defended his world title 11 consecutive fights.

Actor-producer Sylvester Stallone attended workouts in Las Vegas, using the promotion to help publicize his latest boxing fable, "Rocky III." When I met him, after shaking hands, he immediately said, "I bet you thought I was bigger." Stallone photographed like a heavyweight in his films, but he was really less than 160 lbs. and shorter than six feet tall.

Four days before the fight, I was working with a tape crew for ESPN at Cooney's workout. The 6-foot, 6-inch, 225 pound lefthander from the New York City suburb of Huntington, Long Island was wrongly depicted as "The Great White Hope." There had been no Caucasian World Heavyweight Champion since Rocky Marciano and that became the drumbeat of the multi-million dollar promotion. Two years earlier, in Atlantic City, Cooney gained widespread prominence knocking out Jimmy Young in the 4th round of his first nationally televised bout and his 54-second demolition of former

WBC champ Ken Norton was frightening. The alert and forceful intervention by referee Tony Perez saved the life of Norton who was trapped in a corner and Cooney became a national name.

Gerald Arthur Cooney turned professional in 1977, a tough kid from a large working class Irish family on Long Island. He originally called himself "Irish Gerry Cooney." Joe Flaherty of the Village Voice once asked him where his family came from, specifically which county in Ireland. Cooney responded sarcastically "Suffolk." While some of his buddies went to college and others took jobs, Cooney went to the gym because he figured he could make good money in the ring as a hard-hitter. He was always bigger than his opponents and he could really bring it with the left hook. But, this was graduation day because he was challenging an alltimer, the best man in his division, with an accurate and powerful jab and a solid chin. I had too much respect for the hand speed and upper body movement of Holmes to pick against him. Cooney was a standup boxer, a stationary target for a marksman like Holmes. Also, Cooney was over protected with only six rounds of work in the previous two years. Despite mean and ruthless in the ring, Gerry was really a friendly guy who hadn't matured yet. He grew up watching my sportscasts on New York television and he was always gracious regarding interview requests. However, at the beginning of his workout in a fancy hotel ballroom with crystal chandeliers, he wiped the smile off my face when he walked over to me and mentioned he heard my prediction on ESPN the night before. Cooney said "This is for picking Holmes." He spit on my right shoe. Sorry, Gerry, but in boxing I never pick with my heart.

The 25-year-old challenger was managed by the so-called "Wacko Twins," Dennis Rappaport and Mike Jones who shrewdly guided Cooney avoiding any top-10 opponent en route to a title shot. The affable and sweet Cooney was strongly influenced by the tough talking and outspoken Rappaport, who chanted on his way to the ring on fight night . . . "Gerry, win it for America," as if Holmes was a foreigner.

Rappaport was a laughingstock in Vegas a week before the bout. Because he was Cooney's manager, he was staying in a plush suite at Caesar's Palace. His first night in town, Rappaport was picked up by two women, who took him back to their apartment for some fun. Once there, he suggested they continue their party in his hotel suite with all the room service they desired. The trio switched locations and the next morning, Rappaport awakened with a headache and minus his cash and jewelry. He called Caesar's security and then the Las Vegas police and told them he remembered where the women lived. When they arrived at the apartment house, they discovered it was the kind of place you can rent by the day. Locals know it as "the Storefront Trick." The scam is as old as the Las Vegas Strip. Rappaport needed some cash until some money was wired to him. He asked rival manager Lou Duva for a couple hundred bucks and Lou agreed. But, Lou spread the embarrassing story, gleefully.

Besides his racial taunts, Rappaport made himself more of a clown by carrying a paper mockup of a clock to the ring to indicate that time was running out on Holmes' championship reign. One of Rappaport's boorish and tasteless statements to the press was "If Holmes thumbs Gerry, I've instructed him to knee Holmes in the groin."

In the still heat of a summer night in Las Vegas, the outdoor stadium crowd was buzzing with anticipation. From the opening bell, Cooney was determined and showed a tough chin but he was bewildered by Holmes' movement and his whiplash jab which was the best in the business. Cooney was awkward because he threw punches off-balance and he seldom hit with leverage. His jab had little power but his left hand was wrecker. Cooney could bang with the best of them. Opponents were very wary of his left hand so they tried to box him.

In the second round of his 26th pro fight, the undefeated Cooney was knocked down for the first time. Cooney was up at the count of 5 and spent the rest of the steamy Friday night taking a beating from Holmes. Cooney resorted to fouls and he hurt Holmes with several low blows. Referee Mills Lane kept warning him in vain. Because of low blows in the 9th round, Lane deducted two points. Holmes was allowed a brief rest period because of the pain in his groin. After the same infraction in the 11th, Lane took a third point away from Cooney. Late in the 13th round, Cooney was bleeding from his closed left eye and his nose, taking a two-handed barrage, not throwing a punch, when he spun toward the ropes and hooked the top one to keep from going down. But, he sagged. Holmes retreated to a neutral corner and Lane's count was to four when Cooney's trainer/surrogate-father, Victor Valle jumped into the ring and urged the referee to stop the slaughter. Lane called it a disqualification because he had not stopped it when Valle entered the ring.

There would have been a huge controversy if the fight had gone the distance, 2 rounds and 8 seconds more, leaving the matter to the three judges. Their view of the fight was mystifying. Most of the 32,000 in the outdoor stadium at Caesar's Palace and most reporters at ringside saw it as a one-sided fight. Using the 10-point must-system, after 12 rounds, one judge, Jerry Roth saw it that way. Ford had Holmes in front 115-109. If the three points had not been deducted, the two other judges, Mike Moretti and Duane Ford, would have had Cooney ahead after 12 rounds, 113-111. In other words, the judging was odd. Despite Holmes' dominance and Cooney's loss of three points, those two judges had Cooney winning seven of the 12 rounds that were completed. This is not to say Cooney didn't try and didn't hurt Holmes, he rocked Holmes with rights in the 2nd, 6th and 13th rounds, but over all those rounds, the champion was the master. Cooney never delivered his freight train of a left-hand. The judges overrated Cooney's aggressiveness and ignored Larry's jab that kept scoring. If Moretti and Ford had carried the voting, it would have been a scandal.

Cooney was especially disappointed and he apologized to the spectators on the ring microphone saying "I'm sorry." He had earned $8.5 million for his beating and he learned more about boxing in 13 rounds against Holmes than he did in his 25 previous professional bouts.

Immediately after the fight, I had arranged for an exclusive interview with Holmes in his trailer. When I was allowed in, Holmes was wincing in pain while dabbing at his bloody feet. He had made a foolish mistake, wearing new athletic shoes and he suffered throughout the fight with bleeding blisters on the soles of his feet.

Holmes, at 32, improved to 40-0, his 30th win by knockout, extending his four-year championship reign with his 12th consecutive successful defense of his World Boxing Council title. The affable Holmes, who endured the added burden of following Ali across the heavyweight division landscape, yearned for acceptance and respect. Holmes earned his bones in boxing but he could never match Ali's charisma. Then again, who has? At the ensuing news conference, Holmes said, "I see no color. I'm not a racist. I'm not prejudiced. When I see Gerry Cooney, I see a human being who was trying to take my head off." Cooney's eyes were puffy and filled with tears when he said in a raspy voice, "I did my best, I'm very sorry."

The flight to New York was humming and seatbelt lights were off when I moved back toward the familiar Ray Arcel. He was 82 years old. Holmes was the 22nd world champion he trained. His list of guys read like a Who's Who in pugilism . . . . Barney Ross . . . Benny Leonard . . . . Tony Zale . . . Kid Gavilan . . . James Braddock . . . . Ezzard Charles . . . Roberto Duran.

In 1923, his first world champion was a flyweight named Frankie Genaro. In 1949, Arcel was in Charles' corner when he defeated Jersey Joe Walcott for the heavyweight title vacated by Joe Louis. In 1972, he was in Duran's corner when he knocked out Ken Buchanan for the world lightweight championship.

Ray didn't carry the pail for David against Goliath, but he had a Masters Degree in punching and avoiding blows from that hallowed hall of fighting knowledge, New York's Stillman's Gym. For some 2,000 fighters, he had been teacher, psychiatrist, dietician and protector. He stressed discipline and rigorous training. Arcel once said the secret to success in the ring was "brains over brawn." Twice he had been voted "Trainer of the Year" by the National Boxing Writers Association. His proper manners and natty attire made him appear professorial, but this was one cunning old man. Arcel grew up around 106th Street, in Manhattan and was a "dees-dems-and-dos" "Noo Yawker" who pronounced one of his favorite words, as "woik."

I asked the Hall of Famer trainer, who had been in boxing since he was 17, if I could sit beside him for a few minutes so we could talk. For all his boxing notoriety, Ray was friendly and polite. I treasured our conversations about boxing and was very pleased that he watched my sportscasts in New York through the years and critiqued my blow-by-blow calls on the weekly ESPN fights.

"Ray, what you did between the 10th and 11th rounds last night . . . how many times have you done that?"

He turned toward me, his eyebrows arched and he smiled. After a long look into my eyes, he answered, "If I tell ya, will ya not tell anyone until after I die?" I said, "Of course, you have my word."

Arcel said, "You've got a good eye. Where were you seated?" I said, "On the apron to the left of your corner, the third guy down the line."

Arcel said, "How many times? . . . . big fights?" I nodded yes. ". . . about 500 times."

Arcel was admitting to something against the rules but the octogenarian got away with it and his guy, Larry Holmes, still wore his crown.

Holmes dominated the fight but Cooney was game and had the ringside crowd on his side. Holmes was clipped several times in the 10th round and with less than 10 seconds left, Cooney, who was a natural lefthander, caught Holmes with a left to the head. Holmes was hurt but didn't go down. When the bell rang, the obviously fatigued Holmes shuffled to his corner. With five rounds left, the champion looked stale. He was on the take and the low blows were taking effect.

Eddie Futch, his other elderly trainer and another Hall of Famer, jumped into the ring spraying Holmes face with a sponge full of cold water. Holmes sat in the corner on his stool. Outside the corner, slightly to the right of Holmes, Arcel was yelling into his ear. My eyes never left the Holmes corner. I didn't want to blink. Boxing's Gold Dust Twins, with decades of experience, helped their fighter while fooling everyone in attendance and watching on television. Futch waved a towel about six inches from the champion's face, cooling him. Suddenly, Futch stopped and held the towel upright, obscuring Holmes' face. In that instant, Arcel's right hand came under the top rope and he covered Holmes' nose and mouth with a hand towel. Larry's head bolted back. Arcel's right hand moved back under the top rope and into the right pocket of his white smock and Futch resumed fanning Holmes. It took a few seconds while the crowd buzzed about the prospect of a comeback by Cooney who was 7 to 5 underdog.

A sleight-of-hand trick by two old pros, a waker-upper for a groggy champion, thanks to "poppers," amyl-nitrite, concealed in a hand towel. Because of his 65 years experience, Arcel had loaded up, while Holmes stumbled to his corner. What was in Arcel's hand rag gave Holmes' heart a rush of adrenaline. Arcel yelled, "Don't let this bum take your title away." Holmes was alert when he answered the bell for the 11th round and he pounded Cooney into submission for two and a half more rounds before the slaughter was stopped in the 13th. Futch and Arcel were skillful in their execution of deceit.

The day after, on that plane flight home, Ray Arcel was content that he had protected his guy. So, he broke some rules, what else was new after more than six decades in the cruelest of sports? Didn't the other guy hit his guy below the belt a couple of times? His guy needed some help.

When Arcel died of leukemia in 1993 at age 94, I remembered his words, on that flight after Holmes' victory, "How many times? . . . . big fights? . . . . About 500 times."

A GIANTS DIARY

It is early Sunday, July 11, 1971 and dawn breaks east of Brookville, Long Island. A soft rain stops falling on the campus of C. W. Post College. A white Volkswagen camper rolls through the entrance gate, jumps a sidewalk and stops at the edge of the football practice field. The driver steps out, lies on the wet grass and falls asleep. He's Fred Dryer, defensive end for the New York Giants. He has driven from Los Angeles, arriving ahead of the rookies and free agents who report the next day. Dryer is one week ahead of the Giants' returning veterans because "I want to get an early start on our trip to the Super Bowl."

Monday, July 12th . . . . 42 rookies and free agents check into the Giants' training camp at Post. They're joined by Dryer and two reserve linemen on the bubble, Dennis Crane and Vernon Vanoy. Head coach Alex Webster welcomes them and introduces his assistants and team staff. The players are issued rooms and football gear. Later, all of them bus into Manhattan for physical examinations.

Dryer is wide-eyed about New York. He has eagerly taken to the big rush in the big city and yearns to experience its endless possibilities. He thought playing professional football in New York would be a double whack of good fortune. The San Diego State Aztec was selected in the first round of the National Football League Draft by the Giants, the 13th player picked overall. In his first two seasons, #89 led the team in tackles. Because of his relentless pursuit of ball carriers, teammates nicknamed him "Fearless."

The 6-foot, 6-inch, 225 pound combination of speed and strength was the product of Southern California's bountiful football talent pool. The emergence of the aerospace industry attracted families from all over the country and the baby boom eventually strengthened the school systems. His father, Charles, had migrated from Kentucky and Ohio to California in 1936.

He served in the Navy in World War II and then met Genevieve Nell Clark, a native Californian and they wed. Fred and his brother, Charlie, grew up in a sun-kissed paradise playing with their German shepherd, Rex, and biking to Manhattan Beach to bodysurf.

At Lawndale High School, Dryer preferred baseball but, because of his size, coaches urged him to also play basketball and football. In his senior year, Fred adapted quickly and successfully to football. He understood the tactics of defending against offenses. He was especially strong and quick and pursued ball-carriers like a panther on the hunt. After Lawndale High School, he went to El Camino College for two years. Then, Dryer was recruited by John Madden, at the time, the defensive assistant to Don Coryell at San Diego State, a teachers college. Coryell's football guru was Sid Gillman, the innovator of pro football offenses while leading the San Diego Chargers in the old American Football League. Madden drove from San Diego to Dryer's home in Hawthorne, near Los Angeles, and spent an afternoon with Fred's mother, Nell, discussing her son's collegiate future. After they agreed on San Diego State, Madden drove Fred back to San Diego and he became an Aztec.

In two seasons at San Diego State, Coryell's Aztecs were so deep and talented, Dryer played in only one defeat. Practicing against Coryell's "throw without fear" offenses was extremely rewarding for the Aztecs' defensive unit. Dryer's football teachers were vastly experienced and were still innovating.

However, he felt his progress was blunted as a professional with the Giants, a middle tier team. New York's coaching was inferior and the organization lagged behind the times in scouting and drafting. He was shocked how slow his teammates were. He was sure the franchise owner, Wellington Mara, had the best intentions but he hired too many cronies because he was excessively loyal. They weren't necessarily the best available people in football.

Dryer especially loved game-days at Yankee Stadium in the Bronx. Its familiar gothic structure set peculiar shadows as the light slanted in the late afternoon toward left field. The Giants' dark blue game jerseys and helmets were classic. Dryer liked the feel of his cleats on the same turf that was the stage for so many baseball and football immortals. He appreciated the roar of the New York crowd, a deafening sound unlike any other in sports stadiums. The slow, deep, perfect diction of longtime public address announcer Bob Shepherd was almost religious sounding.

After home games, there were Sunday night parties, on Manhattan's swinging Eastside, at teammates' apartments. Eligible bachelors like Tucker

Fredrickson and Bobby Duhon attracted dozens of pretty models and airline
attendants.

As much fun as he was having, Dryer knew he was stalemated. He felt
that his team at San Diego State could have beaten his Giants of the NFL.
All that stuff he said about going to the Super Bowl was just for the sports
writers to print.

So, Dryer began his third year in New York appropriately stuck in rush
hour traffic. The waiting at the medical clinic was long and tedious. The
players didn't return to the C.W. Post campus on Long Island until 10 pm.
A long, uneventful, first day, but no one flunked his physical.

Tuesday, July 13th . . . . it's hot and humid . . . . two-a-day workouts
begin minus the Giants' 1st, 3rd and 4th round draft choices. Wide receiver
Rocky Thompson was the 18th selection overall. But, he's with the third
round pick, linebacker Ron Hornsby, at the College All Stars training camp.
Only two weeks ago, 4th round pick Dave Tipton, a huge defensive end from
Stanford, broke his leg in the Coaches All-America game. Tipton never put
on a Giants jersey and he was done for the season, the team's first loss in what
would be a list of many.

Wednesday, July 14th . . . . Webster and his assistants focus on 2nd
draft pick, tackle center Wayne Walton, from Abilene Christian. He's 6-5,
245 lbs. and he moves quickly. Walton is getting special attention from Pop
Ivy, the new offensive line coach. In less than two hours, Walton must have
been imposing. Following the morning workout, center Joe Zigulich from
Northwestern packs his bag and leaves, muttering "I've had enough of pro
football." After his hasty exit from the dorm, there are jokes about the Big
Ten, among the players in the hallways.

During the afternoon workout, word reaches camp about a wire service
report that has the Giants moving from Yankee Stadium to a proposed new
stadium in New Jersey. As usual, team owner Wellington Mara is at the
practice. Wellington is a solid family man and devoutly Catholic. He attends
mass everyday and would father 11 children. He's extremely loyal to those
close to him and those who perform their duties without sin or scandal.
Named after the Duke of Wellington, he's a pug nosed Irishman and speaks
with a New York accent. He is "Mr. Mara" to most, "Well" to family and
close friends and "Duke" to his inner circle. He is an everyday attendee at
practice, staying on the perimeter and he doesn't interfere. He's a serious man
but when he smiles, it's big and broad and crinkles his face.

Wellington's father, Timothy, acquired the team for $500 in 1925. Legend has it as the payment of a gambling debt, but that has never been confirmed. Wellington was a 9-year old ball boy for the Giants. In 1930, when he was 14 and his brother Jack was 22, their father turned the ownership to them. In 1965, when Jack died of cancer at age 59, his son Tim inherited the other half share in the team. Wellington made the Giants his life's work, attending all practices and overseeing the business as president.

The 35-year-old Tim Mara may own 50 percent of the franchise and is vice-president, but he isn't included in the football decisions. After graduating Iona College, Tim served in the Navy and the Giants have been his only business career endeavor. Publicly, Tim isn't critical about the Giants. Privately he fumes to friends, especially late in the evening over cocktails at P.J. Clarke's or Mr. Laffs. He laments that his team is behind the times because other NFL teams are scouting better players. Tim is loyal to his uncle "Well," but he spends more and more time complaining to buddies about the team's old school practice of hiring buddies for aides and scouting players without firsthand scouting.

Wellington always wears a sweat suit to practice and keeps in shape by running and doing calisthenics. Well is very visible with his Giants but he doesn't seek publicity. A television crew arrives and a TV news reporter, looking for Mara, walks right past him on the sideline. The TV guy asks Publicity Director Don Smith if Mara is in camp. Smith says "No" and proceeds to give a minute of double talk on camera while Mara strolls across the field to the dormitory and his room.

Thursday, July 15th . . . . from his platform, 20 feet above the field, Jim Trimble scans the players on the field. He is the Giants' Director of Player Personnel. Trimble was a head coach in Canada and the NFL. He was a longtime scout for the Giants. He's called "Super Scout" or "Jungle Jim." Trimble is a handsome man, with a broad chest, and muscular with huge hands. His voice is resonant and he's famous for his offbeat descriptive imagery. Discussing a wide receiver from a West-Coast small college, Trimble says he rejected him because "He's dainty-boned." Looking at the sleek, well-built body of defensive back Pete Athas, Trimble remarks "I'm sure envious of those wiry guys. Look at Pete's behind. It looks like two pebbles on a shingle."

Late in the day, the Giants trade an undisclosed draft choice to San Francisco for 10-year defensive tackle Roland Lakes. Dryer says "Another stopgap deal by Trimble."

Fred Dryer at Giants training camp, 1971

Dryer's football pedigree was better than any other defensive player on the Giants who weren't being taught any new tactical philosophy except the obvious X's and O's. "This game," says Dryer, "is about speed, covering the 50-by100 yard field, coordinating the flow of pursuit angles and aggressively attacking offenses. I'm not learning anything here and things won't improve in the near future. We don't have enough playing talent because the scouting is inferior and the team is being out-coached by opponents. What the Giants need are younger and quicker players, not guys hanging on, after 10 years in the league."

Friday, July 16th . . . . wide receiver Coleman Zeno, a 17th round draft pick from Grambling, loses his defender and glides under a pass for an easy touchdown. Offensive backfield coach Jim Garrett, effervescent like a freshman cheerleader, yells: "Offense, way to percolate!" When Garrett was head coach at Susquehanna, he was known for his lengthy itineraries. One of them ended, "Following our total team victory, return to campus with horns blowing!"

During one-on one drills for linemen, Webster stares at defensive lineman named Bob Winchell. He has the dimensions, 6'5" and 290 lbs., but he never played football, he was a shot putter. Trimble spotted him on a practice field at the University of Indiana and talked him into trying out. Winchell is quite a physical specimen, but no football player. He's lined up at tackle and also at end. Offensive linemen manhandle him and look like all-pros. After every whistle, Winchell takes off his helmet because it hurts his head. It's hot and humid and Winchell airs his expansive belly by raising his jersey. Webster orders Winchell to keep his helmet on and his jersey down. At the end of the day, a very sore and almost dehydrated Winchell is asked to leave.

Saturday, July 17th . . . . The first sense of urgency . . . this is the day for the first player cuts . . . . after an intensive, steamy morning workout, the players are free, but still must make curfew at C.W.Post College. Seven free agents are told by Trimble they aren't talented enough to stay.

Dryer goes to off-campus dinner with Matt Hazeltine, his closest friend on the team who is 38, 13 years older than Dryer. Hazeltine was an All-American linebacker at the University of California. He was a standout player with the San Francisco 49ers. He retired after the 1969 season, but was convinced to return with the Giants by former teammate and onetime Giants quarterback Y.A. Tittle. Hazeltine agreed to be a player/coach with New York.

As the weak side linebacker behind Dryer at right end, they proved to be quite an effective tandem during the 1970 season. Dryer possessed speed and Hazeltine had the experience. They created odd fronts and rushing schemes to cause blocking problems for opposing offenses. They made a lot of tackles and Hazeltine felt like a teenager again.

Good-looking Matt capped his 13-year NFL career with spectacular play on and off the field. Most of the young women he met in Manhattan were transfixed by his good looks and quiet, confident demeanor. Matt continually reminded them that he had a wife back home in Palo Alto where he had a second career in insurance. Hazeltine told Dryer his season with the Giants was the most fun he had in football, even though he injured a knee in practice when he was hit oddly by receiver Coleman Zeno. The injured knee deteriorated and Hazeltine became a fulltime linebacker coach for the '71 season. The younger players envied his easy success with women their age. Pete Athas nicknamed him "Matinee Matt at the Laundromat."

Sunday, July 18th . . . Everyone is off, but Dennis Crane is running. The reserve center was told by Webster in the off season to report at 260 lbs. Crane tipped the scales at 287. Webster fumed it'll start costing Dennis 25 dollars a pound on Monday, the day the veterans report. Crane puts in an exhaustive day and eats only two pieces of meat. Two weeks before training camp, he stopped drinking beer and switched to soda pop. He is discovering there are more calories in the sweet stuff.

The interest and energy that went into Crane's weight problem became a team joke and symbolic of its misdirection. The Giants were coming off a 9-5 season. But, this year's Giants were already regressing. Dryer felt the instability. What had worked the year before had lost its momentum. He had just negotiated his third, one-year contract. His initial deal in 1969 was $30,000 for the season with a $60,000 signing bonus. Dryer wanted an increase in salary to $70,000. The Giants refused and he accepted $47,000. "I am not a troublemaker. I just want Wellington Mara, a good and reasonable man, to wake up and recognize the failings of this organization. We need better players."

Dryer was slowly accepting the fact that he was the only quality player drafted in three years and he had to leave to play on a better team. "I don't have enough playing time left to wait." (The Giants' inability to adapt to contemporary football systems and philosophies was borne out by their subsequent 4-10 record.)

Monday, July 19th . . . the dorm is livelier because of the joking among the veterans who haven't seen each other since last December. They were a 9-5 team that finished second in the NFC East under Webster. Two of them are missing. Ron Johnson's attorney has advised the Giants that their first 1,000 yard gainer in franchise history wants his salary doubled to $100,000. Johnson won't report until a six-figure is agreed upon. Defensive lineman Bob Lurtsema doesn't report and a telephone call to his wife brought the news that "Lurts" broke his small toe due to a falling piece of furniture.

Her explanation to the Giants was complicated and puzzling because her husband would like to earn more money from the Giants. So, Lurtsema is considered a holdout.

Crane is weighed. Despite his day of running in the sun and eating only two pieces of meat, he's gained three lbs. Crane is 290 lbs. and owes Webster $750. The veterans take the same long bus trip to Manhattan for their physicals and return late, too. Crane enters Dryer's room and plops on a bunk perplexed by his dilemma. Dryer offers him a piece of pie. Later, there are whispers in the dorm that Crane went to the Mug N'Ale down the road and gorged on hamburgers and beer.

Tuesday, July 20th . . . . Weighing heavily on the mind of Crane is the arrow that points to 292 lbs. and he owes Webster $800. Crane is tortured. He hasn't lost any significant weight. Dryer offers help, promising he can help

Dennis lose 20 lbs. in about a half-hour. Crane asks how, and Fred says, "I'll tie you to the back of my camper and drag you all over campus."

After another visit to the Mug N' Ale, the bloated Crane quietly checks out. He is symbolic of the failing of the Giants organization. Crane should have never been there, taking a spot on the roster.

Dryer says, "This is a weird and screwed up training camp, but not mean-spirited."

Wednesday, July 21st . . . . After morning and afternoon practices and dinner, the Giants listen to a seminar on drugs and gambling delivered by a representative from the NFL Commissioner's staff. He's Bernie Jackson and a black. For some unexplained reason, the talk offends Wes Grant, a defensive end out of UCLA who missed his entire rookie season because of a back injury. Grant demands a private talk with Webster and his anger is puzzling because the team had been fair to a promising player who still hadn't played a minute while getting full pay. He's projected as the left defensive end to compliment Dryer's hard-charging style at right end. Grant tells Webster he's really offended by his salary, that he wants more money. Right after the meeting, the Giants put Grant on waivers and trade him to Miami.

Thursday, July 22nd . . . . The workouts are brisk. Running back Joe Morrison is back for a 13th season. This offensive jack of all trades is the only Giant left from a team that last won a division title, in 1963. He's an ex-teammate of Webster. They're buddies and chain smokers. Morrison wasn't big enough or fast enough, but he always won a job as running back or wide receiver. Webster will try Morrison as a backup tight end behind Bob Tucker.

Friday . . . . July 23rd . . . . more hot and humid weather . . . . rain would be welcome . . . . Fran Tarkenton's passes have zip . . . "I'm throwing as good as I've ever thrown." Asked about rookie quarterbacks Jim Plunkett, with New England and Archie Manning with New Orleans, he says, "It's much too early to rate them. It's going to be tough enough for them in their rookie seasons and for the next couple three years. They're playing for teams that aren't strong." As for the Giants' multiple offense, Fran says "It's geared to our type of people. We're not overpowering because we don't have big running backs. Hopefully, multiple sets will distract because defenses are dominating the game and taken it over. Dallas was a forerunner in this respect. Tom Landry, who's a defensive genius, recognized this a few years ago. He's done more in-depth study than anyone else."

With Giants Fred Dryer and Fran Tarkenton NYC 1971

Saturday July 24th . . . . after practice, the players are free until curfew Sunday night. Fred Dryer drives to Manhattan in his white Volkswagen camper. Grand Funk Railroad is playing on his radio. He's chewing a carrot. The cotton bed sheets on his camper bunk are the Disney characters "Snow White and the Seven Dwarfs." Thanks to newspaper photographs of his Volkswagen camper and several newspaper stories about his southern California, surfer boy style, the popular misconception is that Dryer lives in his camper parked at Yankees Stadium. In fact, he shares a four-bedroom luxury apartment in Manhattan with teammates Matt Hazeltine, Ray Hickle and Tim McCann, in the Lyden Gardens building on East 64th Street. Fred drinks no alcohol and eats no red meat. While growing up in Southern California, Fred's mother raised him on a macrobiotic diet. For breakfast he prefers oats and honey. When the Giants are served beef at team lunches, he prefers vegetables and grains plus a lot of water with no ice. The Giants maintain that he should be heavier and encourage more carbohydrates and supplemental food drinks. Dryer is in perfect physical condition and will not change his diet. He has never owned a sports jacket until coming to New York. He wears clean white T-shirts and blue jeans and sometimes his favorite, size 13, green-and-red bowling shoes. After he appeared at his first Giants charity luncheon in white T-shirt and jeans, it was suggested to him by Tim Mara that he buy a wardrobe more appropriate for New York's social life. He did.

In his off time, Fred prowls the city's museums and art galleries. He is friendly with pop artist Andy Warhol who published a cover story about Dryer in his weekly pop art "Interview" newspaper. The gay Warhol was smitten with Fred who made him understand he preferred women as sexual partners. Still Warhol was very hospitable at his so-called Factory in lower Manhattan where he collaborated with artists, socialites and magazine front-cover models, discussing paintings, sculpture, movies and books. Warhol hosted luncheons for Fred in his studio and showed him with great pride his bins and bins of personal mail, including every commercial letter he received, along with the hundreds of instant photographs he took and saved. Warhol's obsession with keeping a personal history through his mail is unique and offbeat, but Dryer considers the collection of correspondence indicative of the pop culture artist's insufferable narcissism.

Fred is not only the best defensive player; he's popular with most of his teammates because of his well-meaning humor. His ability to mimic almost anyone makes him the team clown. His laugh-riot imitations of Wellington Mara are accurate but good-natured. One day, after practice, Webster, says to him, "Freddie, when I come back, I want to come back as you."

Monday, July 26th . . . . Tight end Bob Tucker answers to the nickname "Roman" because he's built like a muscular Roman centurion with a sturdy and handsome face. Naked in the locker room, Tucker looks like a classic sculptured statue. Tucker wants to prove his rookie year, last season, was no fluke. He hung on as a free agent out of the Atlantic Coast Football League and became the starter, catching 40 balls including clutch receptions in comeback wins over the Jets and Redskins. No more Pottstown, Pennsylvania, or Lowell, Massachusetts, for him. "It's my job now. I've got a family to worry about. You're only as good as your last play." Tucker is a tough blocker and he holds on to Tarkenton's passes. Most importantly, he knows how to shake a defender when Fran scrambles. He breaks the bridge of his nose in a scrimmage but Tucker refuses to take a day off.

Tuesday, July 27th . . . . Webster doesn't know what kind of team he has. Right now, they're a mixture of veterans, fringe players, rookies and free agents. One of his main projects is with the offensive line and their new blocking schemes. Last season, they were dominated too much by opposing front-sevens. To keep the opposition guessing, Webster has added variations on his I-formation and man-in-motion attack. But, all of this takes time to learn.

Wednesday, July 28 . . . . Close to the 11pm players' curfew, Dryer seeks out Coach Webster and finds him walking down a dormitory corridor dragging on a cigarette. Dryer asks Alex to let him leave the dorm for an hour so he can meet a woman who's waiting for him in the parking lot. He promises not to leave campus. Alex says, "Damn it, Freddy, go ahead but get back in your room as soon as you can." She's a Pan Am stewardess known as "The Body." They walk to the nearby practice field and in the darkness make love under the goalposts.

Thursday, July 29th . . . . Maybe it's the intense heat, maybe the grind of training camp, probably a combination of both. The players are lethargic and lacking focus. Coach Webster and his assistants try to rouse them, but to no avail. Finally, the exasperated Webster blows his whistle and yells at them for their inattentiveness. Alex takes a long pause and says softly, "Damn it . . . get off the field . . . all of you . . . . go out and have a beer with each other and we'll start out again tomorrow."

Monday, August 2nd . . . . All eyes are on Rocky Thompson . . . . he arrives sporting a huge Afro hairdo. He missed the first three weeks of training camp because he was at the College All Stars camp. Thompson was a running back at West Texas State and because of his blazing speed, converted into a wide receiver. The 5-9 Thompson looks undersized for either position, but when he isn't wearing helmet, appears taller because of his Afro hairdo. Former Giants Most Valuable Player Frank Gifford is on the field filming for WABC-TV's Eyewitness News. Gifford plans a feature on Thompson's first day as a New York Giant. Gifford was an all-pro running back and receiver. He asks for a football and tells his cameraman to roll while he plays catch with Thompson. After Rocky grabs Gifford's third toss, Frank turns and says, "My God, he catches the ball the wrong way . . . all fingers . . . instead of gathering it in."

Tuesday, August 3rd . . . . Vernon Vanoy is an impressive physical specimen . . . 6'8" . . . 270 lbs. . . . a 24-year old who played defensive end at the University of Kansas. He was drafted in the third round by the Giants two years earlier, but, instead played in the Canadian League for Toronto and Vancouver. Last year, Vanoy came to the Giants and was exiled to the taxi squad of reserve players. The Giants need him to plug the hole at defensive tackle. Webster says Vernon will get every opportunity to make the team. Vanoy is worried about the switch from outside to inside on the defensive line. The trade for Roland Lakes, who played right defensive tackle for the past eight years with San Francisco, and the play of Jim Kanicki, Willie Townes and Bob Lurtsema, lessen Vernan's chances. He confides to Dryer that he doesn't know how he'll make a living after football. Dryer says he could rent himself to the Giants as a girder at Yankee Stadium.

. Wednesday, August 4th, Coach Webster knows about fresh legs. He once was a gritty workhorse carrying the ball for the Giants. So, in the pre-season opener Monday night in Houston, Alex has decided that backups Ernie Koy and Bobby Duhon will start in the backfield. Tucker Fredrickson has a sore ankle, Ron Johnson, a charley horse and Junior Coffey, a pulled hamstring muscle. Most of the players like Webster because he's on their side. A New Jersey guy who was lucky to play for a high profile team when the Giants were the darlings of the New York media and the NFL was gaining national prominence. "Big Red," as he was known to his teammates, was a hero to the fans. That proved to be Webster's greatest strength to an organization that allowed two obscure Jim Lee Howell assistants get away. If either Tom Landry or Vince Lombardi had been promoted to head coach, the Giants course of history would have been changed for the better.

Sunday, August 8th . . . the Giants are in Houston for their first pre-season game. Johnson and Lurtsema settled their salary problems and the team is intact, but not for long. Fran Tarkenton checks out of the hotel and owner Mara breaks the news that his quarterback has retired because of a contract dispute. Lurtsema is the Giants player representative and he takes a vote. Most of the players feel that management isn't "credible." Lurtsema takes the results to Mara. "Lurtsie-burger," as he is called by his teammates, is on a naïve suicide mission. The Giants place Lurtsema on waivers. This is odd, because they need defensive linemen.

Monday, August 9th, before a national television audience, the Houston Oilers humble the Giants 35-6. Tarkenton's backup, Dick Shiner, is ineffective. The coaches are spared viewing the debacle because the game films are accidentally destroyed in processing. Mara says he has no plans to contact Fran who wants a high, six-figure business loan for an unspecified new venture, in addition to his $100,000 salary. Mara says, "It wasn't us who left Fran. I won't negotiate with someone who isn't in camp."

Tuesday, August 10th . . . . After a late flight from Houston, the players are off . . . most sleep late and then scatter. Reached at home in Atlanta, Tarkenton says "There is no next step as far as I'm, concerned. I will be here until something is resolved."

Wednesday, August 11th . . . . It's past the 11pm curfew at C.W. Post but punter Bill Johnson is in Assistant Coach Jim Garrett's dorm room, despondent over his kicking against the Oilers

While rookie Tom Blanchard, a 12th round pick out of Oregon, almost hit the top of the Astrodome with his punts. It was Garrett who brought Johnson to the Giants last year. Garrett doubles as the Giants special teams' coach and Johnson wants out so he can get latch on elsewhere. Say so long to Bill Johnson.

Thursday, August 12th . . . . the Giants trade offensive tackle Rich Buzin to the Los Angeles Rams for veteran offensive tackle Joe Taffoni.

Late in the evening, Tarkenton slips into the dorm to pick up his gear. He's just come from a taping of the Dick Cavett TV talk show. He asks Mara for a private meeting. Close to midnight, Tarkenton comes down the hall from Mara's room, up to his room on the second floor and tells some of the guys he's agreed to Mara's terms. There are shouts of joy up and down the darkened hallways. Tarkenton's nickname is "Rodent" because he's always in the dorm hallways, visiting with teammates and schmoozing.

Late that night in Fred's dormitory room, Tarkenton says, "I've been in this game a long time and don't have a lot of time left. I'm out of here after this season. I'm gonna try to get back to Minnesota. You're a young player on the rise. You have to come to a realization. Do you want to stay in New York and be on a mediocre team or get a chance to be on a winning team?

Dryer answers, "I got it. I'll be leaving too."

After the long and difficult contract negotiations and his reluctant agreement, Tarkenton is so mind-weary, he needs to sleep immediately.

Friday, August 13th . . . . one more practice before the Patriots exhibition game at Foxboro . . . . Shiner is told he's a backup again. He becomes enraged and leaves. A Giants spokesman tells the beat reporters, "We don't know where Shiner has gone and. frankly we don't care." Tarkenton says, "My immediate plans are to play this year for the Giants. I don't think any pro football player can plan beyond the year he's playing in. You never know what's going to happen."

Sunday, August 15th . . . . the Giants and Patriots inaugurate New England's Schaefer stadium, the team's new home in Foxboro, Massachusetts, between Boston and Providence. There's a crowd of more than 60,000 and the traffic snarl is of mammoth proportions. Rocky Thompson runs a kickoff back for a 90-yard touchdown, but the rest of the game is controlled by the fired-up AFL Pats who win their first-ever game over an NFL team, 20-14. The Giants are 0-2 and their offense is dull. Tarkenton's absence due to his contract holdout affected the offensive unit's timing.

Monday, August 16th . . . . Offensive tackle Joe Taffoni quits with no explanation. The trade with the Rams stands, so the Giants get nothing in return for Rich Buzin who was a starter. Coach Webster scoffs at getting nothing in exchange for Buzin, wisecracking, "We end up with 45 less yards in holding penalties."

Dryer is asked about the Giants prospects. It's obvious the offense isn't threatening enough and the defense allows too much. "Listen, offense compliments defense and vice versa. There's no way any defensive team, an ordinary one to boot, can continually bail out the offense. This isn't a cop out. It's frustrating to take the field and the other guys have a first down on our 45-yard line. The opposing offense is within a first down of getting at least 3 points throughout the game. Let's face it. A team must get points and good field position so that the front-4 can loosen up and take off. Also, our defensive philosophy is antiquated. Today's defenses are structured for attacking offenses, not just defending against them. Once you start playing catch-up and take away the defensive attack, the eleven defensive players are on their heels. The front four are catching blocks, the linebackers are back-peddling before the snap and the defensive backs are playing 10 to 15 yards off the receivers. The ideal is for the front-four to attack with abandon, the linebackers going for interceptions and the defensive backs playing tighter and attempting interceptions. In this situation, opposing offenses have to be careful and alternate their game plans. Let's get real. Every playoff team has four great bodies up front and our front line isn't good enough yet. Linebackers and defensive backs don't win games, they keep from losing them. Defensive linemen win games and that's why teams can't trade for great defensive linemen. Overpowering guys are never on the trading block. The Giants' only hope is through the draft. Until I was drafted out of San Diego State in 1969, who was the last defensive lineman, the Giants drafted, who ended up a regular?"

Tuesday August 7th . . . . In the evening, Dryer organizes the rookie show in the small theater at C. W. Post College. The entire team and coaching staff attend along with the Maras. On most teams, the first year players are ordered to stand in front of their teammates and sing their school songs. The humorous self-mockery draws players closer and helps distract them from the grind of training camp.

Instead, Dryer writes a 10-skit play about the controversial events and oddball characters during training camp. He cast team members Pete Athas, Willie Williams and Willie Young. Using his comedic and mimicking skills, he impersonates the squinty-eyed Wellington, the deep-voiced Trimble, and the affable chain-smoking Webster and certain oddball players. It's a parody of the team, with the silent square-jawed part-owner sitting in the first row. The nervous tittering from the audience becomes bellowing laughter. Webster smiles broadly but tries not to belly laugh at his boss' expense. Alex is depicted as a good guy, friendly to all and not exactly a taskmaster. In his seat, Wellington alternately chuckles and frowns.

In the background of every scene, Tucker Frederickson sits in a whirlpool reading the Wall Street Journal. Fredrickson was a hard-charging running back, out of Auburn who was burdened with leg injuries and he was intent of becoming a business mogul. Also, in every scene Dryer portrays Wellington, wearing sweat clothes and doing jumping jacks and mimicking "You're just a bunch of bums on the Bowery. But, this is a new year."

The departed Dennis Crane is portrayed as an overweight fool, which he was, and Trimble as an old school enforcer who is infatuated with players' physical dimensions. Tarkenton's pleading for more salary has the players howling. Down front, Mara's expressions are obvious. He doesn't take kindly to Dryer's interpretation of him. When it's over, the players and coaches cheer and Wellington smiles and applauds and then says, "Freddie, nice job. I don't fully understand everything you did but everybody seemed to have a good time."

As for Dryer, "It was a release of nervous energy. The guys laughed and hugged each other and we went down the road for a few beers and laughed some more. It was like the family that doesn't talk about the elephant in the room and decides it can't move forward unless the elephant is discussed. The elephant is Well. We are an old team with many players whose best days are behind them. The Giants employ scouts and talent evaluators who aren't as sharp as the men who plot the futures of the Dallas Cowboys and the Minnesota Vikings. Well is a very decent man who looks at his team as a family and expects loyalty no matter what. The truth is, the Giants need a complete overhaul. Our record of 9-5 last year obscures our regression as a team. We're mortgaging future draft choices for older players to stay competitive but that's short changing tomorrow. Well needs to hire a competent general manager, better scouts, a dynamic head coach and catch up with contemporary pro football. In my two years with the Giants, on the defensive line, I haven't played alongside the same guy for more than three games in a row."

Wednesday, August 18th . . . . The Giants are eating their evening meal in the ground floor cafeteria at C.W. Post when a fire erupts in the kitchen. Players jam the only door out of the first-floor dining room, while others smash windows with chairs and jump out. Offensive lineman Charlie Harper finds the 4-foot drop too difficult. He suffers a hairline fracture of his right ankle.

11-year center Greg Larson is calm. He follows the wave of panic-stricken players, carrying his tray of food through the door, saying, "I didn't want my steak to get too well done." After the fire was quickly extinguished, place kicker Pete Gogolak emerges from a closet. Gogo mistook the closet as an exit, and once in the closet, decided it was the safest place.

Thursday, August 19th . . . . Pete Gogolak is feeling more comfortable with Tarkenton as his regular holder on placekicks, instead of Dick Shiner. The Hungarian Gogolak introduced soccer style place kicking to American football. He was a sensation at Cornell University with his side-of-the-foot technique instead of straight ahead off the toe. Gogolak set an Ivy League record of 44 straight extra points and his longest field goal was a 50-yarder. He kicked for two winning teams in Buffalo before jumping from the American Football League to the National Football League and the Giants in 1967.

He holds the Giants record for the longest field goal at 54 yards. Pete has written an instructional book on his specialty entitled: "Kicking Soccer Style." But, there is no chapter on how to conquer a slump. That's what's happening to Gogolak, this training camp and he's second guessing himself. "I think I did too much running and too little kicking in the off season. I'm very proud I completed the team's 2-mile run in less than 12 minutes. It meant I was in condition, but perhaps I should have kicked more. My timing is off. I've asked Coach Webster for more live action in practice. You know, rushing linemen to simulate game conditions. Physically, I feel good, but mentally it's starting to bother me. Let's face it, in this business you've got to put the ball between the uprights."

Dryer figures he'll try something to break Gogolak's kicking slump. While Pete shampoos his hair in the shower, keeping his eyes shut, Fred urinates on his leg.

Friday, August 20th . . . . Coach Webster switches Rocky Thompson from wide receiver to a running back position, which he played at West Texas State. Team scouts mistakenly projected him a receiver, where the Giants are shallow. Thompson is having problems with two elemental skills at the position, running routes and holding onto the ball. The no. 1 draft pick makes the startling remark, "I haven't had a chance at playing receiver yet in a game." Adding to the misuse of their top draft pick is Thompson's inability as a kick returner. He continues to drop kicked balls, some bounce off his helmet.

Saturday, August 21th . . . . After a morning, intensive workout at C.W. Post, the entire team and coaches ride buses to New Haven, Connecticut. For the first time, there is a sense of urgency, like a mid-season game. The rival

Jets are waiting and so are thousands of New York football fans who clog the hotels and restaurants of the Yale University town.

Sunday, August 22nd, ... The third game in the newfound-rivalry for local bragging rights and its 98-degrees on the field of the Yale Bowl in New Haven, Connecticut. Before a sellout crowd of more than 70,000, the arch rival Jets dominate the Giants and whip them 27-14, with Al Woodall, at quarterback, subbing for the injured Joe Namath. Both Weeb Ewbank and Alex Webster play their regulars virtually all game. The Jets led 20-0 before the Giants score in the fourth quarter. The Jets don't throw a single pass in the second half because guards Dave Herman and Randy Rasmussen easily trap block the Giants defensive line. Matt Snell, Emerson Boozer and John Riggins hit the holes for a combined 230 yards. Webster says, "The way they were running, I wouldn't throw a pass either." Safety Spider Lockhart spits out the words, "We had absolutely nothing!." The Giants manage only 33 yards rushing, their third straight game under 100 yards. Tarkenton passes for 93 yards but gives back 41 yards because of five sacks. Johnson is ineffective and quits in the second quarter, admitting to an unusual ailment. An off-season injury to his right thigh didn't heal. Dried blood next to his leg bone has caused a knot and only surgery will repair it. Not only do the Giants get drubbed by their rivals, they lose their 1,000-yard running back.

Saturday, August 28th . . . . In their annual pre-season game, at Princeton University, in New Jersey, the Giants look ragged against Philadelphia. At halftime, New Jersey Governor William Cahill gets a mixed reaction from the 45,000 fans when he gets on the public address system and calls them "The New Jersey Giants." The Eagles crush the Giants 26-7, their fourth straight defeat. The Giants cross the midfield stripe only 3 times. They rush for 84 yards, a pre-season high, but inadequate, and their fourth straight game under 100 yards. The offensive unit is flagged for 85 yards in penalties, repeatedly nullifying gains and Tarkenton is sacked three times. Tarkenton can barely speak to reporters. He's visibly disgusted, "We've got a long way to go . . . . we're just not getting . . ." He broke it off and turned away.

After the game, Governor Cahill hosts a dinner at his nearby home for the Giants' brass. Tim Mara and finance officer Ray Walsh are the point men in secret negotiations for a Giants franchise move to the Garden State. The Giants are enduring an expensive lease at Yankee Stadium. They don't benefit from parking or concessions receipts and Mayor John Lindsay refuses to help re-negotiate. Also, they must play all their pre-season exhibition games on the road because of the Yankees baseball schedule.

Meanwhile, most of the team travels back to New York by bus. A friend drives Dryer and Pete Athas to New York City. They intend to have dinner at their favorite Italian restaurant, Il Vagabondo on East 62nd Street. Pete likes to call himself "A Jive Ass from Miami," a very nimble athlete who could cover any receiver but is weak against the run. His longhair extends out of his football helmet and Wellington doesn't like the disheveled look. Trimble paid tribute to Pete's wiry, muscular body calling him "The Greek God." One late night, Trimble was on curfew patrol in the in the dorm when he spotted Pete walking nude to the toilet. Trimble was stern. "Pete, I don't want to see you walking around, nude, again, you're a threat to the men."

As the car carrying Dryer and Athas heads north on the New Jersey Turnpike, Athas is sitting in the front seat next to the driver and Dryer crouched in the backseat. Athas is vomiting out the open window. He ingested too many amphetamines, known as "bennies" or "speed," which are stimulants to the central nervous system. Many of the Giants defensive and offensive linemen take stimulants, including coffee, before games. It was a psychological motivation because it isn't easy to "get up" for every game. Stimulants don't improve speed or dexterity, but "bennies" help raise anger and rage. Usage of stimulants is frowned upon by the National Football League and coaches look the other way.

Swallowing a couple more at halftime extended Athas' feeling of euphoria. Now, hours later, Athas is still "high" and dehydrated and he's throwing up. The wind is in his taut face and his long hair is swept back. Dryer looks at him and says "Pete, you look like the Indian head on a Pontiac."

Saturday, September 4th . . . . A night game against Cleveland and the Giants drop their 5th in a row, 30-7. There is little positive about the Giants. It's a team slump. In their five losses, they've managed only 55 points while giving up 138. In the pre-season, Gogolak with only 3 field goal attempts, made 2. "A place-kicker needs more game-situation conditions than that." Generally, there are few smiles, the outlook is grim and the 14-game schedule is about to begin.

Monday, September 6th . . . . The Giants cut five players and are down to 44 on the roster.

Tuesday, September 7th . . . . After five pre-season losses . . . after walkouts, cop-outs and holdouts . . . . the Giants view the films of the Browns disaster. Garrett gives the entire squad a moving, eloquent speech. He implores them, "You're like bums on the Bowery. Nobody can help you, you can only help yourself."

The Giants of 1971 staggered through the 14-game schedule, finishing 4-10, outscored by the opponents 362-228. The Giants lost 6 of their 7 home games while losing 4 of 7 on the road. In half of their losses, five defeats, they scored 7 or less points. They dropped 3 of their last 4 games. Ron Johnson, who had rushed for 1,027 yards the season before with 8 rushing touchdowns and 4 receiving TDs, didn't bounce back from his thigh injury. Johnson ran the ball only 32 times for 156 yards, scoring only one touchdown. Under-sized Bobby Duhon was the Giants best rusher with only 344 yards and one score. Tarkenton passed for 11 touchdowns but was intercepted 21 times. Tight end Bob Tucker was the main threat with 59 receptions for 791 yards and 4 touchdowns. Gogolak made only 6 field goals in 17 attempts. Thompson made little impact with only 177 yards rushing and 2 touchdowns while catching 16 balls for only 85 yards. Blanchard, the rookie punter, kicked too many times, 66, but averaged 41 yards. The defense allowed 42 touchdowns, 2,059 yards rushing and 2,458 yards passing.

After the 1971 season, Tarkenton and Dryer threatened to play out their options and were traded. Fran received his wish and returned to the Vikings, in a swap for quarterback Norm Snead. Eight NFL teams inquired about Dryer and he was dealt to the New England Patriots. But, general manager Upton Bell reneged on a very lucrative contract offer when Patriots owner Billy Sullivan balked at $80,000 a season for 3 years. When Dryer's attorney, John Thomas, threatened to sue the Patriots, they traded him to the Los Angeles Rams.

After three losing years with the Giants, Dryer played 10 years for the winning Rams and was on their Super Bowl team in 1980. Dryer says, "For all of my success with the Rams and how that led to my business investments and acting career, I've always wondered what could have been with the Giants and what could have occurred in the city I love, New York."

Webster's Giants of 1972 improved to 8-6, but after a 2-11-1 record in 1973, he retired and was replaced by Miami defensive coordinator Bill Arnsparger. The Giants struggled through 8 consecutive losing seasons. Their bright spot was moving to their own stadium in East Rutherford, New Jersey. Between 1963 and 1981, the Giants failed to qualify for the playoffs because of 12 losing seasons and three 7-7 seasons.

During their drought, the Maras were shaken by what they saw in the sky above Giants Stadium one game day. A small plane towed a banner in full view by more than 75,000 mutinous Giants fans. It read "15 years of Lousy Football, We've had enough."

Nephew Tim and Uncle "Well" hardly spoke to each other because they disagreed about the team's construction and management. Trading away draft choices for veterans was not the way to rebuild. Drafting collegiate players on newspaper account reputations, instead of intense in-person scouting was not the way to stock a roster. Not keeping up to date with computerized summaries of opposing teams' tendencies was not the way to formulate game plans.

Because of the importance of the New York franchise to the rest of the NFL, the feuding Maras reluctantly agreed to find a solution elsewhere for the team's futility. In 1979, Commissioner Pete Rozelle strongly suggested George Young, the Miami Dolphins' talent evaluator. Young was hired as General Manager and became the architect of 2 championship teams. Coached by Ray Perkins and then Bill Parcells, the Giants were restored as one of the NFL's premier franchises. The first step was returning to the playoffs in 1981. After a 9-7, 3rd-place record, they qualified as a wildcard team.

In between the Giants glory days of the '50s and their comeback in the '80s, for most of the '60s and '70s, the Giants were a monument to pro football mediocrity. Wellington Mara had the zeal of a saint. This religious and proud man believed in loyalty as the bedrock for his life. Most of his players and staff loved him for that. But, Mara was too paternal in a professional sport that changing. He hired too many cronies instead of more intelligent football people from outside the organization. It cannot be denied, when the Giants won their championships, in the late '80s, Young was the reason for their success not the bickering owners. Young had to be stuffed down their throats by the league. In 1991, Tim sold his half of the ownership to co-owner Robert Tisch. Like his father Jack, Tim died of cancer.

Wellington was inducted into the Pro Football Hall of Fame in 1997. His football legacy was the insistence as owner of the New York franchise that he and his partners in the NFL share equally in the television revenue. That notion proved to be the bedrock of the NFL and its huge success. As for the team, Wellington never wanted cheerleaders at the games and steadfastly refused to sell the stadium name to a business entity. Under his watch, it was always "Giants Stadium." He remained the reigning patriarch of the Mara family and the Giants until his death because of cancer at age 89 on October 25, 2005. He was survived by his wife Ann, 11 children and 40 grandchildren. Wellington's sons, John, Chris and Frank were already involved with the management of the Giants.

Dryer studied acting with veteran actress Nina Foch, while playing a decade for the Los Angeles Rams. After his retirement, in 1981, he began a successful acting career. His signature role, as Sgt. Rick Hunter, in the popular NBC cop series "Hunter" lasted seven years. He not only starred in the hit series but he became its executive producer, forming Fred Dryer Productions. The young man who organized a rookies show at the Giants training camp in 1971 evolved into a film producer, starring in movies seen by audiences all over the world for decades. The Hunter series was dubbed into Chinese and has played for years on Chinese television. As of this writing, Fred Dryer is the most popular film star in China.

His "Hunter" series was brought back by NBC for the 2003 season and Dryer reprised his leading role. It was the first time in the history of television, a popular weekly series returned after an absence of a decade.

ESPN AT THE START

Sports televised all day, everyday on one channel, was as wild an idea in 1979 as a four-legged chicken. In that long ago of lesisure time, before the proliferation of personal computers, the Internet, videogames, laptops, cell phones I-Pods and video on demand, consumers could only select from channels two through thirteen. With battery-powered clickers in hand, they were ready to be served and the birth of cable television caused an explosion of specialty channels.

In June of 1980, I was hired by the Entertainment and Sports Programming Network, ESPN, the fledgling 24-hour all-sports television network, to host its sports news program, Sportscenter, and do boxing blow-by-blow, as well as college football play by play.

Chet Simmons, the former NBC Sports boss, ran the new operation for the Getty Oil Company. Simmons' right hand man was Scotty Connal who had been in charge of production at NBC Sports. The Programming Chiefs were Steve Bornstein, Bill Creasy and Joe Valerio.

Chet was the father of ESPN. His rights acquisitions and visionary decisions laid the groundwork for what later evolved into a television titan.

If ESPN had been in the suburbs of New York City, it would have been paradise. To avoid the jurisdiction of talent and technical unions, the ESPN complex was established and remains in Bristol, Connecticut. The land, in the remote hills of the Nutmeg State, was cheap. Bristol is a rural suburb, southwest of Hartford, a bleak town on the decline because its manufacturing plants for brassworks and mattress springs closed and new major industries didn't evolve. Bristol is a nice family town but boring for the young employees at ESPN. It was the only television network with a batting cage and golf range on the same road.

The adjacent town of Plainville is aptly named. If you were an escaped convict, it would be easy to hide in Bristol. First of all, Bristol isn't a destination city. It's just another exit off Interstate 84 and the odds are very long you would run into anyone you know. It's a two hour drive to New York City, but it may as well be Iowa.

A New England sportscaster named Bill Rasmussen was smart enough to lease one of the first transponders on an orbiting satellite. Rasmussen thought that he'd televise Connecticut sports all over the state. Working with the NCAA, he agreed to televise less popular sports to get football and basketball packages.

Taped events lineups included Australian Rules football and go-cart racing. Rasmussen figured out this could go national. He convinced venture capitalists at the Getty Company to catch the first wave of the satellite technology that allowed new networks to bounce signals off orbiting stations back to earth stations that beamed feeds to individual cable boxes in homes across the United States.

As the '70s were ending, the big three of ABC, CBS and NBC yawned at the notion of a 24-hour-a-day sports TV network, the way they scoffed at CNN, the new 24-hour-a-day all-news TV network. They were wrong and it was only a matter of time before America was wired for cable television. By the end of the '80s, ESPN became as familiar as the light that goes on when you open your refrigerator door.

This tiny technological village, with a single administrative building, ringed by muddy parking lots, on a rural two-lane road deep in the Connecticut woods, became a billion dollar holding. Along the way, it was acquired by ABC for nearly $300 million. ESPN spawned secondary networks like ESPN-2, ESPN Classic, ESPN News, ESPN Radio and ESPN The Magazine. The company went global with broadcasts in several languages. In 2002, ESPN's revenue exceeded $2 billion and its market value was estimated at $15 to 20 billion. Cable operators consider its basic package an essential. Because of its familiar brand, ESPN expanded into radio, publishing and sports bars.

ESPN became the first network to televise all four major professional sports simultaneously. Over the years, Sportscenter blossomed into the nightly TV sportscast of record. Its theme music became so familiar, high school and college bands play it at games.

When I joined ESPN, Sportscenter was a difficult program to host because of a lack of financial commitment to news gathering. There were no correspondents and tape crews assigned to major events across the country. No satellite feeds of stories from regional bureaus and no expert analysts. The cheaply-paid anchors were mostly entry level guys with a sprinkling of veterans from the New England region. Among them were sports gamblers, boozers and drug abusers. One gay guy constantly tried to get others to travel with him to sporting events.

I was hired because I was familiar and credible to the advertising agencies in New York. My first assignment, my first day, was taping a presentation for time buyers on what was known as "Madison Avenue." After my salary became known, at ESPN, I was nicknamed "Six Figure Sal" because I was the only Sportscenter host earning more than $100,000 a year.

Working at the ESPN complex in Bristol was odd. It took months to pave the parking lot, so mud was tracked into the building. TV sets and other electronic gear were grabbed by greedy hands because security was so inept. The Sportscenter guys were cramped into a modest-sized room. There was a news ticker, some telephones, typewriters, paper, pens and little else. Someone bought big red vinyl chairs, probably at a discount, and they looked out of place.

I refused to move to the Bristol area. I kept my apartment in Manhattan and bought a house in Westport, Connecticut, which was an easy 40-minute drive through the woods to Bristol. As a matter of fact, there were only two red lights between my home and the ESPN complex. My daughter was able to stay in school in Manhattan and we used the Westport home as a weekend retreat.

As more American homes became wired for Cable-TV, ESPN became a viewing habit. Soon enough, the unknown sportscasters developed inflated egos because some friend or relative in another part of the country telephoned to say "Hey, I saw you on ESPN." The more they were infatuated with themselves, the more they believed they were sports experts. Betting on games became rampant. Predictably, they lost more money than they won.

When certain partial scores were read on the air, there were many inside jokes, because money was riding on the final score.

A production guy was "the candy man," the house dealer of drugs. I saw cocaine used and pot smoked in the building. There was sex in the stairwells and one well-known anchor copulated with a secretary in her office. Connal told me he had a female employee say to him she was lonely working at ESPN, because she had no social life and no sexual experiences. Connal said he knew of no way to answer her. There were off-campus frat-house type parties. It was something to do after 12-hour work stints. Nearby Hartford was an insurance company town and lacking in interesting nightlife.

In 1982, Chris Berman asked me for some counsel. He came out of Connecticut radio and television and wasn't yet 30 years of age. Chris confided to me he was considering working at ABC's KGO-TV in San Francisco for a boost in salary to $100,000. It was a dream job because he was a big 49ers and Giants fan. I thought Berman was the most knowledgeable and charismatic anchor on the roster and advised him to ignore the opportunity and grow with a network that would eventually dwarf any local TV position. Berman stayed and became ESPN's star personality and its best-paid performer. "Boomer" is better known by sports fans and more liked than other TV personalities because his constant enthusiasm and unbridled love for sports is evident in his work. Critics are way off the mark when they describe his "act" as contrived. Chris is the same off the screen. He's the kind of guy who sits next to you on an airplane or next to you at a bar and shares the subject of sports as a wonderful diversion.

When Berman began, he and Tom Mees were especially effective on the 2:30 am Sportscenter because their personalities meshed well. It was tragic when Tom Mees later drowned.

Of all the co-anchors I was teamed with on Sportscenter, Greg Gumbel was the most even-natured. He came from a major TV station in Chicago and like me had a disdain for the triviality of local TV newscasts. Greg graduated to much deserved success with CBS Sports. In those early days of ESPN, he was a delight to work with. That's why when we run into each other, there are smiles all around.

Calling the ESPN fights on the road was a blast. Two and a half hours every Thursday night, twice a month in Atlantic City and once a month in Las Vegas. The other Thursday telecasts came from charming places like San Juan, Puerto Rico, Panama City, Panama, Lake Charles, Louisiana, Bristol, Tennessee, Dallas-Fort Worth, and Reno, Nevada. The first weekly, prime-time boxing series on cable television, "Top Rank Boxing," was guided by promoter Bob Arum. It drew ESPN's largest audiences. The matchmaker was Bruce Trampler. On site, Top Rank's Akbar Muhammad ran the shows which grew and grew in popularity. A typical telecast was two and a half hours live and the card included pro debuts and four-rounders, involving local heroes before the main event. Top Rank Boxing drew a cult following, like the old Friday Night Fights on NBC-TV, in the '50s. The lead analysts were Sean O'Grady, the former lightweight champion and then, Al Bernstein, a Chicago sportswriter. During that period, we also worked world championship bouts on pay-per-view, including Marvin Hagler's 15-round epic match with Roberto Duran and Sugar Ray Leonard's one-eyed comeback over Tommy Hearns.

Muhammad Ali's fighting days were over, but boxing was buzzing again because of a rush of talent. The weekly Top Rank Boxing programs drew enough of a big audience to attract advertisers and generate more income for ESPN.

My experience at ABC, learning at ringside from Howard Cosell, primed me well. We took club fighters and made them personalities. Not every match-up was terrific, so we filled the boring rounds, stressing fundamentals and offering constructive criticism of the fighters' techniques.

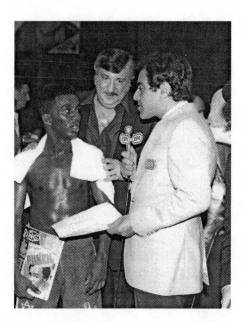

Ringside in Atlantic City 1980.

Many unknown fighters became national names because of their appearances on ESPN. On April 2, 1981, Lightweight Ray Mancini debuted on an ESPN program promoted by former heavyweight contender Ernie Terrell, in Chicago. Ray was a white, 20 year old, 135-pounder, from Youngstown, Ohio, raised in a middle class family. He was president of his senior class in high school and had a scholarship offer to attend Xavier University in Cincinnati. He was an excellent baseball player, talented enough to draw the interest of the Toronto Blue Jays. But, Ray was on a mission to attain something that was denied to his father, 40 years earlier. Ray's father, Lennie, was a tough lightweight whose boxing career was cut short by military duty in World War II.

Ray said, in the pre-fight interview, "I want to regain the glory my father didn't get."

Ray had a picture of his dad in his wallet. We enlarged the photo of him in a boxing pose and showed it full screen, while we told the tale of Lennie "Boom Boom" Mancini and his frustration. Lennie was a relentless, hard-hitting, crowd-pleasing lightweight, whose upper body was bigger like a middleweight. Lennie fought many times in Brooklyn, New York, in the late 1930s and early 1940s. The closest he came to a world championship was a split decision, 10-round loss to lightweight champion Sammy Angott, in a non-title fight in 1941. When Mancini took the Canadian lightweight championship from Dave Castilloux, in Montreal, he was elevated to the no. 1 contender. In 1942, a title fight with Angott was agreed to and contracts were signed, but Lennie was drafted into the U.S. Army.

Mancini experienced combat against the Nazis in France and suffered six shrapnel wounds because of a mortar explosion that killed others. Four metal pieces were removed by surgery and two remained. In 1945, Lennie was discharged from the Army with a Purple Heart medal. He tried boxing but he had gained too much weight while convalescing, so he retired at age 28 with 73 wins, 2 defeats and three draws, but no world lightweight championship.

Ray dedicated his boxing career to his dad. Ray's slick boxing style and clever counter-punching enabled him to rocket through the 135-pound division. In his debut on ESPN, Ray won a 10-round, unanimous decision over Al Ford, knocking him down once for his 18th straight victory. The pay night for "Boom Boom-II" was $2, 500. In the post-fight interview, Mancini said to me, "I needed rounds. This is exactly what I needed. Ford used to be the Canadian champ. He's one of the slickest fighters I've ever fought. I couldn't have asked for a better test."

The next morning CBS Sports contacted Mancini and made a quick deal for him to be showcased on the network's boxing series on Saturday afternoons. Thanks to a springboard from cable television, Ray "Boom Boom" Mancini became the CBS Sports "house" fighter, eventually winning the world lightweight championship that eluded his father. Ray took the WBA title from Arturo Frias, in 1982, the year after he debuted on ESPN.

The All-American boy carried home the championship belt to his 62-year-old father Lennie, who was retired from his factory job in Youngstown. When he handed the diamond-studded championship belt to his father, Ray said, "This is for you, Pop."

ESPN's weekly Top Rank Boxing series was moved around the country to present a mosaic of the sport in the United States. While unknown fighters gained notoriety quickly, we witnessed mismatches, incompetence and dishonesty away from strong boxing commissions in Atlantic City and Las Vegas. We saw inept referees and outrageous hometown decisions, like the network's first boxing broadcast in Rhode Island in 1983. In West Warwick, a local lightweight named Rafael Lopez was knocked down four times by a New York lightweight named Juan Veloz.

ESPN Ringcard Girl, Las Vegas 1982.

Each time Lopez went to the canvas, referee Martin Tabor ruled a slip. After the first one, Tabor actually reached out to help Lopez up. Three of the "slips" occurred in the seventh round, which under Rhode Island rules would have ended the bout had they been judged knockdowns. The other was in the 9th round. Bernstein and I judged Veloz the winner. But, not only was Tabor's hometown lean brazen, the judges at ringside were corrupt. Lopez was given a unanimous decision, which was popular with the Rhode Island fans at ringside. Instantly, the ESPN switchboard in Bristol was flooded with complaints by viewers. At that point in time, ESPN reached a nationwide audience of 25 million. In the post fight interview in the ring, I excoriated Tabor whose only defense was that Al and I were too inexperienced to know a slip from a knockdown. Tabor ridiculed himself. Al and I analyzed and scored more fights, because of the weekly series, than anyone else in the country and we were backed fully by our superiors at ESPN because they placed a premium on integrity instead of hometown loyalty. Television magnifies everything and that night in Rhode Island was embarrassing to all.

Boxing is an entrepreneurial activity. It has no governing bodies, only alphabet soup sanctioning organizations that must be courted for their ratings, which the television networks use as validation of the matches. The WBA, WBC, IBF, WBO, etc., are hypocritical and self-righteous. Under the guise of legitimacy, they demand sanctioning fees from promoters and exact tribute in the form of lavish business expenses to be "observers" at the fights. Television demands letters of sanction and the promoters have to continue the farce by funding these mock organizations that remain in positions of power. Ratings of the boxers are the key to control of the sport. The ratings from these organizations decide who gets a challenge at a champion. The promoters must lobby and pay for their fighters' ratings. The governing bodies make their own rules. There is no higher court of accountability. By any business standards, this is a Mad Hatter's Tea Party and sitting at the head of the table are television executives.

In the glory days of boxing, there were eight champions in eight weight categories, from bantamweight to heavyweight. Now, each sanctioning body has a champion. So, confused fight fans have become apathetic and boxing is no longer of major interest, unless two better known champions have a rare collision.

Big money fights in arenas were sports events. Now, marquee fights in casino resorts are theatrical. The constant is the public's primal anticipation watching two men punching each other until one dominates the other.

While boxing is a brutal exchange, one has to admire the courage of the young men who chase their dreams when they put up their dukes and expose their manhood.

From bare-knuckling in saloons, to arenas and ballparks, to free television, to pay-per-view television, boxing has been, at best, a tank full of sharks. It is a traveling circus of con artists, swindlers and thieves. Managers find fighters and promoters manipulate them and arrange the match ups to earn significant money. The promoter takes the risks but the rewards are in the millions of dollars, at the championship level, solely because of pay per view. Except for Muhammad Ali's reign, the days of huge crowds at downtown arenas ended when the public became infatuated with television and film evolved from black and white to color. In the '70s, and early '80s, there was resurgence in interest because of Ali, Sugar Ray Leonard, Roberto Duran, Marvin Hagler, Larry Holmes and then Mike Tyson.

There were only a handful of major players. Bob Arum and Don King were the rich pharoahs of the game and everyone else just earned. Arum's Top Rank Inc. spawned the ESPN series because he had a deep stable of fighters and business ties with smaller promoters all over the United States and some other countries.

Those ESPN boxing shows on Thursday nights in the early '80s, sold out their advertising time, so a Saturday night series was added. ESPN didn't have rights yet to broadcast Major League baseball or National Football League games. Boxing was the all-sports network's early signature, attracting new viewers and earning revenue while the network was initially losing much money. ESPN was more than a bottom feeder in boxing, it was developing fighters whose exposure on cable television spring boarded them to pay-per-view television.

Early in the series, after an on-camera opening scene setter, to make the transition to the first commercials, I began using the expression, "we're ready to rumble in (city) and we'll be back with the opening bell after this first timeout." ESPN viewers were familiar with the word "rumble" as a term for boxing. Ring announcer Michael Buffer asked me if he could, in his words, "borrow the line." He not only borrowed it, he trademarked it and has earned a considerable amount of money. Buffer, whose only claim to fame is his "Let's get ready to rumble!!!!," gave me credit in a Sports Illustrated profile but nothing else. Not even a cheesy T-shirt, he sells, with "Lets get ready to rumble!!!" on the back.

Whenever there was a knockout, I said, ". . . 8, 9, 10 . . . good night, sweet prince." I meant it as a compliment to the fighters who had the courage to enter the ring and battle others. The catch-phrase became popular with the ESPN audience. Sugar Ray Leonard said he watched our telecasts and looked forward to it and asked me where I got it. I told him from a guy named "Billy Shakespeare." (Hamlet Act V., when he dies, his friend Horatio says, "Now cracks a noble heart. Good night, sweet prince: And flights of angels sing thee to thy rest.")

I spent a very interesting week in Panama City, Panama where we telecast two championship fights live on a Saturday night. One of our hosts was Luis Henriquez, a New Yorker of Panamanian descent who worked for Roberto Duran. The former lightweight champion of the world was a national idol in Panama until his infamous "No Mas. No Mas" defeat to Leonard.

Roberto Duran, Las Vegas, 1983.

Sugar Ray Leonard, NYC 1984.

In New Orleans, Duran stunned everyone by quitting while defending his world welterweight championship because his stomach hurt and he was suffering from diarrhea. During our visit, Duran's shameful surrender was still fresh in the minds of his countrymen and women. One night, in Panama City, Henriquez arranged a dinner with Carlos Elata, Duran's manager who was also a celebrated powerful businessman in Panama. We dined at a fancy seafood restaurant. During our sumptuous meal, a woman rose at another table. She waved her napkin at Elata and said something aloud in Spanish. There was a hush in the room. Elata made no response and continuing dining. Later, I asked Luis what the woman had said and he winced. Henriquez quoted her, "Mr. Elata, tell Mr. Duran that the women of Panama bleed once a month, but they still get the job done."

One night, after a boxing card in Texas, I heard a Mac Davis country tune on the radio in my rental car. It was "Happiness is Lubbock in my rear view mirror." When I returned to the ESPN headquarters in Connecticut, I substituted Lubbock with Bristol. For those staffers who detested Bristol for its lack of social life, along with its dull people and bad food, the lyric became a rallying cry. After a work shift, we would say goodnight to each other in the ESPN parking lot, shortening the line to just ". . . . Happiness."

When ESPN's CEO, Chet Simmons left ESPN in 1982, to become commissioner of the new United States Football League, there was a big party at a local country club and the employees autographed an ESPN banner as a souvenir. On it, I wrote, "Chet, Happiness is Bristol in your rear view mirror." No one took notice or exception.

Simmons had brought Scotty Connal with him from NBC Sports when ESPN launched. Connal became the interim operating officer while a new CEO was sought. Scotty was an excellent director and production guy, but he had few "people skills." He was engulfed with work and responsibilities, wearing two hats, so he was snarly. Scotty was a tyrant, accustomed to having his way and his temper was short.

After my initial 3 year contract, negotiated with Simmons, was over, Scotty wasn't interested in paying 6 figures to me again. He said he could hire an entry-level-anchor for Sportscenter for $20,000, going as high as $35,000 dollars. But, he wanted me to continue hosting Top Rank Boxing. Jimmy Walsh, my attorney, found Scotty especially belligerent. They were at an impasse, seven weeks past my contract, so I asked to meet with Scotty.

Connal began his discussion with me in a rather hostile and demeaning manner. He sounded like a prep school dean admonishing one of his freshmen. Because of my New York contacts in the ad agencies, I knew that ESPN was earning more than it envisioned because of the boxing telecasts. Connal wasn't only crying poverty but he was insulting to me.

After the shouting stopped, and we negotiated, I agreed to stay at ESPN for boxing alone and would be free to work elsewhere, the remainder of time. We shook hands on terms and I agreed to finish working that week's schedule. But, Connal wasn't pleased with my demeanor in that meeting.

Bob Ley and I hosted that Sunday night's Sportscenter. It turned out to be my final sportscast at ESPN. At the end, Ley said, "I guess there's only one thing left to say." I explained I was leaving Sportscenter but not boxing on ESPN and ended with "Happiness is Bristol in my rear view mirror."

The next morning, Jimmy Walsh telephoned to inform me that Connal had taken the offer off the table and I was fired for "Sticking it up the ass of everyone who works for ESPN."

My remark was an innocuous poke at a remote town in Connecticut that the ESPN viewers nationwide could care less about. As for my fellow employees, what I said was always on their minds because Bristol is culturally barren. When I said it that Sunday night live on ESPN there was raucous laughter in the control room and more than one co-worker told me they laughed so hard, they almost fell off their chairs at home.

Immediately after the remark, a 31-day survey of the town's newspaper, the Bristol Press, revealed not one complaint or even a mention of what I said. So, the remark wasn't disparaging to Bristol or its citizens. An expert on contracts and good faith negotiations advised me that I could sue ESPN and win the salary that Connal had agreed upon for boxing. However, in network television that's bad form. More than one TV executive advised me to walk away and earn another day. The clincher was a meeting with John Martin, a friend of mine who was Roone Arledge's right hand man at ABC-Sports which had become a partner in ESPN. Martin strongly advised me not to sue ESPN, otherwise, I would be blackballed in television. I heeded his advice and did not react in an adverse way. I took a local sports job at WNBC-TV in New York. (Now, ESPN's company policy for immediate dismissal is (1) fighting with a co-worker, (2) transmitting Internet pornography, and/or (3) sexual harassment)

Within a year, in 1984, Connal was replaced by Bill Grimes. He took me to lunch at the "21" in New York and offered me my old job as boxing host at ESPN. He said I should have never been fired and that the series was hurt by a loss of chemistry during the broadcasts and a dozen or so blow-by-blow guys were hired and fired. What Grimes said was a satisfying moment for me, but, it was too late. I had an exclusive, long-term contract with WNBC-TV, worth much more money and I was home with my family much more. So I declined his offer to return to ESPN.

Howard Cosell asked me about my adventure at ESPN and my odd departure. I told him I had a daughter about to begin a rather expensive education at Columbia University and said, "All that matters is to endure and to earn."

Cosell said he understood full well.

THE BIZ

My first job in broadcasting taught me that it is a high wire act that requires a nimble sense of balance for maintaining existence.

While attending Fordham University, I worked nights as a producer at WMGM, 1050 on the AM dial, "The Call Letters of the Stars." In 1960, WMGM added a new football team and league to its roster of major league New York sports broadcasts. Nationally known sportscaster Harry Wismer, who married into the Ford family, owned the New York Titans of the American Football League. There were franchises in Boston, Buffalo, Denver, Houston, Los Angeles and Oakland.

I produced the Titans games for WMGM at the Polo Grounds and on the road. I was responsible for all aspects of the broadcast, including its accuracy and timing as well as commercial copy and promotional announcements for the announcers.

Wismer had been a national football voice in the '40s and '50s, but as a franchise owner, he didn't work the broadcasts. He hired a buddy from Philadelphia, whose only experience was describing the single-wing offense on radio. The Titans' T-formation and its handoffs baffled him, so I had to whisper in his ear and identify who had the ball.

The guy would also "interview" Wismer, the braggart-owner, at halftime. This enabled Wismer to huff and puff and make himself even grander. In 1960, during a Friday night broadcast from Boston, at halftime, Wismer called sportswriter Dan Parker "a liar." The New York Mirror columnist was Wismer's rival and nemesis.

Wismer's play-by-play dunce would say anything I said to him in his ear and he would read anything I gave him. After he signed off with Wismer, he read a note I had just scratched out. In effect, the disclaimer protected WMGM and the sponsors, the Sinclair Oil Company and Loew's Theaters from Wismer's libelous remarks about Parker.

Wismer yelled, "Who told you to read that?" His lackey pointed to me and Wismer fired me on the spot. But, I continued working the broadcast because I was employed by WMGM, not Wismer.

After the game, on the flight home to New York, Wismer came back to my seat and berated me some more, promising to blackball me from the broadcasting business.

Monday morning, I was summoned to the office of Art Tolchin, the general manager of WMGM. I was nervous with anticipation and worried that I had lost my job and ruined my career. Tolchin calmed me down and said I had protected WMGM and the sponsors properly and that I hadn't lost my job. He gave me a check for $200, as a bonus. Wismer didn't speak to me or look at me the rest of the season.

Three years later, Wismer was divorced and he declared bankruptcy. The franchise was purchased by Sonny Werblin and his partners and the Titans became the Jets. In 1967, Wismer died at age 56 of a skull fracture, suffered at home in mysterious circumstances.

Working at WMGM during my schooling at Fordham University helped pay the tuition and provided a basic broadcasting foundation. I began in the record library, stacking records and pulling commercial copy for the next day's programs. I worked in the newsroom as an assistant and learned how to write and structure a newscast, intergrating sound bites. Occasionally I drove the white WMGM station wagon that roamed the metropolitan area's highways in the morning with a traffic reporter. Besides learning how to prepare sportscasts at the elbow of Marty Glickman in the sports department and producing the AFL New York Titans football broadcasts, I graduated to the production staff for Ted Brown's morning drive program. When WMGM became WHN in 1962, Bob and Ray replaced Ted Brown who had moved on to WNEW. Bob and Ray's wry and witty humor was so prodigious they scoffed at playing music recordings and in fact defied management's orders. I programmed what little music they used and they described me as their "musicologist." Bob and Ray put me on the air one morning and in a long laugh filled skit inquired in detail, with tongues in cheeks, how I went about choosing a certain Kirby Stone-Four long playing album.

In 1963, after graduating Fordham University where I majored in Communication Arts, my first on-air job was drive-time sports on WJRZ-radio in Newark, New Jersey. My first interview was Giants Head Coach Allie Sherman at their training camp.

**Giants Head Coach Allie Sherman, Training Camp,
Fairfield University Connecticut July 1963.**

It didn't take long for my introduction into the competition between the established print media and broadcast reporters.

Tony Lema had just won the Thunderbird Classic at the Westchester Country Club. I sat at his feet, my tape recorder running, as he met with the press, treating each one of us to a glass of champagne. This victory ritual had earned him the nickname "Champagne Tony." A newspaper guy asked me to turn off my recorder. Of course, I balked and the happy scene became grim and quiet. The scribe was Dana Mozley of the New York Daily News. He said he was the president of the Metropolitan Golf Writers Association and he wasn't letting the news conference continue until I shut off my recorder. He wanted the print media to have sole access to Lema's victory remarks.

To this day, I don't know what struck Lema. I guess he had a strong sense of justice since he had been an unknown from nowhere who found fame and fortune in golf. Lema said to Mozley, "The kid stays or I leave." Mozley backed down and what happened in the locker room of the Westchester Country Club that summer day in 1964, was indicative of the broadcast media gaining on the print media, in terms of access.

Certain sportswriters resisted the presence of more and more radio and TV reporters and crews by purposely getting in the way. Many a post-game sound bite was purposely ruined by a head blocking the shot of the subject and loud obscenities.

My favorite sportswriter was Jimmy Cannon. While traveling to and from St. John's Prep and Fordham University on the subway trains everyday, I read all the New York newspaper sports sections. Cannon, Red Smith, Milton Gross, and Arthur Daley, were extraordinary writers and dogged reporters. Cannon was a New Yorker from Hell's Kitchen who dropped out of high school at age 15 and was hired by the New York Daily News as a copyboy. He never left the business, writing in the jargon of the streets in his byline column for the New York Post. Most importantly, Cannon was a master at describing the human spirit which fueled all athletes. He profiled every big name athlete and made it personal. I felt I was in the dugout with Cannon and Willie Mays, or having breakfast with Rocky Marciano after a big fight, or shooting the breeze with Eddie Arcaro. Comparing his area of expertise to the rest of what was written in the newspaper, Cannon said he worked for the "toy department."

While at Fordham, I called the Rams basketball games on the university's FM station, WFUV, and worked nights at WMGM, 1050-AM, as a production assistant. That's how I paid my tuition.

Cannon's sports columns were the daily Bible to me. I read them and reread them, all through my formal education. He wrote about the winners and losers in sports and Broadway society. He could take you into Bob Feller's head as he reluctantly came to grips that his fastball had lost velocity and he could take you backstage to a chorus girl's mirror, as she reluctantly came to grips that her prime years were over and "stage door Johnnies" no longer waited with roses. Cannon took the reader to the heart of the matter.

I had a classic Jesuit education at Fordham, but I learned a lot about life, reading Cannon. After graduation in 1963, my first professional sportscasting job was at WJRZ-AM in Newark, New Jersey. I hosted the drive time sports, mornings and afternoons, and called high school football games. I covered the Mets, Yankees, Giants and Titans/Jets carrying my tape recorder everywhere. After I became a familiar reporter on the beat, I shyly introduced myself to Cannon. He was short with a handsome face and dark piercing eyes. I could sense in our conversations that he had spent all his adult life answering the basic journalistic questions, "Who, what, when, and why?" He was inquisitive and analytical. His manner was quiet, but if provoked, he would spit out candid opinions like peanut shells.

One Sunday morning before a Giants football game at Yankee Stadium, we sat in the press room sipping weak chicken broth, as provided by the Maras. The team's chaplain passed our table and extended a warm greeting. Cannon blurted, "Why aren't you consoling some widow today, or helping the poor, instead of hanging out with a football team? You're a priest, not a cheerleader!" The football chaplain scurried away.

Cannon never married. In a live television interview on the Dumont Network, Mike Wallace, the host of Night-Beat, asked him why. Jimmy said, "For the same reason you just divorced Buff Cobb."

One night, I drove him to his modern apartment building near Sutton Place, on Manhattan's fancy East Side. Cannon's home was quite an upgrade from his childhood in Hell's Kitchen, on the grim West Side. He invited me up for a drink and proudly showed me an oil painting of a clown by Frank Sinatra which was a gift from the singer. Cannon allowed me to read some of his original drafts of columns. What read like butter in the newspaper was heavily edited with a black pen in its original form.

I mentioned to Cannon that I read Joe DiMaggio, in his rookie year with the Yankees, was his roommate and Cannon showed him around New York's nightlife. Jimmy said it was true. I asked Cannon, "What's the bottom line on DiMaggio?" He didn't miss a beat, spitting out, "THE MAN READS COMIC BOOKS!"

In 1965, I went national for the first time, reporting sports for UPI Audio. In May, I was in Lewiston, Maine, for the Ali-Liston rematch and the great Cannon taught me a lesson firsthand. Sonny had lost his championship to Ali, 15 months earlier in Miami, refusing to get off his stool after the 7th round, claiming he had a shoulder injury. But, Liston had been out-punched because Ali was too fast with his fists and too elusive. Until that night in Miami, Liston was the most-feared of heavyweights. But, he clearly was psyched by Ali who nicknamed him Sonny "The Bear." Liston called Ali "a nut."

There was an ominous aura surrounding the rematch. Cassius Clay had embraced Elijah Muhammad's black separatist Nation of Islam. He spoke out against the so-called white power structure in America. The American public was surprised. Their world heavyweight champion was against the Vietnam War. Their controversial black champion criticized the government and made headlines in the front of newspapers and at the start of television newscasts.

Four days before their first encounter, on February 21, 1964, Malcolm X of the Nation of Islam, was assassinated. There were rumors of further violence and Ali was protected by several bodyguards, called the Fruits of Islam.

The afternoon of the rematch, on May 25, 1965, at the Poland Springs Hotel, in Lewiston, Maine, I was chatting with Cannon in the lobby when Liston came down from his suite to have his lunch in the dining room. After Liston walked past us, Cannon said to me, ". . . HE LOOKS LIKE

HE'S GOING TO THE ELECTRIC CHAIR!" Being inexperienced at age 24, I said, ". . . He looks serious because he's fighting tonight." "NO," answered Cannon, "HIS FACE IS ASHEN. THAT MAN IS AFRAID OF SOMETHING!"

That night, at St. Dominic's Arena, an ice hockey youth center in Lewiston, Liston didn't last the first round. A lightning quick right-hand lead by Ali sent Liston down. Referee Jersey Joe Walcott botched the moment, by trying to get the celebrating Ali to a neutral corner. Liston stayed down for at least 17 seconds. Wolcott was confused and never counted for the knockdown. When Liston got up, Walcott attempted to get them fighting again. At ringside, Nat Fleischer, the publisher of Ring Magazine, shouted to the inept referee, who once was the world heavyweight champ for a little over a year, "It's over. He's out." Walcott turned and stopped the fight.

Ali retained his world heavyweight championship and called his 3rd blow of the fight, his "Anchor Punch," developed by Jack Johnson the first black heavyweight champion. Ali took great pains to describe the chopping, turn-of-the-wrist right hand to the chin, delivered when an opponent is advancing. Whatever it was, Liston, who was never knocked out before, looked like a buffoon rolling around the ring on his back and the joke among reporters was that it should be called "The Phantom Punch." At any rate, the savvy and wise Cannon was right. Liston was fearful and he quit against Ali a second time. This is the worst thing you can say about a fighter. Who knows why Liston "went into the tank"? Maybe his upset loss in his first encounter with Ali, when he quit because of an injured shoulder, pissed off someone who laid the 7-1 odds? Maybe, Liston had to make amends. Sonny "splashed" with everybody watching and I got a lesson, from a master observer, to look deep into a fighter's eyes, the mirrors of his soul.

In 1966, Earnest "Bud" Lamoreaux, a lead producer at CBS News, hired me and that was the biggest break in my career. Bud taught me much about writing and editing for television. He produced the weekly profiles and essays by the erudite Haywood Hale Broun. I sat in screening rooms and editing rooms watching them produce their stories and it was TV Sports Reporting 101.

At the 1968 World Series in St. Louis, I was on assignment for CBS News and I managed an interview with Roger Maris of the Cardinals during batting practice. Within earshot on the field were dozens of sportswriters from all over the country. Maris was on his way out of baseball and he allowed me a quick interview. Seven years earlier, Maris had broken Babe Ruth's single season home run record with 61 wallops and he suffered so much mental stress, some of his head hair fell out.

I asked Maris about the status of the World Series against Detroit and then, "What are you going to miss the most and what will you miss the least?" Maris answered he would miss his teammates the most and interviews the least. Adding, he was never comfortable talking about himself with reporters. The next day, in the New York Daily News, sportswriter Red Foley, who wore a fedora in the press box and smoked a pipe, wrote: "Before the game, a TV guy pushed his mike into Roger Maris' face and said "What are you gonna miss the most and the least? Maris said I'll miss my teammates the most and YOU the least." Foley purposely misquote Maris to take a jab at a broadcaster.

In 1970, the Knicks were in the stretch drive of their first championship run. The night the Knicks eliminated the Milwaukee Bucks in the 5th game of the best-of-seven, to advance to the NBA finals against the Los Angeles Lakers, I had to literally fight for the right to equal access. That afternoon, Madison Square Garden officials, including the team's public relations director, Frankie Blauschild, informed the radio and TV reporters that, at the insistence of the pro basketball writers, only they would be allowed into the locker rooms after the game for 15 minutes. Broadcast reporters would have to wait.

The writers wanted their own player quotes because their newspaper editors didn't want the post-game interviews on the 11pm TV news and subsequent radio newscasts. The next morning, they wanted their readership to see quotes for the first time. The Garden suits caved in. Since the inception of pro basketball, the teams needed the daily publicity the newspaper industry provided. But, times were changing. Less people were reading newspapers and more were using television as their primary source of news.

After the Knicks defeated the Bucks, I was at their door, waiting for us to be welcomed inside. I was ignoring the power play by the sportswriters. The New York Daily News beat guy challenged my presence. He yelled the new rule and pushed me in the chest. At that moment, someone opened the Knicks door and our confrontation spilled into the Knicks locker room. We grappled as Cazzie Russell laughed. Someone grabbed me from behind and shoved me into Coach Red Holzman's room. Red told me to calm down and I said, "This isn't where I want to be." I wanted to be in the other room with the players." Holzman insisted I calm down and he offered me an exclusive, one-on-one interview.

After subsequent arguing with Madison Square Garden officials and sportswriters, the15 minute ban was dropped. I was one of the new wave of broadcast reporters who insisted on equal access.

Before the 1969 World Series, I represented the broadcast media at a Shea Stadium meeting presided over by Frank Slocum of the baseball commissioner's office. Dick Young of the New York Daily News represented the sportswriters and Harry Harris of the Associated Press represented the still photographers. Young and Harris had hoarded all the press box positions.

I argued for positions for network and local TV cameras as well as reporters. Slocum, speaking for the Commissioner, told me to advise the broadcast outlets to buy tickets. I telephoned my superiors at CBS, along with ABC and NBC and the local TV stations. At the time, World Series games were in the afternoon and the filmed highlights were seen on all the evening local newscasts, as well as the national newscasts hosted by Walter Cronkite on CBS, Chet Huntley and David Brinkley on NBC and Murphy Martin on ABC. The two first rows of the third deck behind home plate at Shea Stadium were purchased by the broadcast media. That was the only way to gain access.

I asked Harris why his photographers needed so many positions. He said, "Because our pictures are seen all over the world, even in Timbuktu." And, and I said, "By the only guy who knows about baseball there."

Two days earlier, in Atlanta, after the third game of the first-ever National League Championship series, Young had been in a brawl in the jubilant and crowded Mets locker room. He was still hot about it. A CBS-News three-man crew out of the Atlanta bureau, known as the Pierce crew, named for its cameraman, was impeded in its coverage of Mets players talking with a knot of reporters. Young kept putting his head in front of the subjects, so the CBS light man applied a hot hand-light to Dick's neck. A fistfight ensued. This was playtime for the Pierce crew. They had been assigned the baseball playoffs as a reward for their dangerous work in race riots and civil unrest of the time. The brief scuffle was controlled by the many men in the room.

(Young wrote in the Daily News, the following day, Oct. 6, 1969, "There is a long standing concept that radio and TV men should not stick their mikes in the middle of a newspaper interview to parasite on the newsmen's questions.")

Although uninvited, Cosell arrived at that meeting with Slocum and Young carried on his vendetta with Cosell. They hated each other. By the end of the stormy meeting, Slocum accepted my suggestion that a hundred reporters crowding one dressing cubicle to interview a World Series game hero was now an impractical situation. Why not copy the NFL's switch to news conferences at the Super Bowl? Equal access was easier for everyone, including the players. This infuriated Young, but Slocum, to his credit, saw the merit of the suggestion. Major League Baseball switched to mass interviews, still allowing all media personal access, leaving the decision about individual interviews up to the athlete. Even Young had to accept that there weren't only "men" and newsmen" in those locker rooms. Credentialed women began asking questions, too.

In the spring of 1967, I won an audition for the weekend sports on WCBS-TV. My first broadcast was the first Saturday in May. Just before the 6pm news, on channel-2, anchored by veteran CBS News correspondent Robert Trout, CBS broadcast the Kentucky Derby, won by Proud Clarion. As nervous as I was, little did I know that would begin a run on New York TV news spanning five decades. However, in horse racing terms, I almost didn't make it out of the gate. Frank Gifford, who was the main sports anchor and had arranged my audition, showed me a personal memo from Robert D. Wood, the president of CBS. Gifford and Wood had been classmates at the University of Southern California and were close friends. Wood saw my first telecast and wrote that I had a fraction wrong in the timing of the race, so "We should be still looking for a weekend sportscaster." Gifford scoffed at the memo and reminded me we were the local station for the CBS bigwigs and at CBS every broadcast had to be perfect.

While at WCBS-TV, I learned how to film and edit sports events and how to interview personalities. I took lessons in personal demeanor from Gifford who was a private person despite his sports notoriety. He was extremely loyal to his handful of friends. The former Giants hero lectured me about being professional, polite to others and to carry oneself as a representative of CBS, the so-called "Tiffany of TV Networks." With "no. 16," you had to earn the right to call him "Frank" and happily we developed a warm friendship.

With Frank Gifford, NYC, 1971.

It was amazing how many celebrities wanted to know him. In the seven years we worked together, his telephone messages were from a "who's who" list of dynamic and successful Americans. It was common for the celebrated to drop by our tiny office. Among them, Don Meredith, Paul Hornung, Jerry West, Dave Marr, Pat Summerall, Phil Rizzuto and singer Gordon McRae. We were on the first floor at 524 West 57th Street in a block-size red brick building that was nicknamed "The Milk Factory" because it had been a dairy distribution center before CBS acquired the space and built the most up-to-date broadcasting facility in the world. The commissary in the basement was a gathering place because most of the employees spent some part of their day there. The food was diner variety and the facilities were clean. The people were especially interesting because office personnel and technical workers mixed with news people and the actors and actresses from the daily soap operas that were produced in "The Milk Factory." There was so much flirting going on, it reminded me of a high school cafeteria.

At WCBS-TV, I was surrounded by very experienced broadcasting personalities and there was much to emulate. The CBS TV newsroom was down the hall. Its stable of journalists included Eric Sevareid, Charles Collingwood, Howard K. Smith, Walker Cronkite, Mike Wallace, Robert Trout, Morley Safer, Dan Rather, Andy Rooney, Charles Kuralt, Harry Reasoner and Douglas Edwards. Dozens of correspondents, assigned all over the world, eventually passed through the newsroom. My personal favorite was Ike Pappas whose range was enormous. He could report war news from Vietnam or cover the World Series.

The CBS News room and studios and those of WCBS-TV were housed in a half-block complex on West 57th Street between 11th and 12th Avenues. It was the former Sealtest Milk depot. The entrance at 524 may have been used by some of the most famous people in the country. Once past the revolving doors the entranceway featured a plaque on the wall honoring the late Edward R. Murrow, who set high standards in broadcast journalism. You never knew who you would encounter in the hallways of "The Milk Factory." In the basement, I had my shoes shined by Lonnie whose two elevated chairs were situated down the hall from the commissary. Lonnie was a short, amiable black man who always smiled. Sometimes while getting a shine, I'd be sitting next to one of those esteemed network reporters chatting about the day's events and, yes, some sports too.

The WCBS Sports office was a favorite hangout, especially for lead anchor Jim Jensen who had been a minor league pitcher and organized the Channel-2 softball team that played in charity events all over New York, New

Jersey and Connecticut. (Jensen showed a lot of class when he was asked by management to report the Mets' first ever clincher of a division title in 1969. Jim insisted that I get the assignment because I had covered the team all season.) Jim loved talking sports with visiting CBS personnel like Jerry Coleman, the one-time Yankees second baseman who was beginning his broadcasting career. Win Eliot was a daily visitor. He was the best sports anchor on CBS radio, also located down the hall. Win was so talented and versatile; he hosted a network radio comedy program called "Can You Top This?" while calling the Kentucky Derby live and doing the play-by-play of National Hockey League games. Win advised all to learn more vocabulary and use descriptive terms and always be humorous. Win did the sports with a wink and a smile.

Jack Whitaker hosted the 11pm sports on WCBS-TV while working for the network on NFL football and professional golf events. No one wrote for television better than Whitaker. He was an essayist whose phraseology and timing were impeccable. He voice was distinctive and his delivery charming and urbane. I could listen to Whitaker read the telephone book.

Chris Shenkel, one of the first TV play-by-play guys, visited Gifford and stunned me by calling me by name. We had met four years earlier and Schenkel had an uncanny ability to remember people's names even if he met them once.

Former Yankees shortstop Phil Rizzuto came by every afternoon to record his daily network radio program which was written by Herb Goren who also wrote for Gifford on TV. Herb was the father of Ed Goren who cut his teeth in Florida local news before coming to CBS news. Ed enjoyed a meteoric rise through CBS Sports and now runs Fox Sports. His dad, Herb, had been a sports columnist, known as "The Old Scout," with the Brooklyn Eagle and later was the New York Rangers publicist for many years.

The night of the first Ali-Frazier fight in 1971, Herb was hospitalized with a broken leg. He suggested that Rizzuto use the CBS Radio credential for the bout and write down his eyewitness impressions for his sportscast the next day. "The Scooter" went to Madison Square Garden but could not write his script. The next morning, Herb asked for a typewriter and the morning newspapers. In his hospital bed, Goren wrote a script that was hand delivered to Rizzuto at CBS in time for the broadcast. Like many ex-jocks in broadcasting, Rizzuto was a strong personality who was tolerated and accommodated by the network.

Thanks to John Chanin at CBS Radio Sports, I took a side assignment, writing Pat Summerall's nightly five-minute sportscast on the network. Pat blotted out anything controversial I tried to sneak into his commentary.

Summerall was a former Giants place-kicker who didn't want to make any enemies. Biting and critical slants on sports weren't for him as he developed into a first rate play-by-play guy on NFL games and professional golf. Summerall's understated reportorial approach, though bland, became his signature. He was arguably the voice of the National Football League, which required stressing the positive not the negative.

One of the production guys at WCBS-TV was Bob Stenner, who graduated to CBS Sports and became its lead football producer, nicknamed "The Midnight Rambler." Stenner teamed with Summerall and John Madden on the weekly games and Super Bowl telecasts. Bob also produced the Daytona 500 for CBS.

When Fox acquired the NFL, Bob switched networks and brought along his longtime director Sandy Grossman and the technical crew that had produced games for CBS for a couple of decades.

In the late '60s at CBS, the mail was delivered by teenagers in gray uniforms, pushing carts of letters and inter-office correspondence. One of them had a constant smile and a courteous manner. Also, he couldn't keep away from any piano in a deserted rehearsal room or studio. He was Barry Manilow, who was eventually promoted to a production assistant.

With Roger Grimsby, WABC TV, 1971.

Three years later, in 1970, Gifford took me with him, when he switched from CBS to ABC. For the next decade, WABC-TV Eyewitness News changed the way local newscasts impacted not only New York viewers but the rest of the country, too. Up till then, TV news was presented by rigid, stone-faced white men, in a cold, austere manner. Visionary Al Primo was a young news director who cast the Eyewitness News team to reflect the community. His choices became an ensemble that was ethnic, co-ed, chatty, and offbeat, but charming. We looked and sounded like New Yorkers who rode the subways and the buses. The viewing audience related to the cast of characters and Eyewitness News, for all its frivolity, was the most watched newscast in New York by a wide margin, winning awards and becoming a franchise asset for the American Broadcasting Company.

The stars at the anchor desk were the experienced and authoritative looking Roger Grimsby and Bill Beutel whose distinctive voices were honed in radio. They were triple threats. Grimsby and Beutel were excellent reporters, writers and ad-libbers. Whacky Tex Antoine did the weather, Rona Barrett was the first-ever entertainment reporter while Cosell did the sports. At that moment in time, Cosell's caustic thunder and lightning made him a network star and he asked off to devote his full time to ABC's Wide World of Sports. Roone Arledge of ABC Sports lured Frank Gifford away from CBS Sports to be part of a new Monday Night Football series. In its second season, Gifford replaced Keith Jackson on play-by-play. Gifford insisted on anchoring the nightly local sports in New York, as he did at WCBS-TV. The former Giants football MVP hosted the early sportscast on WABC-TV and former Yankees pitcher Jim Bouton did the 11pm sports. I anchored the weekend sports and covered the sports beat during the week.

Hispanic Geraldo Rivera was an aggressive, award-winning street reporter. He was a controversial "hire" by Primo that proved to be a wonder stroke. While he had his detractors for being a self-promoter, Geraldo was a provocative journalist and eventually evolved into a network star, with his producer from the start, Marty Berman. Most of the other street reporters were veterans, like Bill Aleward, Doug Johnson, John Johnson, Bob Lape, Milton Lewis, Gil Noble, Roger Sharpe, Carol Jenkins and Gloria Rojas. Primo banked on their experience for the daily routine stories but insisted the stories be filmed differently. Instead of long, steady shots and close ups, Primo wanted the cameramen to move and show the entire scene, from all angles. The resulting firsthand approach brought the viewing audience "into the story." Eyewitness News looked different than the opposition and it attracted a bigger audience.

Primo had the foresight to hire a Brooklyn social worker named Roseanne Scammardella. He pushed her into television and the girl next door became a local television phenomenon. Gilda Radner shaped her character, "Roseanne Roseanna Dana," after her. The parody was a weekly feature on NBC's comedy program, Saturday Night Live.

Melba Tolliver was a young black secretary at WABC-TV. Primo put her on the air and New Yorkers embraced her. She was an African American reporting the news and that was a big deal for the new black consciousness. When Melba changed to cornrows in her hairdo, it was Page-3 in the New York Post!

Primo ordered black blazers for everyone. On the left lapel, we wore the golden Circle-7, the logo of WABC-TV. We looked like ushers. While that was accurate in person, on TV we had a distinctive and neat look. Tex Antoine refused to wear a black blazer, saying the artist's smock he wore for decades on WNBC-TV had become his signature. Primo said, "Tex, either we all wear black blazers or we all wear white smocks. Which is it gonna be?"

The Eyewitness Newsroom staff was young, brash, and aggressive.

Primo's assistant was Al Ittleson. The lead producer was Ron Tindigla. The assignment desk was run by Bob Davis and Joe Coscia. The mandate everyday was to be informative about New York City and its suburbs, while entertaining.

Primo wanted participation in the story by each reporter. There were confrontational scenes and dangerous episodes. Citizens were given a chance to tell their stories. Many times there was outrage. New York's minorities saw themselves on TV and they felt this was their channel. The filmed stories were hustled back to WABC-TV by motorcycle to expedite breaking news. That group of bike jockeys, headed by "Joey D.," were like "The Dead End Kids." They were street-tough New Yorkers who were also helpful as security men on dangerous assignments. In the all-important audience ratings, the channel-7 newscasts zoomed from third to first place. Its success was astounding and the "Happy Talk" Eyewitness News format was copied by TV stations all over the country. The face of local television news changed forever and that's why Al Primo is the "Godfather of Eyewitness News."

In the autumn of 1973, Jim Bouton's contract wasn't renewed and I was switched to the 11PM sportscast on an interim basis. As 1974 began, WABC-TV hired veteran sportscaster Guy Lebow to replace me on the 11pm sports, bouncing me back to weekends. Lebow had the look and sound of an informed reporter, but his reputation was questioned because he concocted stories. He claimed exclusivity, which was true, but his fantasies weren't.

Frank and I traveled to Houston for Super Bowl VIII between Miami and Minnesota, while Lebow was left to anchor in New York. The first night in town, in a restaurant-bar filled with players from both teams, Dolphins safety Jake Scott gave me a scoop. Defensive coach Bill Arnsparger, on the flight to Houston, revealed he would be new head coach of the Giants. At media day, the next morning, I went straight to Arnsparger and filmed an exclusive interview, confirming the hiring. We put the film on an airplane to New York easily making the 6pm newscast. Lebow refused to air it and I had to get the new news director, Al Ittleson, to order him to air it. After my piece, Lebow said, "Anyway, I reported about Arnsparger a week ago," which was untrue.

When I returned from Houston, I told Lebow he was a phony and a fraud. Within months, he was fired by WABC-TV for faking a controversial filmed interview with Rangers captain Vic Hadfield. On a night off from hockey, Hadfield was interviewed on film at Channel-7. After he left, Lebow changed a question on a close-up of himself from a reverse angle and edited a fraudulent question into the interview. Hadfield's response to another question made it sound like rookie coach Larry Popein was losing control of the Rangers team. This infuriated Madison Square Garden officials who confronted WABC-TV executives. After a careful examination of the film and its alteration, the WABC-TV management waited until July before releasing Lebow. After six months of chaos, normalcy returned to our Eyewitness News office and our sportscasts.

In the past 30-odd years, dozens of sports anchors caromed into and out of New York. Of all of the sportscasters who stayed awhile, Dan Lovett was the most talented. He came out of Houston to join Eyewitness News when Gifford left WABC-TV to work exclusively for ABC Sports. Danny, with a loveable squint in his eyes, was excellent writer and reporter with a strong voice. He later found his broadcasting happiness in Washington, D.C. and San Francisco.

One summer night in 1972, after the early WABC-TV Eyewitness News, Gifford was giving me a ride home to Manhattan's East Side with Ethel Kennedy in the front seat. The widow of Robert Kennedy was helped in her grief by friends like Frank. On the car radio, we heard a Rolling Stones song. I mentioned they were appearing at the Garden that very night. She asked if we could go. At the nearest phone booth, I called the Garden and asked Joe Acquafreda for help. Joe was the head of security. About an hour later, we sat in the photographers' well in front the Rolling Stones on stage. Dick Cavett was in the pit, too. Only in New York!

ABC Sports Update Studio, NYC, 1972.

In the '70s, I free-lanced assignments for ABC's Wide World of Sports, as a studio host and correspondent. I called major league baseball games and college football games. I did the blow-by-blow of amateur and professional boxing. I learned as Cosell's backup. I hosted ABC-Radio network and local sportscasts. I traveled all over the country and to the Soviet Union and the Philippines for boxing telecasts.

After a 3 year stint at ESPN, in 1984 I was hired by WNBC-TV News Director Jerry Nachman to anchor the weekend sports and backup Marv Albert. Nachman and I had worked at WCBS-TV when he was a street reporter. Nachman was from Brooklyn and was obese because he ate too much Chinese food. He was a tabloid guy with street smarts and an extraordinary ability to write and report. His assistant news director was Bob Davis and we had worked together at WABC-TV's Eyewitness News. For the next 10 years, the offices and studios in Rockefeller Center became my broadcasting home. This was especially sweet because when I was a teenager and obsessed with broadcasting, I used to roam the halls and sneak into NBC's empty studios. There was hardly any security at 30 Rock and it was easy to drift away from the guided tours.

Now, NBC was the hot network and 30 Rock was bulging with talent, from the Today Show, the Nightly News with Tom Brokaw, Late Night with

David Letterman, and Saturday Night Live. In the hallways you could bump into Bill Cosby, John Belushi and Billy Crystal. The Letterman taping was across the hall from our studio for the Newscenter-4 programs. Letterman did ambush walk-ons during Live at Five. Often in his opening monologues, his control room put correspondents, like me, on the screen waiting to do remote reports and Letterman joked about our appearance and demeanor. In the same building on WNBC-Radio, Don Imus and Howard Stern were emerging as talk-show megastars.

In the '80s, the Newscenter-4 news operation was a well-oiled machine with immense local credibility. The reportage was aggressive and solid. Live at Five was entertaining, as well as informative. The senior correspondent was Gabe Pressman, who already was in his fourth decade covering the New York beat for television news. Channel-4's daily and nightly top-rated newscasts were anchored by Chuck Scarborough, Sue Simmons, Pat Harper and Jack Cafferty. In addition to Marv Albert, Len Berman and me with the sports, the weathermen were Dr. Frank Fields and Al Roker. Among the reporters were Mary Cavillo, David Diaz, Tony Guida, Jane Hanson, Ralph Penza, Mike Tiabbe, police beat specialist John Miller and entertainment reporter Pia Lindstrom.

Nachman was an old school newsman who collected newsroom all-stars for every position and they had to know New York City. Nachman did not tolerate out-of-towners who couldn't figure out the subway system and didn't know a bagel from a blintz.

During the 1986 National League playoffs, televised by ABC, the Mets beat the Houston Astros in game-5 in the 12th inning on a Gary Carter game-winning single for a 3-2 lead in the best of seven series. It happened about 10 minutes before six p.m. The ABC network went off the air quickly and Channel-7's Eyewitness News began. So, did WNBC-TV's Newscenter-4 and I led our newscast at Shea Stadium with a live interview with Carter on the field. I had grabbed Gary in the runway leading to the clubhouse and he was nice enough to return to the field. When we were finished, a technician in the WNBC-TV satellite truck had a message for me to call Nachman's office. When he answered his telephone, Nachman, who won a Peabody Award, an Edward R. Murrow Award and an Emmy for his journalistic talents, yelled "Sal, you just made me come in my pants."

Over 3 decades, working for the three owned-and-operated television stations in New York, I enjoyed many special sports happenings. The first time champion Mets of 1969 sprayed me with champagne and so did the champion 1986 Mets.

Mets Captain Keith Hernandez and MVP Ray Knight after the World Series victory over the Boston Red Sox, Shea Stadium, NYC, Oct. 1986.

I reported about the Yankees championship teams of the '70s and '90s. Red Holzman's two-time champion Knicks teams were a joy to watch and interview. In the '80s, I covered the Islanders who won four consecutive Stanley Cups. Assembled by general manager Bill Torrey and coached by Al Arbour, the Islanders were the nicest bunch of guys I ever interviewed. Bill Parcells' two Giants championship teams were a talented bunch of characters, led by the greatest defensive player ever, Lawrence Taylor.

Joe Namath was a controversial figure and so was Mickey Mantle. They were bigger than life to sports fans. They ran 1 and 1-A, as the most charismatic of New York sports figures. The rest of those champion Jets were interesting studies, from Brooklyn's Harvard-educated John Dockery to a down-home, good old boy like Curly Johnson.

In those days, pro athletes weren't affected by too much money. They needed off-season jobs. They were accessible and cooperative. I socialized with many pro athletes including the Berras, the Seavers, the McGraws, the Kranepools, the Gilberts, Fred Dryer, Rusty Staub, Jim Fregosi, Walt Frazier, and Namath.

On January 12, 1969, working the postgame at Super Bowl III and filing a live report with filmed interviews for the 11PM WCBS-TV Newscast was a thrill. Live switches between cities, like between New York and Miami, were rare and reserved for the biggest of stories. I interviewed Namath about the Jets victory and his "guarantee" and a picture of the moment hangs in the Pro Football Hall of Fame in Canton, Ohio.

Mets Manager Yogi Berra, Shea Stadium NYC, Sept. 1973.

I covered the first 11 Super Bowls and dozens of world championship fights. I was at ringside for all three Ali-Frazier fights. I covered dozens of World Series games and I witnessed one of the last great day games in post-season history. On October 2, 1978, at Boston's Fenway Park, it was a one game playoff for the American League East championship. The Yankees had caught the Red Sox for a tie for first place at the end of the schedule. It is a game that lives in Red Sox infamy. Light-hitting Yankees shortstop Bucky Dent, who hit only four home runs all season, became a curse word all over Red Sox Nation when he lofted a 7th inning, two-out three-run home run off Mike Torrez, over the Green Monster wall into the net. What struck me was the silence from the sellout crowd at Fenway Park. It was so quiet, I could hear the shouts of joy from the Yankees dugout and from George Steinbrenner and his friends in the adjacent box seats. Reggie Jackson added a solo shot and the Yankees won the one-game playoff 5-4 and and captured the American League East Title. Red Sox fans were stung again by the Yankees.

Over the summer of '78, the Yankees had lagged behind and then stalked the front-running Red Sox. In early September, Boston led by four games when the Yankees went to Fenway Park and beat the tar out of the Bosox, winning four straight outscoring them 42-9 to tie for the lead. It became an early autumn all over England when The Boston Collapse became complete on Bucky Dent Day at the Fens. I watched from a photographer's overhang just short of first base. My buddy Jonathan Schwartz, the New York radio personality, sat with me. As anyone who has ever listened to his program knows, Jonathan is a lifelong, very intense Red Sox fan. In broadcasting's caveman days, Jono would park his Volkswagen near 96th Street and the FDR drive. That was the best spot in New York to pick up the Red Sox broadcasts on AM radio from Boston. Schwartz would sit and listen to full games, sometimes doubleheaders, at 96th and the Drive.

The night before the game, I offered my extra press credential to my best friend Les Davis, who was old Yankee fan. Because of his radio commitments, Lester declined. After nervous negotiations by telephone, Schwartz grabbed the brass ring. He had spent another gut-wrenching baseball summer and the only place to be was at Fenway Park. We caught a Monday morning Eastern Airlines Shuttle flight from LaGuardia Airport to Boston's Logan Airport. Jono was extremely grateful for the press credential. He had done this before, tagging along with me as a credentialed "producer" at Celtics' playoff games, for example.

Everything that pristine October afternoon at Fenway Park was fine until Dent's home run. Schwartz simply rose from his chair, turned from me without a word and climbed the tiny ladder out of the photographer's well to the second deck and disappeared into the mostly silent crowd. Les Davis told me Schwartz took the defeat so badly, he went into seclusion in Palm Springs, California. He didn't resurface for three months.

Meanwhile, I had to get downstairs. In the Yankees' clubhouse, there was a champagne spraying celebration and I hosted a live broadcast, interviewing the players for WABC-TV.

In 1973, I stroked the brow of Secretariat and saw him win the Belmont Stakes by 31 lengths. The mighty Secretariat was the first Triple Crown winner in 25 years, since Citation. I was privileged the see Affirmed nip Alydar at the finish line of their mighty stretch run in the 1978 Belmont Stakes for the Triple Crown. With the crowd of more than 80,000 roaring and 18-year-old Steve Cauthen riding the 3-year old chestnut colt, Affirmed's sweep of thoroughbred racing's Triple Crown was complete by only a head at the wire. The game Alydar had also finished second in the Kentucky Derby and the Preakness, but in their later years in stud Alydar sired more stakes winners than Affirmed.

The New York Islanders of the early '80s should have been more celebrated. Except for the cantankerous Billy Smith, their spectacular goalie, and a couple of other odd types, the Islanders were a class act in their relationships with the media. They didn't act arrogantly while winning a record 19 playoff series in a row and four straight Stanley Cups. One of the greatest teams in all of professional sports placed seven men into the Hockey Hall of Fame in Toronto. They were General Manager Bill Torrey, Coach Al Arbour and players, Bryan Trottier, Mike Bossy, Denis Potvin, Billy Smith and Clarke Gillies. Other key components to their championship run were Butch Goring, Bob Nystrom, John Tonelli, Lorne Henning, Stefan Persson and Anders Kallur.

A routine interview put me in a courtroom and a landmark broadcast legal case. In 1971, the Giants were 4-9 with one game left in their dismal season. On December 14th, Gifford asked me to interview Giants head coach Alex Webster about what went wrong and what did the Giants needed to improve next year. Webster answered those questions candidly. "Big Red" wasn't a successful head coach but he was a standup guy. He and Frank were in the backfield of the Giants' fabled teams in the '50s and '60s. That night, during Frank's 6pm sportscast on Eyewitness News, we aired a portion of that interview. On his 11pm sportscast, Bouton characterized Webster as a clown of a coach and played a sound-bite backwards to make Webster appear evasive and foolish.

The next morning, I went back to Yankee Stadium and before I could say to Webster I didn't have anything to do with Bouton's cheapshot, he waved me off. Webster understood my non-compliance, but didn't appreciate how the telecast saddened his wife and children. Wellington Mara told me he would fund a libel suit, on behalf of Webster against Bouton. Mara warned me I would be part of it, so that I would have to testify that Webster gave me honest answers.

Soon enough, Bouton was sued for a million dollars, so was I, and the American Broadcasting Company. After that was published in the local newspapers, I visited my immigrant grandparents in Brooklyn. My grandmother didn't bother to say hello. In Sicilian and with a wave of her hand, she moaned to me "I always knew you would be the ruination of this family. Where are we going to get a million dollars?"

I said, "Grandma, in America, it's a good thing to be sued for a million dollars because of the publicity." She countered, "You Americans are crazy." I assured her I was protected by the company.

The litigation dragged on until 1976, when a New York state judge ruled that Bouton did not defame Webster because newscasters and sportscasters are as much entertainers as they are reporters. The Honorable Martin Stecher added, if Public Broadcasting could parody President Richard Nixon, a TV sportscaster could parody a football coach.

Frank and I shared an office with Jim and our relationship with him was icy. I relayed a message from Webster warning Jim that if he encountered Alex in public, he should expect a beating. Jim said, "Doesn't he know he could get sued if he punches me?'

Frank wisecracked, "The last guy who sued Alex for punching him was in P.J. Clarke's when Alex pulled him out to the sidewalk and gave him another beating. Jim, you insulted Alex and got away with it. Don't push your luck."

Bouton wrote a tattletale book about his baseball career, "Ball Four" and the subsequent controversy catapulted him into a broadcasting stint. The respected and quiet Elston Howard told me he wished he could corner Bouton alone and smack him for writing that the Yankees catcher cut the baseball, enabling Whitey Ford to throw an illegal pitch.

One afternoon at Yankee Stadium, at the end of a Giants workout, Bouton posed on the goalposts for a Eyewitness News publicity photograph. A bunch of Giants grabbed footballs and hit Bouton with a shower of them. I saw Billy Martin throw Bouton out of the Yankees clubhouse despite his press pass. Three decades later, Bouton was invited by the team to his first Yankees' Old-Timers' Day.

At Eyewitness News we were instructed to be aggressive and air exclusive reports. On March 26, 1974, George Foreman knocked out Ken Norton in the second round in Caracas, Venezuela, to retain his world heavyweight championship. The new Venezuelan government refused to allow Foreman to leave until he paid a special "tax" of $250,000. Norton was ordered to pay $50,000. The contract with the original government was null and void and the world's heavyweight champion and the man he beat were detained for two days until the bill was paid by the local promoter.

Detaining and then releasing the world heavyweight champion was extraordinary. When Foreman's jetliner arrived at JFK Airport in New York, I was waiting with a film crew. Promoter Don King, who was wooing Foreman for future business, stood by with a dozen long-stemmed roses. Foreman didn't come into the terminal. He walked off the plane onto the tarmac. The airline representative told me special arrangements were made for George to quickly make a connection for a flight to Houston. My camera crew and I ran to the terminal jetport and the attendant told me Foreman was on the flight, which had a stop in Atlanta. I whipped out my American Express card and paid for four round trip tickets to Atlanta. My cameraman, light man and soundman and I went aboard and in flight we filmed an exclusive interview with Foreman. Foreman's publicist, Bill Caplan, exclaimed. "Kid, I like your style!"

We returned from Atlanta in plenty of time to air the interview that night. The next day, I was asked by News Director Al Primo to come to his office. He wanted to know why I had submitted an expenditure of over a thousand dollars for a trip to and from Atlanta. I told him why, showed him the story about the Eyewitness News exclusive in the New York Post and reminded him of his desire for us to be different. He smiled and said, "Next time, keep it local."

Along the way I lost two jobs in 14 months, at WABC-TV and WCBS-TV, to Warner Wolf. His dynamic high-energy kaleidoscope of sports video highlights endeared him to viewers who loved his trademark, "Lets go to the videotape." Warner was simply the best act in New York and I considered what happened as business. We remain close friends to this day.

Reggie Jackson once asked me, "How can you be that man's friend? He took your job twice." I told him Warner was considered by management a better act than me, he didn't TAKE my job. Our relationship is about truth and friendship and I would rather not live with anger on my mind and malice in my heart.

No one was more imitated than Warner. The hybrid versions of his style are stupid because they think it's about yelling over the highlights and making dumb jokes. Warner has deep sports knowledge to back his strong presentation. Through the decades, watching oddballs who can't write compound sentences and the phonies who act like game-show hosts, it seems there are only two professionals who need no experience, prostitutes and sportscasters.

A stations' division executive once told me he preferred the "entertainer" type of sports anchor who regularly shows elephants playing soccer, polo on camels and crashing skateboarders because the news program audience, that doesn't care about sports, has to be held attentive during the sportscast. I said, if that's valid, to keep the attention of viewers, who don't care for the nightly financial reports, we should show colliding stockbrokers and bankers competing in foot races. His theory was nonsense because television cannot fully satisfy all of the audience, on every topic, during every segment. The executive and I had a heated debate, but hucksters who put the sizzle ahead of the steak don't back down because they are myopic.

In the last 40 years, I've worked for many news directors, most of them very competent, a few were know-it-all tyrants. One actually walked around the newsroom everyday with a plastic baseball bat in his hands. Another was always nattily dressed with a fresh flower in his lapel and preferred nothing on his desk. The most incompetent was a corporate assassin at NBC, whose previous experience was producing TV game shows. His assignment from the new ownership at General Electric was to fire many workers to save as much money as possible. That was understandable and the company's prerogative, but for someone who never covered a fire or a state house, his demeanor toward news people was arrogant and despicable.

In 40 years of encountering good and bad news directors, the best was saved for last. The news director with the most ability to extract the most from her staff is Karen Scott at WPIX. She has an innate ability to lead and instruct kindly and her journalistic and programming decisions add luster to the CW-11 News-at-Ten. Starting in 2001, four of the past six years our nightly program has been voted the Emmy Award for best TV newscast in New York.

My pet peeve in television news is the word "unbelievable." It is an adlib crutch for broadcasters and it should never be used by a newsperson. Newscasts aren't Ripley's Believe It or Not.

I've watched thousands and thousands of games on television to prepare nightly highlight tapes for my sportscasts. TV's technical evolution made the action in sports more vivid. Slow motion replays, isolated views and close-ups of athletes are riveting. But, for my generation, TV's "reality" of a typical game has become too busy with an excess of shot changes, confusing graphics and endless network promos that interfere with the flow. The video and audio onslaught is very intense, lasting throughout the 3 or 4 hour telecasts. The technical toys in the trucks are over-used and the expanding commercial load makes suckers of all advertisers because audiences are using the commercial breaks to channel-surf.

It's about spectacle now. At halftime of football games, the networks present musical entertainment instead of analyzing the first half and discussing team adjustments. The games and the sports are disrespected. The networks distract in order to hold the audience.

The defining moment of halftime nonsense was NBC promoting its primetime game show by staging a mini-version during the halftime of a Los Angeles Lakers-Philadelphia 76ers championship round game in 2001. One of the "contestants" was WNBA star Lisa Leslie, whose games were on NBC. The moderator asked Leslie which President Roosevelt was a Republican. Leslie, who supposedly was educated at the University of Southern California, blurted, "JFK?"

The networks are enslaved to the demographic of men, 18 to 34. So, like the general culture, sports fans are fractured and polarized. I can understand dressing in a contemporary way and the use of modern music, but for the most part, sports history is avoided. Fans beyond the age of 34 are ignored.

For "name-razzle-dazzle" and authenticity, networks hire ex-jocks and sportswriters. But, a reach is hiring a comedian for sports telecasts, like ABC did with Dennis Miller for Monday Night Football. It's lame. Sports fans don't stand around the water cooler the next day clucking snappy patter about jokes they heard the night before during a football game. Executives responsible for this silliness probably never sit in the bleachers of stadiums with the rest of America. Sports fans root for their teams and athletes, not broadcasters and the technical wizardry.

One of the worst programming ideas ever was HBO concocting a boxing series with rap artists, singers and dancers who were framed in artificial smoke and flashing lights. The fights were ordinary and the series failed.

After years of ignoring women, networks began hiring females to cover sports. Several evolved as solid reporters, but in not so subtle ways the younger ones were given a mandate: dress provocatively because the networks want to attract the young male demographic. Females, working sidelines at football games, are framed full-bodied while males are in tight close-ups.

Women who pose nude in magazines are given auditions and jobs. Sex appeal is what catapulted Lisa Guerrero from modeling to a local TV gig in Los Angeles to Fox Sports to ABC Sports. She posed in scanty outfits on her web site and ended up as the sideline reporter on Monday Night Football where she failed because of her lack of football knowledge. Fox Network's sports commentator Leeann Tweeden posed in lingerie in the men's magazine FHM and there was no objection from her employers who exploited their young male audience that obviously does not hold the same standards for "hot babes" as they do for expert reporters, whether they're male or female.

Sports journalism no longer exists. Networks that pay huge sums for rights fees make sure their telecasts are clean of controversies and real issues. Games are considered "the product." Advertisers and teams must be protected. For instance, there is no way CBS would air a provocative essay on the racial bigotry at the Augusta National Golf Club which determines the Masters annual TV contract. That happened in the late '60s, when Heywood Hale Broun of CBS News excoriated the old south bluster at the Masters. CBS Sports was embarrassed, but CBS News wasn't compromised. CBS managed to hold the rights. Now, the piece would never be produced and aired because television is more about business than truth. More than ever, the viewer must choose his television programming carefully because too much "eyeball cotton candy" is bad for the brain.

A half century after Alan "The Horse" Ameche, of the Baltimore Colts galloped into the New York Giants end zone and into America's hearts to win the NFL championship in overtime, known as "The Greatest Football Game Ever Played," televised sports has become an entertainment staple.

Over the ensuing decades, these "minstrel shows" became more expensive, but the bellowing summertime crowds at Fenway Park and Wrigley Field don't seem to care. Neither do the frostbitten acolytes in football stadiums and the howling students in steamy basketball gyms. Americans love their games and television pumps the product. Millions continue to watch despite the clutter of commercials, promotional announcements and the noisy sound effects. Televised sports remain our national pastime in the evenings and on weekends while the cost of tickets and cable subscriptions spiral ever upward.

Why the consistent popularity? Steve Bornstein, the executive who led ESPN to the top of TV sports, said the smartest thing about televised sports, "You can't go into Blockbuster and rent tonight's game."

As for those of us fortunate enough to be in the arena, whether we are athletes, coaches or reporters, my favorite anecdote involves Digger Phelps. The Notre Dame basketball coach was in New York recruiting high school prospects, handing out tiny Imaculate Conception Medals to their parents, when I asked him this question: "What's it like in the runway just before a game with your team, while you're wearing your green carnation and they are playing the Notre Dame fight song on the floor? Digger answered: "It's better than sex."

ENCOUNTERS

I have two distinct memories of Thurman Munson, one trivial and one profound. During the 1977 season, the Yankees catcher and captain approached me with a gruff demeanor in the Yankees dugout before a game and demanded to know what I meant about a teammate of his, the night before on the late news on WABC-TV. I explained that his team had called up a shortstop from Syracuse named Mickey Klutz and his error in the 9th inning cost the game. I said on the air, "Klutz was a klutz." In "New Yorkese," a klutz is someone who makes mistakes. Thurmon said he understood and managed a smile. More importantly, he knew he could not intimidate me. Munson liked to do that with beat reporters. I never had another problem getting an interview from him even though he usually wasn't gracious to the press especially broadcasters.

My other memory of the Yankees captain was in their locker room at Dodgers Stadium after they had clinched the 1978 World Series. Munson had played all summer with painful knees, but he helped carry the team to a remarkable comeback. In that clinching sixth game of the World Series, Munson had caught what proved to be Jim Catfish Hunter's last start before he retired. Rich "Goose" Gossage relieved to close the door on the Dodgers and Munson had squeezed a foul pop for the last out. Later, in the Yankees clubhouse, long after the champagne celebration and long after the interviews, Munson sat in his no. 15 jersey hugging the championship trophy. His satisfaction was so immense, he embraced it. He wouldn't let it go. It proved to be Thurmon's last moment of baseball glory.

The next August 2nd, he was killed in his private twin-engine plane, while practicing takeoffs and landings in Canton, Ohio. He was 32 years old and the father of three children. Two days later, all the Yankees and team officials attended his funeral. WCBS-TV flew me and a camera crew by private jet to Canton to cover it. It was the saddest assignment I ever experienced. The champion Yankees openly grieved their beloved teammate and captain.

My most interesting encounter was with Frank Sinatra. His close friend, Dennis Stein said the famous singer brought up my name during dinner with Los Angeles Dodgers manager Tommy Lasorda the night before at the 21 Club. Sinatra said he noticed my sportscasts while watching TV in his Waldorf Towers apartment and would like to meet me. I was stunned. When we met, Sinatra's first words while shaking hands were, "I'm from Hoboken, where are you from?" I answered ". . . . Brooklyn." It was a gracious gesture to set me at ease. He wanted to know about my family and my education. He was a big sports fan and that was much of the conversation in subsequent meetings. It always amazed me that I was talking with Sinatra and how even natured he was. When Jilly tried an East Side version of his popular West Side saloon, over Rocky Lee's restaurant on Second Avenue, there was an opening night party. When I arrived, Stein met me at the door and motioned that Sinatra was in the back. At that moment, he was putting a slice of pizza in his mouth. I went to the bar instead. When I approached the table about 20 minutes later, Sinatra said, "You saw me eating when you came in and didn't come to my table. That's why I like you."

He said he found me intriguing while watching on TV because I didn't change my name to some Anglo-Saxon, non-ethnic name like so many others in the entertainment business. He was proud of his heritage and said, "When I started out as a singer, someone suggested I change my name to 'Frankie Satin' I insisted I was Frank Fucking Sinatra!" He was well known for his perfect diction while singing. He offered the opinion that most newscasters didn't speak well enough, but complimented me about my diction. He wanted to know if I took lessons and I told him I spent two years with a private teacher.

In our first meeting, after he asked sports questions, Sinatra asked me what I wanted to talk about and I replied that I read mostly biographies and the film industry was interesting. I mentioned I had just finished reading Montgomery Clift's unauthorized biography. We discussed Clift who had prepped Sinatra for his Oscar-winning role as "Angelo Maggio" in the acclaimed motion picture, "From Here to Eternity."

Sinatra's voice rose and he became angry. He lectured me that people shouldn't talk about the dead, especially revealing their private lives in books. Sinatra said in disgust, "They're all in the book . . . . Elizabeth Taylor, Marlon Brando . . . . not me. Monty was a very troubled man who sank to embarrassing depths. This gifted actor had extremely low self-esteem which is nobody's business."

(A couple of years after Sinatra's death, his daughter Tina, in her memoir, "My Father's Daughter," wrote about his health problems in his last years).

Sinatra praised Clift for helping him develop Maggio's character and how to say the dialogue properly and move naturally. He expressed his gratitude for Clift's intense, private coaching. Sinatra's portrayal of "Maggio" was so powerful, he received an Academy Award for Best Supporting Actor in the 1953 production that won eight Oscars, including best film. The impact of Sinatra's role and the critical acclaim revitalized his singing career. After our first meeting, Sinatra said to Stein, "I like him, bring him around again."

I was Sinatra's guest at Carnegie Hall and Madison Square Garden concerts and was able to speak privately with him for a few minutes. At the glittering Boys Town of Italy dinner that honored him at the Waldorf Astoria, he was especially kind to me, promising, and "I'll put in a good word with your boss Bill Paley." In the late 70's, my wife Bernadette and I saw Sinatra at a New Jersey concert in an outdoor bowl off the Garden State Parkway. Dennis Stein came to our seats and invited us to dinner afterwards at Jilly's in Manhattan. Over coffee and dessert, Sinatra moved from the head of the table to opposite me at the end. I complimented him on the use that night of a sextet in the midst of his usual big band presentation. It was the first time I heard him in person with a small instrumental group. Sinatra sang a jazzy version of "Lover Come Back To Me," a classic ballad. Proving that everyone needs a compliment once in a while, the great Frank Sinatra said, "You really liked that? Thank you. I use a small group for charity appearances. Tonight, I thought I'd break up my big concert routine. Thanks for noticing."

Sinatra told me he tried to influence George Steinbrenner into hiring Leo Durocher as a coach, but the Yankees owner refused because "Leo the Lip" was too old and he would be disruptive. At the 1977 World Series in Los Angeles, Sinatra sat behind the Dodgers dugout and gave me an exclusive television interview.

In the spring of 1985, after Don Mattingly's breakout season with the Yankees, I visited with Sinatra backstage after a Carnegie Hall concert. He said to me, "Tell me about Don Mattingly." I offered the opinion that Mattingly was the best Yankees first baseman since Lou Gehrig. He could hit for average and for power and he was slick with the glove. Sinatra wanted to know his age. I said he was 24. Sinatra said, "Would you believe, I'm gonna turn 70." He looked at the ceiling and said it wistfully, as if it was a song lyric.

Sinatra laughed long and loud when I told him about a New Yorker's sidewalk reaction to me after a Sinatra concert. As I hopped into a friend's chauffeured Rolls Royce, a guy, assuming it was mine, yelled out, "Hey, Sal, you get this for reading scores!"

Sinatra was very kind to me and always supportive. For an Italian-American from Brooklyn, meeting and knowing Sinatra was a genuine thrill. He represented success for those of us who yearned to assimilate into American life.

I met Rocky Marciano in June of 1969, at a Madison Square Garden ceremony inducting him and others into its Hall of Fame. I interviewed the former world heavyweight champion for WCBS-TV. Afterwards, he said he heard about "an Italian guy on New York television" and asked me about my Italian heritage and if people presumed we were relatives. I said, "I get that all the time, but I tell them the truth, we're not relatives."

Rocky was Rocco Francis Marchegiano, known professionally as "The Brockton Blockbuster." The son of a shoemaker in Brockton, Massachusetts, was the idol of Italian-Americans because he had been the king of boxing from 1952-56.

After winning all of his 49 professional fights, 43 by knockout, Marciano retired as the only undefeated world heavyweight champion at age 33.

Former Undefeated World Heavyweight Champion Rocky Marciano, Madison Square Garden, NYC, June 1969.

I was thrilled to meet him and realized his hands were massive, the fingers thick, the palms huge and his wrists oversized. Rocky was on the short side for a heavyweight fighter. He was about 5'10", and 185 lbs. Rocky's arms were short, only 68 inches. But, Marciano had powerful hands and a fiery determination. His short arms forced him to get inside an opponent's attack. To get there, Rocky took many punches and was knocked down, but he never lost a professional fight. Marciano disdained the jab. He was a hooker, bending at the knees for a crouched attack. His sweeping left hook was devastating and he nicknamed his lethal right hand, his "Susie Q."

On September 23, 1952, in Philadelphia, Marciano suffered his first knockdown in the opening moments and was behind on all cards when he unleashed his "Susie Q" in the 13th round to take the world heavyweight championship away from Joe Walcott. In the next four years, Marciano successfully defended his title six times and became an international celebrity, appearing on the nationally popular variety programs, hosted by Bob Hope, Ed Sullivan, etc. Later, Marciano hosted a filmed, syndicated program of sports interviews.

In our conversations, I found the Boxing Hall of Famer easygoing and genuinely interested in my TV career. As for our similar names, Rocky advised, "Tell them we're related. Make it cousins. Good luck, kid."

Four months later, on August 31, 1969, "The Brockton Blockbuster" died in a small airplane crash in Newton, Iowa. My "cousin," Rocky Marciano, was a day short of his 46th birthday.

If there's such a thing as an awful kiss, it happened one night in Las Vegas. Muhammad Ali, 38 years old and on the decline physically, in his first fight in two years, was two days away from trading punches with 30-year-old Larry Holmes, on October 2, 1980, in a temporary arena in the parking lot of Caesar's Palace.

I was there for ESPN and we had videotaped Holmes' last workout. Later, in the hotel coffee shop, Ali's trainer, Angelo Dundee, sat down at my table and flat out asked me if we would give him a copy for Ali to look at. I suggested a trade. How about the videotape for a one-on-one interview with Ali? This is what they don't teach you in journalism courses.

Within an hour, I was in Ali's suite at Caesar's Palace, along with my cameraman Jeff Israel and producer Tom Riles. While Jeff set up the lights in the spacious living room, Riles and I were taken to Ali's huge bedroom. I gave him the videotape and Ali slammed it into the playback machine. Then, he shadowboxed to the image of Holmes sparring at the workout. Ali spat out, "I'm gonna get you Larry Holmes!" He raised a sweat and then spun the tape back and shadowboxed again. Tom, Jeff and I watched Ali trying to psyche himself by firing phantom punches at a image of Holmes.

It was startling. Arguably, the world's most famous man was naked and yelling, while punching in the direction of his television set. We couldn't stop laughing. Classic Ali, in the buff, as few have seen him.

After Ali cooled down, showered and dressed, he joined me on the couch in the living room for the interview. While we taped, there was a moaning outside the door. The man's voice grew louder and Drew Bundini Brown stumbled in. He was Ali's special trainer, a jack of all trades who inspired the champion. His loud obscenities forced us to stop taping. Not only did he interrupt us, Bundini hovered over me and gave me a wet kiss on the mouth. It was disgusting. Ali jumped up and slapped him in the face. Muhammad grabbed the drunken Bundini, dragged him to the front door and threw him into the hallway, telling him "You're fired!"

Ali returned to the couch and apologized for Bundini's behavior. We started taping again and he resumed telling me how he would "DESTROY LARRY HOLMES."

As happened many times, Bundini didn't lose his job. Two nights later, Ali was hammered by Holmes. At 217 lbs., Ali was the lightest he'd been since facing George Foreman and winning back the title. Holmes was 211. Ali was fatigued from the start. It was an execution. In the 9th and 10th rounds, Ali took a total 125 punches. Each judge awarded Holmes every round until the slaughter was stopped at the end of 10 rounds.

Four days later, Ali checked into UCLA Medical Center. Two days of tests revealed the presence of Benzedrine in his system. Benzedrine is a stimulant and the user becomes more fatigued when it wears off. According to the medical history taken from Ali at UCLA, he had been ingesting several drugs for weeks before the bout, including Thyrolar for his hyperthyroid condition. Thyrolar is a potentially lethal drug and no one should use it while involved in a professional fight. Ali foolishly considered it a vitamin. Instead of a one-a-day dosage, he took three. All of this compounded his weak condition. From round one, he felt fatigued and short of breath. His body couldn't cool properly and his temperature rose. Considering the debilitating medication he used and the pummeling he took from Holmes, Ali could have been killed in the ring.

So, even shadow boxing to a secret tape couldn't help Ali beat Holmes or Father Time. What we had witnessed in Ali's bedroom wasn't so funny, after all. He was a desperate man.

When Bernie "Boom Boom" Geoffrion extended his All Star hockey career and became a New York Ranger in 1966, I met the dynamic right wing from the famed Montreal Canadiens at Rod Gilbert's apartment in Manhattan. Although I was a stanch Rangers fan my entire adult life, no. 5 in Montreal's rouge, bleu and blanc jersey was to me the most fun player in the old six-team National Hockey League when they didn't wear helmets. Geoffrion played from 1950-64, retiring before taking New York's money to play again. The Montreal native broke into the NHL as the Rookie of the Year, playing with a certain determination. He was voted the Most Valuable Player once. He was a two-time top scorer in the league and played on six Stanley Cup championship teams. He was fiery and fearless and he invented the slapshot that blazed past goalies' furtive grasps. He and fellow future Hall of Famers Maurice Richard and Jean Beliveau formed Montreal's longtime first line. In a business suit, Boom Boom had the demeanor of a movie wiseguy. He was Jean-Paul Belmondo before the French New Wave actor became a celluloid gangster. Loud but charming, Geoffrion filled a room with his natural charisma. He boasted of the old Les Habitants and their Saturday night games at home and how "da boyz went out after to da clubs and da wives had to go HOME." He said "Da cash" was the only reason to play professional hockey and he was having one last go round in New York. One night at a Westchester County party, the well-heeled host lit a marijuana cigarette. He was told to put it out in respect for Geoffrion and the other Rangers. The Boomer smiled and took the joint in his right fingers. He beckoned to teammate Phil Goyette and said, "Hey, Phil remember dis . . . . dey used to call dis 'maryjane' . . . right?" The hockey icon took a long drag, laughing out loud.

My biggest faux pas happened backstage at a fashion runway show. In the late 70s, my circle of friends included some people in the fashion industry. Esme, one of the top fashion models of the moment, invited me to a showing. Afterwards, a guy walked up to me and said he was a big Yankees fan. He asked me some baseball questions which wasn't unusual. It happens all the time to sportscasters and because most fans are nice, it's easy to be friendly and polite; all it takes is a little conversation. After a few minutes, I asked him, ". . . . And, what do you do?" The man answered, "What do I do? This is my show. I'm Perry Ellis." To his credit, the fashion icon laughed heartily.

My second favorite faux pas was the night I went to a party at the Mayflower Hotel. I had been invited by Joe Pesci who shared an apartment with Robert DeNiro, after they starred in Martin Scorsese's classic "Raging Bull." I met DeNiro and Al Pacino, among others. Some guys DeNiro knew, who had just flown in from London, wanted to hear a typical American lounge singer. We all went to Tres Amici, an Italian restaurant on Third Avenue. As we listened to the crooner in the bar area, one of the British chaps wanted to talk American sports with me. Then, I asked him, "And, what do you do?" He was astonished. ""What do I do, we're The Clash!" I answered, "Who in-the-fuck is The Clash?" Pesci couldn't stop laughing.

I'll never forget the Yankees of 1978. On July 19th, they were in fourth place, 14-1/2 games behind arch-rival Boston. But, the Yankees went on a rampage the rest of the summer while the Red Sox suffered the team collapse that ranks with the 1951 Dodgers and the 1964 Phillies, in terms of squandering double digit first place leads.

First, the fiery Billy Martin was fired by George Steinbrenner and replaced with the placid Bob Lemon. His low-key manner was a welcome change for the mostly veteran Yankees. With Captain Thurman Munson leading the way and key contributions from Reggie Jackson, Graig Nettles, Willie Randolph, Lou Piniella, Ron Guidry and Goose Gossage, the Yankees won 48 of their last 68 games. Their winning percentage of .706 tied the Red Sox on the last day of the regular schedule, forcing a one game playoff in Boston to determine the American League East championship. During batting practice for the Red Sox, reporters crowded the batting cage and when their leader, Carl Yazstremski, finished taking his licks someone shouted "What ya think, Yaz?" His gaze never left the ground as he walked away from us and muttered, "Anything can happen."

Bucky Dent's name became forever more an expletive-deleted in New England because his three-run home run off Mike Torrez in the seventh inning put the Yankees ahead for good and into ALCS. A jammed-pack, excited crowd at Fenway Park was suddenly quieted as the Yankees shortstop trotted out his damage and Yazstremski sagged at the knees and then kicked the dirt in disgust as the base of the Green Monster wall in leftfield.

The Red Sox fold of '78 was complete and utterly disappointing to their diehard fans, who hadn't enjoyed a championship in 60 years. Maybe there was something to the supposed "Curse of the Bambino." The Red Sox ownership made the monumental mistake of selling Babe Ruth to the Yankees and the last Boston championship was in 1918.

(Every summer, my daughter Sam and I are joined by close friends Marvin Cohen and Bob Pronovost and we make a pilgrimage to Boston. We buy Fenway Park tickets for a Saturday afternoon Yankees-Red Sox game. After the game, we have dinner in the Italian North End with Eddie Andelman and his wife, Judy. Win or lose, the most respected radio sportstalk personality in Boston and all of New England treats us to dinner. Eddie hates New York and playfully ridicules "New Yawkers." I love trading verbal jabs with Andelman. To his credit, he is a kind philanthropic person. But, it's fun to be parochial in sports. Before 2004, and the first Red Sox championship in 86 years, at our annual Yankees-Red Sox game, I walked through the aisles asking Boston fans cruelly, "Can you tell me where the Red Sox trophy room is?"

As the '78 Yankees celebrated their comeback American League East championship, I hosted the beginning of Eyewitness News live from their tiny clubhouse, sprayed by champagne. I interviewed the principals.

NY Yankees Closer Rich Gossage after Clincher in Boston 1978

That evening, I was on the same shuttle air flight to New York with Yankees' owner George Steinbrenner and a dozen of his cronies who included Larry and Zack Fisher, Bill Fugazy, Bill Rose Jr., and Mike Forest. (I was familiar to them because for many years, my daughter Susan and I were frequent guests of Larry Fisher in his luxury suites at Yankees and Giants games. The New York real estate tycoon called my daughter his good luck charm and she grew up knowing Larry's brother Zack and Larry's son Arnold.) After the clincher in Boston, when we arrived at LaGuardia Airport, Larry suggested I join them for a celebration at Jimmy Weston's saloon. Steinbrenner hosted a dinner party for his pals. I was the only media person at the table. The principal owner of the Yankees was toasted with champagne. Off to the side, George said to me, "Now, you're one of us." I said, "No, I'm not, But, congratulations and thanks for the drinks."

An insight into Steinbrenner's temperament occurred at the end of a night game in 1978 in Larry Fisher's private box. Lou Piniella struck out at the end of the game. George was so incensed over the defeat he loudly cursed his favorite player.

Fisher stood up to Steinbrenner and admonished him for his lack of loyalty. Georger blurted out "You know me Larry, it's what have you done for me lately."

A unique interview was with actor Paul Newman about his passion for participating in auto racing. One afternoon, in the mid-'70s, women were yelling for him in the outer hallway at Tavern on the Green in Manhattan's Central Park as we filmed a conversation for WABC-TV Eyewitness News.

The door had to remain locked while he calmly answered my questions. He managed to drain a couple of canned beers while we talked. It was disconcerting to hear the muted shouts of his female fans while trying to maintain focus with the international film star. Newman had more than a fan's knowledge of auto racing. He told me about his races at small tracks, his challenges and feeling of accomplishment.

When I moved to Westport, Connecticut, I discovered that Newman was a badminton enthusiast. Once in a while, at the Westport YMCA, the gym was sealed off so Newman could play badminton with his buddy and fellow actor, Robert Redford. The head of the YMCA allowed me to peek through a gym door window and watch "Butch Cassidy and the Sundance Kid" attack each other, in a gentleman's game.

Joe Namath has been a dear friend for years and his gracious hospitality led to a memorable afternoon, in 1982. While I was staying at Joe's Beverly Hills home, he suggested we play golf at the exclusive Bel Air Country Club. Before we teed off, he asked two others to join us to make a foursome, actors James Garner and Mac Davis. What a treat! As what usually happens while playing golf, our conversation became friendlier. Garner was a huge sports fan and we hit it off immediately. By the 13th hole, we were arguing boxing. Garner addressed the ball on the par-3 and then backed off. He yelled to me about something he didn't like about Sugar Ray Leonard. I waved my hand at him and yelled back, "Enough . . . hit the ball." Garner re-took his stance and swung his 6-iron. The ball flew to the green, glanced off the edge of a bunker and caromed across the green into the hole for an ace. Garner jumped for joy because of his first-ever hole-in-one in more than 30 years of playing golf. He declared me his good luck charm. Joe couldn't stop laughing and Davis was incredulous. Afterwards, the star of "Rockford Files" bought champagne for everyone in the grill at the Bel Air Country Club. He said to Joe, "Where did you get this guy? That had to be the strangest round of golf I ever played."

Willie Mays was the greatest baseball player I ever saw. He was the first player to hit 300 home runs and steal 300 bases. Arguably, the best-ever centerfielder with a dozen Gold Gloves. The only outfielder with 7,000 putouts was a fearless ball hawk with a strong, accurate arm.

**Willie Mays of the San Francisco Giants at the 1967,
All Star Game, Anaheim California.**

The "Say Hey Kid" had a lifetime batting average of 302 and his 660 homers ranked him third behind Hank Aaron and Babe Ruth. He could have topped them, if he hadn't missed 21 months serving in the U.S. Army in 1952-53. Over the '50s and '60s, Mays did everything on the baseball field fluently and with flair. He's still the best first-to-third base runner that ever played the game. He is baseball royalty.

On September 25, 1973, the Mets gave the 42 year old Willie a party at Shea Stadium because he had announced his retirement after 22 years, 21 of them with the New York and San Francisco Giants. Mays had been traded to the Mets who were willing to pay him well for his popularity, but he had stayed too long at the fair. His final season back in New York was a fitting ending but he was late to fly balls and stumbled on the basepaths.

Mays' emotional speech included, "Baseball and me, we had what you call a love affair. Willie, say good-bye to America." He walked off, to a standing ovation. My WABC-TV camera crew and I were allowed to follow directly behind Willie. The cameraman locked on to his no. 24 as Willie hastened his steps down the runway from the dugout, up and down a corridor and across a hallway into the Mets locker room. Turning right, past a rack of bats and row of open lockers, Willie walked quickly to the corner stall and his stool as if he had an appointment. He sat down and put his hands to his face . . . he was crying . . . . and moaning . . . "It's over . . . . it's over." Then, Willie's sobbing increased and we left him alone in the clubhouse. He still hadn't removed his cap. It was a profound experience, to witness an individual who is the best ever at his skill, stop doing what is his essence. As John Updike wrote, "Retirement for an athlete is a small death."

My most "dangerous" interview occurred in the late '80s when Billy Martin was rehired by George Steinbrenner to manage the Yankees. It was mid-season and WNBC-TV flew me to Arlington, Texas, where Martin would return that night against the Rangers. Billy used to call me "Dag" (short for Dago, which was a term of endearment in baseball because Joe DiMaggio was "The Big Dago"). I never cared for the ethnic slur but I understood what it meant in baseball. I interviewed Billy on the field during channel 4's LIVE AT FIVE. The Yankees were taking batting practice as an electrical storm brewed overhead. I noticed the microphone I was holding in my left hand became heated. A technical crew member circled behind Billy, out of camera view, and gave me the "cutoff" sign. I put the microphone in my right hand while still asking Billy another question. Then, two technical crew members were frantically signaling me to get off the air and the microphone was hotter. I wrapped up the interview, threw it back to Sue Simmons and Jack Cafferty in New York. I immediately dropped the microphone and stepped back like it was a live snake. Billy looked at me as if I was crazy. I blurted that the air turbulence was the reason. He looked at me funny. Then, there was a bolt of lightning. If it had happened a minute earlier, I would have been electrocuted. I would have been "Toast on Live at Five."

My most contentious moment with an athlete occurred in 1987 when the NFL players were on strike and the league continued with replacement players. Lawrence Taylor, the Giants' all-pro linebacker, crossed the picket line of his teammates outside Giants Stadium because he needed his huge salary. LT's first day as "a union scab" attracted every news organization. The Giants locker room was filled with reporters and videotape crews. Taylor stood in front of his cubicle and answered many questions. I waited till everyone seemed to have enough quotes because I knew he would object to my question and maybe stalk off. In my best Peter Falk, "Columbo" imitation, I said to LT, "I'm confused . . . . are these the Giants in here or are those the Giants outside?" LT went ballistic, shouting, "You're just trying to fuck me up!" He abruptly ended his mass interview and stomped off to the trainer's room. I hung around and soon enough, someone tapped me on the back of my shoulder. I turned and it was LT. He resumed shouting curses at me, sticking his index finger in my face. I calmly reminded him that no cameras and microphones were on and that I wanted a simple answer to the question, "Are these the Giants in here, or, are those the Giants outside?" LT couldn't answer the question and didn't talk to me for the rest of the season. One night in Atlantic City, at a Mike Tyson fight, we met at a Donald Trump party and to his credit LT laughed about the episode and agreed to be interviewed.

Because of my friendship with stock broker and art collector Richard Weisman, I met Andy Warhol. The pop artist had made a can of Campbell's Tomato Soup into a pop art icon. His "Orange Marilyn" portrait of Marilyn Monroe later sold for $17 million. He wasn't a sports fan, but he told me he was mesmerized by televised sports because he considered the slow motion replays "art." In 1977, Weisman conceptualized and marketed a series of sports personality portraits by Warhol called the Athletes Series. "To bring together two of the most popular leisure time activities: art and sports."

Weisman was the son of well known art collectors Frederick and Marcia Weisman, and the nephew of Norton Simon, the founder of the famed Pasadena, California museum that bears his name. Weisman convinced eleven of the leading athletes of the time to pose for the pop artist, including Chris Evert, Rod Gilbert, Muhammad Ali, Willie Shoemaker, Dorothy Hamill, Kareem Abdul Jabbar, O. J. Simpson, Pele, Jack Nicklaus, Tom Seaver and Vitas Gerulaitis. The most well-known was Muhammad Ali.

Warhol took a photograph of the subject and then used his familiar technique: silk screening the photograph onto canvas, adding paint to highlight edges, textures and shadows. He created four oils of each subject, each measuring 40-by-40 inches. The deal was this: the subject was given one of them and the other three were sold for $25, 000 apiece. Warhol didn't know a hockey puck from a baseball bat, but he captured the athletes in a new vision.

Weisman had a problem sending Ali his oil portrait, trying in vain for a year. Weisman asked me if I could help deliver the oil to Ali. I agreed and it happened the day of the weigh-in at Madison Square Garden for Ali's world heavyweight championship fight with Ken Norton at Yankee Stadium in 1977.

That morning, I went to Weisman's duplex apartment at the U-N Plaza. When I arrived, Warhol was studying the four oils of Ali. He came to the decision that the red one was the most eye-catching. Of the three remaining oils, Warhol decided the green one was the least appealing and he selected that for the world heavyweight champion. Richard and I took it to Madison Square Garden. After the ritual weigh-in, I asked Pat Patterson, Ali's head of security, if I could see the champ alone. We were escorted to Ali's dressing room. We took the outer wrapping off the frame and placed the portrait on a bench for Ali to study.

Andy Warhol and Richard Weisman with the Ali portrait behind them.

He liked it very much and stunned us when he said he had no knowledge of Warhol or memory of posing for him at Ali's Deer Lake, Pennsylvania, training camp the year before. Weisman told him that this portrait belonged to him and, soon would be worth at least $100,000. (Today, it's estimated at a million dollars in value) That's why it wasn't mailed or trusted to any member of his entourage. To make the point emphatic, I added that he should hang the portrait in his home and have it insured. I said, "The way you will be remembered for sports, a hundred years from now, he'll be remembered for art."

Ali understood but still couldn't remember posing for Warhol. I started to describe Andy as a short guy with gray hair wearing glasses and Ali suddenly smiled broadly and gave us a bent wrist with his right hand. Yeah, he remembered Warhol. For doing this favor of delivering the painting, Warhol gave me an autographed large lithograph of his red Ali. Later, I had Ali sign it. I will never forget how one icon didn't remember meeting another.

In the '80s, I didn't play golf for more than a year because I had become frustrated with my lack of shot-making progress. I had let my anger get the best of me.

While on vacation at the Turnberry resort in Miami, I had dinner with Joe Pesci, a pal and one of my favorite actors. He had been nominated for an Oscar for best supporting actor because of his gritty portrayal of Joey LaMotta in Martin Scorsese's "Raging Bull." It is my all-time favorite movie. Pesci teamed with Robert DeNiro who won an Oscar for his portrayal of Jake LaMotta, the former world middleweight champion whose anger fueled his boxing career but ruined his personal life.

I declined Joe's invitation to golf the next day and told Joe why. The next morning, he convinced to try again and practically pushed me to the first tee. In his familiar wise-guy way, Pesci advised me to relax and appreciate the natural beauty of a golf course and not to keep score. He added that I should relax my grip, keep my eyes focused on the ball and swing smoothly without trying to bash the ball. Joe said, "When I was in jail, I used to dream about being able to be out in nature in the morning, listening to the birds and feeling the warmth and just hitting a golf ball." Joe was right. When playing golf, it's best to leave your anger with your street shoes in the locker room. Thanks to Joe Pesci, I've enjoyed golf ever since.

A news scoop walked up to my table on the night of November 24, 1986. I was with some friends at the opening-night party of a Mexican restaurant on Broadway and 90th Street. One of the business partners was Dave Winfield of the Yankees. It was about 7pm. I had spent the past two days trying to track down Tyson who had won the WBC heavyweight title two nights earlier in Las Vegas. Iron Mike beat Trevor Berbick and became, at age 20, the youngest heavyweight champion in boxing history. By late Monday afternoon, I stopped the futile telephone calls and Marv Albert, my WNBC-TV colleague, agreed to give up the chase. I stopped at the party on my way home. Tyson walked in, on the arm of well-known black model Beverly Johnson. They were an incongruous couple because he was still a street thug from Brownsville Brooklyn. Mike stopped at my table because I was the only person he recognized at the crowded and noisy party.

I quickly telephoned the Channel-4 assignment desk and a videotape crew was dispatched immediately. Tyson agreed to an interview in the men's room of the restaurant so the boisterous crowd noise wouldn't interfere. Winfield was in the toilet, too. When we finished the interview, I told the crew to hustle the videotape back to our studios at Rockefeller Center for use on Marv's 11pm sportscast.

Tyson had been fighting every two months for quite awhile. Making conversation, I asked Tyson if his handlers were going to allow him a vacation because he won the title.

Tyson said yes and offered this. "I'm going to Tijuana, Mexico. I hear they have a donkey down there that fucks women." Winfield laughed so hard, he slid down . . . his back to the wall . . . onto the floor of the men's room.

In the late '70s, a friend of mine rented the Cole Porter Suite on the 25th floor of the Waldorf Towers for the weekend. I left the Friday night cocktail party at midnight and took a quiet elevator ride down to the street, until we had to stop at the 11th floor. What do you think are the odds that I'd meet someone I knew on the elevator of the semi-private, austere and cathedral-like Waldorf Towers at that time of night?

The elevator bell rang on the 11th floor and when the white-gloved elevator man opened the doors, a woman in a black lace dress strode forward with her male companion behind her. He was struggling to hold a magnum of champagne with two glasses, while asking for the 10th floor. She called me by name and put her arms around me. Her companion's face was beet-red and he was embarrassed. The woman was Martha Haines who was a regular at Mr. Laffs and partied with big name athletes. She introduced me as an old friend to her flush-faced friend who didn't want to meet anyone. Angrily and reluctantly, he put out his right hand while trying to juggle the champagne bottle and the two glasses. After only one floor, as they stepped off, I gave them a cheery farewell that he didn't acknowledge. The elevator man closed the door and we both laughed loudly as we rode down to the lobby. We just experienced an unlikely, late night encounter, with the longtime married Spiro Agnew, the former 39th vice-president of the United States who resigned that office when he was fined for income tax evasion.

Despite 30 years abstention from smoking, I resumed in the mid-90's. Bill Parcells was responsible for getting me to quit again. We played golf in Ara Parseghian's charity event and he saw me light a cigarette. From a distance, others saw the former Giants coach, now the Jets coach, pointing his right index finger at me and lecturing me. Later, they wanted to know what pissed him off. I said he was telling me the stupidest thing he ever did in his life was smoke. It nearly killed him. Bill's candid concern inspired me to stop the filthy habit again.

One afternoon in 1984, I was alone in the sports office at WNBC-TV in 30 Rockefeller Center. Suddenly, Howard Stern walked in with his tape recorder rolling and he was talking about Miss America Vanessa Williams abdicating her title because of her nude photographs published in Penthouse Magazine. He said he was polling opinions for his radio program on WNBC-AM. Assuming I would be part of his sewer of a talk program, he opened the magazine and asked me for my reactions to her vulgar photo layout. I made no sound for a long time, ruining his bit. When he turned off his tape recorder, I told him to leave. Stern's program may be popular but he's never made me laugh. Shock jocks whose "satire" is based on body parts and functions are the lowest form of entertainment, appreciated only by an audience equally as dumb. Stern sounds like one of those suburban, loser nerds who ride the commuter trains, drinking too much beer and shouting obscenities to get attention.

Of all the tales of the road, this one stands out as a one-timer. In 1977, I was in Moscow for ABC Sports to do the blow-by-blow of 11 bouts between the U.S. Olympic boxing team and the Soviet team. I stayed at a grand hotel on Red Square for a week. One snowy day, I went sightseeing, mostly by foot. The traffic was maddening and the people friendly. Repressed life under Soviet rule was obviously stern because most everyone moved about and acted in an orderly fashion. I saw families having fun, swimming in a public heated outdoor pool for the equivalent of 35-cents each.

Moscow had a scruffy appearance except for the stately turn-of-the-century buildings which were stunningly beautiful even in faded splendor. Red Square was expansive with huge portraits of Marx, Lenin and Stalin. While I was meandering, two people offered to buy the blue jeans I was wearing. Russians dressed blandly and their standard of living appeared to me like the depression era in America in the 1930s. Most everyone smoked cigarettes and, because of a lack of dry cleaning, their clothes smelled indoors. After drivers parked their cars, they removed the windshield wipers and stuffed them in their pockets or a carrying bag. I was told there was a scarcity of windshield wipers and Russians stole them from each other.

There were long lines of Moscow citizens at every store that sold food and goods. GUM, the biggest department store, looked like an abandoned warehouse.

Red Square, Moscow, January 1977.

It was so devoid of quality products, I bought nothing. When I left GUM, I bought two ice cream cones from a street vendor. The homemade ice cream was especially delicious. I bought two because I gave one to a man who had been following me all day. He smiled and accepted the gift and walked away. I was told by ABC staffers that every visiting foreigner was routinely followed by the KGB.

And then, there was the night I met Ginger Rogers. In December of 1979, I was dating a Park Avenue socialite named Cathy Tankoos. She invited me to be her escort at a dinner party in the brownstone home of George Abbott who owned Leggs hosiery. It was a black-tie, candle-lit dinner for twenty people. We were asked to change partners for dinner and, by stroke of luck, I sat beside Ginger Rogers. Though in her seventies, she was still a beautiful woman and I was entranced by Fred Astaire's most famous dance partner. Her blue eyes sparkled and she smiled easily. I didn't dare ask her about their 1930's filmed musicals, which are movie classics of elegance and style. Nor did I ask her about her acting range. In 1940, she won the Best Actress Oscar for her dramatic performance in "Kitty Foyle."

Ginger said she looked forward to her upcoming vacation in Acapulco, Mexico. Her passions were sculpting and painting. She was an avid golfer, tennis player and skeet shooter. She tried to keep fit by swimming as much as possible. Ginger asked me several questions about my upbringing, education and career. She was attentive and very easy to converse with. I kidded her that she must have been "Some Hot Babe." She reacted with a girlish laugh.

BROOKLYN

*"Once you've lived in New York, no place
else is good enough."* John Steinbeck

When I met Spike Lee, the black film director, at a Knicks game, he introduced himself as also coming from Brooklyn. (You don't live in Brooklyn. "You come from Brooklyn"). When he told me his neighborhood was Henry Street south of Atlantic Avenue and the nearby Brooklyn Heights, I asked what was his school? Lee said, "Public School 29." I answered, "You must be a lot younger than me because in the '50s we threw guys like you out of the schoolyard at P.S. 29." Spike to his credit laughed it off, "I write movie scripts about Italian guys like you."

I was born on March 3, 1941. The United States had emerged from the Great Depression and its economic recovery was bolstered by Democratic President Franklin D. Roosevelt's New Deal and its reforms. In Europe, glorified thugs like Hitler, Stalin and Mussolini were oppressing people and changing the geography. As if my Sicilian grandparents weren't paranoid enough, they worried that the outbreak of World War II was ravaging the old country they left behind and could threaten their new life here. Nine months after my birth, the Japanese attacked the American fleet and military installations at Pearl Harbor in Hawaii and the United States formally declared war on the Axis powers. FDR called December 7, 1941 "A day that will live infamy" and we joined a world conflict. While I grew to be three or four years old, I have vague memories of gloomy family discussions about food rationing and foreign threats to our security.

Years later, I learned that the summer of '41 was special because of what two Italian Americans accomplished in major league baseball and show business diverted the nation's concern. Joe DiMaggio hit safely in a record

56 consecutive games, a record yet to be broken. "Joltin Joe's" consecutive game hitting streak was celebrated in song as he captivated the country's sports fans who daily checked the box scores of Yankees games. 1941 was also the year Frank Sinatra was named Outstanding Male Vocalist by music trade publications, Downbeat, Billboard and Variety. It wasn't lost on Italian immigrants that two of their boys were standards of excellence for mainstream America.

I remember of lot of music and baseball on the house radio. Everyday I heard the hits and runs and errors on WMGM and the melodies and lyrics of the standard American songs sung by the best singers on WNEW. My mother had her kitchen radio dial set on 1130 AM in the morning at ten to listen to the Make Believe Ballroom hosted by Martin Block. Dance orchestras led by Artie Shaw, Benny Goodman, Tommy and Jimmy Dorsey, Glenn Miller and Duke Ellington were regular entertainment on the radio. Later in the day, 1050 AM was the spot on the dial for Dodgers baseball on WMGM. Red Barber's south-of-Dixie style was lyrical for Brooklyn types who spoke a gnarled version of English.

Spinning 78 rpm audio records were familiar in our home. On special occasions, the rug in the high ceiling living room was lifted and gathered at one end, revealing a polished wooden parquet floor. My parents and my Uncle Sal and Aunt Kay alternately danced the slow Foxtrot and the quick Peabody, smiling all the way.

I was a second generation Italian-American, brought up strictly and religiously. Sicilian was spoken in our home by the elders. Just after the turn of the century, both sides of my family had immigrated to the United States from Sicily, the largest island in the Mediterranean, southwest of the Italian mainland. Sicily's mountainous plateaus slope to the lowlands and the sea. It is an island of fertile soil. Their hometown was Terrasini, a small fishing village, 35 kilometers West of Palermo on Sicily's rocky northern coast. The Gulf of Castellammare was bountiful with fish and the local agriculture provided fruit and vegetables and the families lived simple, ordinary lives.

Like other Sicilians seeking much more, my grandparents boldly journeyed to the United States by steamship from Palermo to Naples across the Atlantic Ocean to New York. In the harbor, the Ellis Island depot processed nearly 12-million immigrants between 1892 and 1954. After my grandparents were questioned and medically examined on Ellis Island, they traveled within eyesight settling on the shore of the Carroll Gardens section of Brooklyn, a borough of New York City. Carroll Gardens was on the southern edge of Cobble Hill. Years later, on the roof of their regal 25-foot wide five-story brownstone building, looking West, they could see Ellis Island, the symbol of America's immigrant heritage, in the near distance. It was a reminder of where they came from and their aspirations. My grandparents kept their citizenship papers in their safety deposit boxes at the local bank on Union Street.

My grandfathers preceded their wives to America, arriving in 1907 at the height of the mass immigration of about 2 million Italians at the turn of the 20th century. Most were from the south and Sicily, escaping poverty, tyranny, diseases and natural phenomena like volcano eruptions and earthquakes. Steerage class on a steamship from Naples to New York was the worst accommodation. It cost about thirty dollars a person or two months earnings in Sicily, to ride in the deepest hole in the ship with little ventilation, in spaces not rooms, with rats crawling in the darkness. Most of the Italian immigrants were peasant class and they were welcomed as workers for America's expansion. Like so many others who were illiterate, my grandfathers had few choices and they were exploited. It was still better than the poverty they fled. They worked on the New York docks hauling shipping cargo and also built railroad systems in the southern part of the United States. They were loaded on railroad cars like animals where they slept after a long day's exhausting work. They endured and saved their dollars. After my grandfathers earned enough money, they sent it home, so their wives could sail in steerage like swine to "The land where the streets are paved with gold."

Carroll Gardens was a working class neighborhood with 19th century charm on the Brooklyn side of New York harbor, only two subway stops and a tunnel ride away from Manhattan's Wall Street business district. Before World War II, thousands of Irish immigrants left the neighborhood and first generation Italians moved in. The tree-lined streets were filled with 3, 4 and 5-story brick and brownstone houses. Some with verdant gardens in front, most with wrought-iron gates, antique style street lamps and stone Romanesque architecture. The trees were so thick with leaves you couldn't see into the upper windows of the homes. The trees were aviaries for the numerous chirping birds. The streets were filled with cobblestones until they were paved with asphalt. Some streets on the waterfront were never paved. The East-West public transportation was electric trolley car and eventually electric buses on Union and Sackett Streets.

The area was named after Charles Carroll of Maryland, a signer of the Declaration of Independence. In August, 1776, during the Revolutionary War, Carroll led a regiment of 400 men against the British on the Gowanus Creek, on the eastern border, sustaining 300 losses. The neighborhood was named after Carroll and a century later, the waterway became a canal because of burgeoning commerce. Later, the creek became the stagnant and polluted Gowanus Canal.

It was the corner of the neighborhood to avoid, especially in the summer. Recently, the Gowanus Canal was flushed. Now, Carroll Gardens looks the same, re-vitalized by young professionals who enjoy its safety and privacy so close to Manhattan. The re-gentrification has increased the worth of many brownstones to seven figures.

My paternal grandfather, Salvatore Marchiano, was in the wholesale and retail fish business near the Brooklyn Bridge. He was married to Vincenzina. My maternal grandfather, Salvatore Lograsso, loaded cargo ships and, in those brutal winters almost a century ago, carried home a burlap bag of coal each night to heat a tiny apartment. He told me it was so cold then, the East River froze in some parts and could be crossed by horse and wagon. Later, grandpa Lograsso owned a general store, at Van Brunt and Union Street, two city blocks from the booming waterfront of New York harbor. On their way to and from the docks, workers could buy fruit, vegetables, canned goods, cold-cut sandwiches, a hot meal, bootleg wine, a parrot or a suit. My grandmother, Grazia, worked alongside him. The Lograsso store was open twenty-four hours a day everyday and because of the cash earnings and the rough house customers, a fulltime bodyguard was brought over from Sicily to protect my grandparents. He lived with the family and was armed with a pair of pearl-handle pistols. Union Street was the main thoroughfare filled with shops and pushcarts loaded with fruits, vegetables and dry goods like clothing and house wares.

During World War II, the Brooklyn waterfront was a life's blood because of the U.S. Navy Yard and the busy docks on New York harbor. Most in our neighborhood were somehow connected to the shipping industry and while there was much activity, corruption caused secrecy. The Longshoremen's union controlled the amazingly lucrative Brooklyn docks. Mobsters threatened to prevent cargo from being loaded or unloaded unless the shipping companies paid tribute. If shipping companies didn't comply, precious cargo was stolen and ships would be sabotaged in the harbor. Strong arm men threatened dock workers to pay a fee for everyday they worked on the ships. My grandfather

Lograsso and then my father Charles, as a young man, went to the docks in the mornings to "shape up." If they were chosen, they had to pay back. Greed, corruption and anger soured the local culture and most took comfort in their families.

In my family, we constantly were told by our elders, "You play by the rules." Of the millions of hard working new Americans, a few thousand became gangsters and that has always obscured the fact that millions labored and prospered honestly, obeying the laws, raising their families and stressing what they were denied back home, formal educations.

South Brooklyn's Little Italy was an enclave for Italians who based their existence in the new world on "la famiglia," the family. Life revolved around one's blood relatives and distant aunts, uncles and cousins. The lineage was traced through paternity. As in Italy, the father was the head of the family but the mother ran the house and exercised strong will in influencing everyone's daily routines. The families lived close to each other and the clans socialized among themselves. There were feelings of solidarity, continuity and tradition with commitments to honor and respect.

Center: My Mother standing with her arm around my father and family, 1952 Brooklyn NY.

My grandmother Grazia Lograsso seemed to always be cooking something. The aroma of fresh food was as ever present as the red votive candles she kept lit under the painting of St. Joseph, Sicily's Patron Saint. She kept the annual tradition of Tavola di San Giuseppe, St. Joseph's Table. This tradition dates back to the Middle-Ages when there was a severe drought in Sicily. The peasants prayed to God for relief and asked St. Joseph, the father of Jesus, to intercede. When their prayers were answered, they honored St. Joseph forever more on his feast day, March 19th.

Every year on that date, my grandmother set a huge table in the dining room of her Brooklyn brownstone with fine linen, chinaware, silver, crystal, candles and floral arrangements. She invited relatives and friends to share in her dinner which featured no meat because it was the Lenten Period. In Sicily, the peasants didn't have much meat, so the traditional dishes were mostly vegetable-based, like stuffed eggplant and artichokes and frittatas made with eggs, cauliflower, broccoli and spinach. There was fried fish, fresh bread, and an assortment of fruit. For dessert, there were platters of honey and almond flavored pastries. Grandpa Sal's homemade red wine was poured out of gallon jugs. At the dinner, the assembled people recited the rosary led by a parish priest, giving thanks for favors rendered. Grandma's devotion to St. Joseph was so intense, she prayed to him everyday of her life and her faith had much to do with my spiritualism.

In the late afternoons, Grandma Grazia listened to an Italian comedy program on WHOM-AM, titled "Pasquale C.O.D." It was a radio version of what would be called "sit-coms" later on television. On Sunday afternoons, the cast from the program performed the same skits on the stage of the Brooklyn Academy of Music and my grandmother and her sisters joined other immigrants and enjoyed what was really Italian vaudeville.

I listened to cops and robbers' radio programs like "Sam Spade," "Boston Blackie," "The Shadow" and "Superman" who represented "Truth, Justice and the American way."

My parents, my sister Vivian and I lived with my grandparents in the first two floors of their five-story brownstone built in the 1890's. Our home was squeaky clean and well furnished. The mahogany staircase in the grand foyer smelled of lemon-oil polish. The upper three floors were rented to three other Italian-American families. My grandmother Grazia had purchased the brownstone during the Great Depression with the cash she squirreled away during her years working in her husband's general store. She hid the cash in her neighborhood bank safety deposit box and astounded my grandfather when she announced the purchase. The brownstone was originally the ornate home of a physician. The high front stone steps were commonly referred to as a stoop. It concealed the ground floor entrance for the kitchen and service areas. The stoop led to the main entrance for us and guests to rooms above street level. The outer doors were glass and wood and led to a reception area with 16-foot ceilings on the second level. The parlor floor was accessed through immense sliding doors whose runners were imbedded in the polished parquet-styled wooden floor. This combination lounge and dining room was originally heated with two massive white marble fireplaces underneath large mirrors with gold-gilded frames. Our bedrooms were downstairs, where the service rooms used to be, with a deck and garden in the rear where my grandfather planted tomatoes and tended his prized fig trees that had to be wrapped in tarpaper and topped with metal cans to ward off the brutal northeast winters.

In the summer, we had more than enough figs to enjoy. We lived comfortably well and our home was a monumental tangible lesson to all in the family about thrift and saving money.

"La via vecchia," the old way, didn't fade quickly as second and third generation Italian-Americans assimilated into mainstream America but kept old age customs.

In that section of Brooklyn everyone shopped in the same stores on Union Street which was jammed with open pushcarts of various goods. The abundance of meat, fish, poultry, vegetables and fruit was a wonder to the first generation. The Italian immigrants enjoyed the communal feeling of a village, like the Old Country. On certain religious holidays, in the summer, most neighborhood people gathered in the streets for what were called "feste," or feasts. Rows and rows of colored lights were strung to brighten the night. Stalls offered toys, sticky candy and local delicacies, like sausage and pepper heroes and pastry. While we ate homemade food and played games of chance, opera singers and comedians entertained on public address systems which could be heard by neighbors, perched on their metal fire escapes, seeking relief from the night heat.

My parents met while riding on a neighborhood trolley car. Charlie Marchiano asked Grace Lograsso to a dance that Saturday night at the local Democratic Party club. They married within two years just before the United States became involved in World War II. During my infant years, my father was in the U.S. Army, participating in The Battle of Okinawa, the bloodiest encounter in the Pacific campaign. Our home life in the brownstone with my grandparents stayed the same except that dad wasn't around.

Pvt. Charles Marchiano, 10th Army, after The Battle of Okinawa, 1945.

After the war, my dad came home to run his father's fish business and made it his life's work, enlarging it. The post war years in Brooklyn were prosperous for our level and there was a feeling of progress and optimism. There was no longer food and gas rationing and the GI Bill allocated funds for education and home ownership. My father took accounting courses. My parents insisted on education and I was the only person on either side of the family to graduate from prep school and college.

Our home at 394 Clinton Street was typical of the neighborhood, marked by well-kept brownstones built at the turn of the century. We were a block East of the Cammarerie Brothers bakery, at the corners of Henry and Sackett Streets, where the Oscar winning film "Moonstruck" was later made in 1987 starring Cher, Danny Aiello, Nicholas Cage and Olympia Dukakis. Our five story brownstone was next door to a branch of the New York Public Library at Clinton and Union Streets. I enjoyed easy access to the joy of reading, starting with Boys' Life magazine and then sports facts and fiction.

The Italian immigrants in our neighborhood raised their families "like the old country." They worked long hours and most kept the laws. Our family had dinner together every evening and on Sunday afternoons, we enjoyed a weekly ritual of a long lunch with relatives and friends. Afterward, there was more conversation about our lives while we nibbled at fruit and nuts and sipped liquors.

Religion was very much a part of our European culture. We belonged to the combined parishes of the Sacred Hearts of Jesus and Mary and St.

Stephen's, a powerhouse that dominated the neighborhood. It was part of the Catholic school system founded and developed in the 1840's by John Hughes, the Catholic Bishop of New York because of the surge of immigrants of the Catholic faith. The parish office helped those in need of apartments and jobs. In the parish grammar school, on Summit Street, we were taught secular and religious subjects by the Mother of Cabrini Nuns. Some of them weren't sweet and benign. Their discipline was crude because most wielded wooden rulers like hatchets. In fourth grade, an obese nun who ate sandwiches during class time flung scissors across a crowded room of children at me and my cousin Joey Gulino because we were talking too much. Thankfully, the scissors struck only the back wall. The incident was never reported to our parents. We accepted nuns' rage as commonplace because physical punishment at home was a fact of life. Yes, slapping and spanking were painful reminders of the old country for unenlightened immigrants.

Most of us boys and girls were Italian and the tuition was free, so public school was out of the question. I was an altar boy at church when responses at mass were in Latin. Senior altar boys helped at wedding ceremonies and we expected cash tips from the grooms. At requiem masses we were tipped by funeral directors. It was part of the altar boy experience to secretly sample the sacramental red wine.

I remember what were called "football" wedding receptions. No one could afford "catering." The bride and groom would rent a large room at the Knight of Columbus and there would be liquor, beer and wine. The food was simply sandwiches in wax paper. They were called "football" weddings because we would trade varieties of sandwiches by tossing them from one table to another

We were told by our elders, "bada ai fatti tuoi" (mind your own business). For kids, the daily challenge, while traveling to and from school, was avoiding the teenage street gangs. I hung out with the "good guys." The young punks respected our group of athletes because we weren't part of the juvenile delinquency of the '50s. To them, we were the neighborhood dance company. The most feared guy in the neighborhood was someone I'll call Philly and he was the head of the Kane Street Midgets. One day we were playing "fistball" in the street on Strong Place and Philly tried to shake us down for some money which had never happened before. Johnny Fiorentino ran in from two sewers away and beat the hell out of him. We stood there, stunned by Fiorentino's fearless sense of righteousness. Years later, Johnny became a career policeman and I heard Philly was a "made" wiseguy.

While gangs liked the Kane Street Midgets roamed around us, our core group was law-biding and crazy about sports. They were Johnny Fiorentino, George Finguerra, his cousin John Finguerra, Donnie Taranto, Ronnie Savoca, Bobby Grana, Johnny Yodice, Rosario Quattrocchi and Ciro Lauro. Our first baseball team was sponsored by the Police Athletic League. Later, we played in the sandlot Kiwanis League and we called ourselves the Majestics. Our games were at the Red Hook Fields and the Parade Grounds. Quattrocchi was the best hitter and fielder and he had a cannon for an arm. "Rossi" made the first cut in a Philadelphia Phillies open tryout at the Parade Grounds. Eventually, he got a track and field scholarship from New York University because he was a stronger than usual shot-putter.

On the asphalt streets, we played stickball and stoop ball using a "Spaldeen," a pink hollow rubber ball. We mispronounced what was printed on the high-bouncer, "Spalding." We played two-handed touch football and enjoyed street games like "Kick the Can," "Hide-and-go-seek," "Johnny-on-the-pony," "Buck-buck-how-many-horns-are-up" and "Ringaleevio." We nailed roller skates onto a block of wood and hammered a wooden crate onto that, fashioning the classic homemade skateboard. We lit illegal fireworks on the 4th of July.

There were no grass lawns in my neighborhood, but Clinton Street was dotted with old maple trees. On November Election Nights, when the windswept leaves in their autumnal colors danced on the asphalt and concrete, we huddled beside our bonfires in empty building lots and roasted potatoes on sticks. In the summer, we swam at the public Red Hook pool and in the winter, we played basketball outdoors in schoolyards with numb hands.

Saturday afternoons, we went to the movies on Court Street. Serials were popular and we cheered for western heroes Lash LaRue, Tex Ritter, the Cisco Kid, Gene Autry and Roy Rogers. We watched The Mark of Zorro over and over again. All of us loved "The Bowery Boys" with pugnacious Leo Gorcey as their leader "Mugsy."

There was a tiny sandwich shop at the "T" intersection where Strong Place ran into DeGraw Street, run by two sisters named Jennie and Louisa. In the summer, we sat on the stoop and ate ice cream called Mello Rolls and in the winter we sat on the same stoop, our mouths sticky with jelly apples dipped in hot flavored red liquid sugar sold by an old street vendor named "Jugamino." In the summertime, he came by daily selling paper cups of lemon ice off his hand cart.

In the early 1950s, in our teens, we bopped with other kids at disc jockey Murray the K's rock n' roll shows at the Brooklyn Paramount and went to

Jahn's Ice Cream Parlor for its specialty, the huge "Kitchen Sink." We roller-skated indoors at Park Circle, rode the subway to Chinatown in Manhattan ("the city") for late meals and hung out on the beach in the summer at Coney Island, especially on Tuesday nights for the fireworks. Of course, we stopped at Nathan's for hotdogs and fried potatoes. In the winter, we went to the Hotel St. George to enjoy its indoor pool. Those frigid January and February nights, at the steamy indoor pool, were very sexy for the adolescent boys and girls of Brooklyn. When we were old enough to drive cars, we petted with girls at Plumb Beach and had prom dates at Club Elegante and Ben Maksik's Town N' Country Club.

After the Allies defeated the Axis of Evil, the Truman-Eisenhower years were tranquil compared to what the previous generation endured through the Great Depression and World War II. New York was the most glamorous and interesting city in the world. Most war-ravaged cities in Europe were still rebuilding while New York was booming with the largest concentration of talent in finance, art, education, show business, fashion and advertising. Broadway was thriving. For world travelers it was a dream trip. For us, it was only a subway ride away under the East River, or across either the Brooklyn or Williamsburgh Bridges.

The boys who used to be The Majestics looked beyond the neighborhood horizon. We went everywhere by subway for fifteen cents. The shiny olive colored long cars, efficient and clean in design inside, brightly lit with cane seats, white iron grab handles for standees and ceiling fans. There was no air conditioning on the IRT (Interboro Rapid Transit), the IND (Independent Line) and the BMT (Brooklyn Manhattan Transit), which my biology teacher, Dr. Loschert, insisted stood for "Burglars, Murderers and Thieves."

The '50s in Brooklyn mirrored the rest of the country. Television was a novelty and free. Motion pictures were becoming less important. On our black and white TV sets, we watched Milton Berle on Tuesday nights, Jackie Gleason and Sid Caesar on Saturday nights, and Ed Sullivan on Sunday nights. While Berle, Gleason and Caesar were entertaining, all Sullivan did was introduce people. But, his variety show was everyone's favorite because his guests were the top variety acts of the time. One of the most popular early TV programs was pro wrestling with host Dennis James. "Gorgeous George" was an outrageous tease because of his blond hair and effeminate style. Antonino Rocca wrestled with bare feet and Italian Americans rooted for him.

My dad introduced me to boxing, watching the Friday night fights on NBC. I'd curl up on the Oriental rug in front of the TV set and my dad sat in his easy chair, spinning tales about the fighters. The theme song for the

"Gillette Cavalcade of Sports" is as familiar to me as the national anthem. Those Friday night TV warriors included Kid Gavalan, Chico Vejar, Tony DeMarco and Chuck Davie. During that period, Rocky Marciano was building his undefeated record and Italian-Americans were prideful when he won the world heavyweight championship in 1952. During the next four years, "The Rock" made six successful defenses, until his retirement with a 49 and 0 record, 43 by knockouts.

During the mid to late 1950s, while we grew into our late teens, our neighborhood fraternity house was the "DeClinton Club" above a garage at the corner of DeGraw and Clinton Streets, in Carroll Gardens. We spent our free time waxing and polishing our cars, weight-lifting and practicing our mambo dance steps in front of a long mirror. On Saturday nights, we dressed up for the club parties which were dimly lit with red and blue light bulbs. We were horny teenage boys, cheek to cheek with the neighborhood teenage girls, "grinding" to the erotic, do-wop beats of "In the Still of the Night" by the Five Satins and "I Only Have Eyes for You" by the Flamingos. The guys were split into two different looking groups. A handful sported crewcuts with white bucks for shoes and khaki trousers, while most greased their hair and formed pompadours. They wore bulging black "peg pants" with black dress shoes and hosiery, "what the romeos wore" as Billy Joel's lyric goes.

The movies shaped our psyche. We were greatly influenced by Elvis' cool, James Dean's quiet masculinity and Marlon Brando's raw passion. (Two decades later when Saturday Night Fever's Tony Manero strutted on 86th Street in Bensonhurst and flashed his white suit and confident attitude at a Brooklyn disco, he could have been the son of one of us).

The girls of Brooklyn were into facial makeup early. They preferred long hair and tight black skirts and "flats" as footwear. Our so-called "sex life" was petting in the balcony of a movie house. Compared to the emerging sexual revolution and drug culture in the '60s, we were innocents.

When my family moved to East Flatbush, I played baseball for the Bisons in the Kiwanis League, coached by a black man in his twenties named Clarence Irving. He was a good teacher of the game and very patient with us. Years later, I realized how good of a man Clarence was. He also taught us to be patient with ourselves and respectful of others.

The holy trinity was your family, your religion and the Dodgers. Because of three major league teams, the Dodgers, the Giants and the Yankees, New York was the capitol of baseball. From April to October, there was at least a game everyday or night. Starting in 1949, for eight consecutive years, a New York team was in the World Series. Five of those years, the World Series was an all-New York affair. Baseball was so much a part of our language. We argued about the merits of our favorite players and imitated their batting stances. The three centerfielders were Willie Mays, Mickey Mantle and Duke Snider, all future Hall of Famers. Many of our fathers reminded us that none of them could compare with the recently retired Joe DiMaggio, "The Yankee Clipper." The Yankees centerfielder, of Sicilian descent from San Francisco, was an idol to Italian-Americans. Joe DiMaggio was successful, so why not us?

My friends and I were year round intense baseball fans. Our opinions dominated our conversations, on front stoops and street corners, in schoolyards and playgrounds. Our interest heightened from spring training through the long spring and summer schedule. Arguing the merits of our teams, defending favorite players and taunting each other, we looked forward to every September, as the pennant races came to a climax. In each league, the eight teams played each other 22 times each season. We were familiar with the rosters and knowledgeable about the players. The two best teams, not the best eight best teams, advanced to the post season which was a best of seven games World Series.

While I was cutting my teeth on baseball, from 1949 through 1953, the hated Yankees won five consecutive championships. So, while the coming of autumn was "Octoberfest" for Yankees fans, it was hell for the Dodgers and Giants fans. All of us shared a common interest with dedication, competitiveness and intensity to top the others. Were we not the grand children of immigrants who had shown us the way to succeed in America?

In October, the World Series was as familiar to us as the falling leaves. In nine years, from 1947 to 1956, when I was six to fifteen years old, there were seven Subway Series. The Yankees played six against the Dodgers, winning five times and taking their 1951 encounter with the Giants. Losing the World Series to a cross-town rival is especially bittersweet, but winning is the best feeling and that's what finally happened on Tuesday, October 4th, 1955.

It was the day the Dodgers won their first and only championship after years of clown baseball and near misses. Although the Dodgers lost the first two games, of the best of seven World Series, they defeated the Yankees in a seventh and deciding game. I was a 14-year-old sophomore at St. John's Prep and I skipped school to nervously watch the broadcast, hosted by Mel Allen and Vin Scully, on our black and white television.

I watched the most intense game of my young life alone, rooting for every Dodger at bat and coaxing every Yankee out. Between innings, to release my nervous tension, I practiced my slide on the slick linoleum hallway floor, hooking my right foot into a pillow (just beating Phil Rizzuto's swipe tag).

Johnny Podres, who turned 23 on the same day, defeated the Yankees in Game-3 at Ebbets Field. He scattered eight hits and threw a 2-0 shutout in Game-7, clinching Brooklyn's only championship. The last Yankee out was made by rookie Elston Howard who grounded to Pee Wee Reese at shortstop and the captain pegged the ball to Gil Hodges for the final out. Hodges was my hero and in that pivotal game he knocked in the only runs with a single and a sacrifice fly. In front of the mound in the shadows of Yankee Stadium, catcher Roy Campanella lifted Podres. On NBC, Vin Scully, the Dodgers' 25-year-old smooth as silk announcer, simply said, "Ladies and gentlemen, the Brooklyn Dodgers are the world champions." He stepped aside to allow the roar of the crowd.

I ran out our door onto our stoop and yelled in glee. I remember from late afternoon and into the night, there was much celebration in our neighborhood. Bells rang in the "Borough of Churches." In Carroll Gardens, Bushwick, Flatbush, Canarsie, Bay Ridge, Sheepshead Bay, Red Hook, and elsewhere, mothers, fathers, sisters, brothers, aunts and uncles, cousins, banging pots and pans like they did when World War-II ended a decade earlier. It was Brooklyn's finest moment. If our ball team was the best in the country, it validated us as assimilated Americans, along with our personal dreams.

We couldn't get enough of our beloved Dodgers so we devoured the sports sections of the fourteen daily newspapers (the tabloids cost 3 cents) and listened to the games on the new fangled transistor radios. The most fun was going to Ebbets Field, the smallish ballpark in Brooklyn's Flatbush section. My buddies and I took three buses to get to Flatbush, but because of two free transfers, there was only one fare of 15-cents. A bleacher ticket to Ebbets Field was 75 cents and a scorecard only a nickel. We carried homemade sandwiches because we just had enough pocket change for soda, peanuts and the scorecard. Every April, I bought only a blue Dodgers cap and a yearbook. Those were the days before team apparel and caps were merchandised.

I can still remember Saturday and Sunday mornings, waiting for the Ebbets Field gates to open and when they did, running up the ramp and at the top seeing the lush green grass of the field and hearing the sounds of batting practice. Our Brooklyn heroes were there, IN PERSON, in their snow white uniforms with blue stockings and caps which had a white "B" in front and white dot on top and a across their chests, the familiar scripted "Dodgers" in blue.

From the Manhattan Bridge, Ebbets Field was about three miles south by southeast down Flatbush Avenue at 55 Sullivan Place. Its entrance behind home plate was a marble rotunda, an 80-foot circle enclosed in Italian marble with a tiled floor stitched like a baseball and a chandelier with baseball bat arms holding a dozen globes shaped like baseballs. Ebbets Field opened April 9, 1913. It was built on a garbage dump and the constricted piece of property was smaller than other major league ballpark footprints. It had a capacity of only 34,000 seats. Sportswriters described it as a "bandbox." After several changes, for the last season. it was 348 feet down the leftfield line, 301 feet down the rightfield line and the backstop behind home plate was 72 feet away. The foul areas were small and we could hear the players shouts and whistles. The huge black scoreboard with tin white numbers above the right field cement wall loomed large. The clock at the top of the scoreboard was round, rimmed by the words "Schaefer Beer." Fans looked for decisions by official scorers in the pressbox by watching for the "H" in Schaefer to light up to signify a hit or the the lighted "E" for error.

At the base of the right field wall, in the middle, there was a 3-by-30 foot advertisement for Abe Stark's Clothing Store at 1514 Pitkin Avenue and it read, "Hit the sign and win a suit." This was very unlikely because right fielders positioned themselves there and Carl Furillo of the Dodgers was a ball hawk.

The high wall beneath the centerfield and leftfield stands had large advertisements for Old Gold Cigarettes, Griffin Shoe Polish and Gem Razor Blades.

Gladys Gooding played the organ cheerfully in an overhang in the girders beneath the upper deck behind first base. In his pressbox perch, the public address announcer, gruff sounding Tex Rickards, sounded like a carnival barker. A ragamuffin band called the "Dodger Sym-phony" paid for their own seats behind first base and serenaded the fans and mocked opposing players. Dotted on the roof, circling the field, were the wind-blown pennants of the other National League teams.

My eyes gazed high behind home plate to the broadcast booths halfway up, marked "WMGM Radio" and "WOR-TV." And, I would imagine broadcasting baseball games, a fantasy shared by many other kids.

A half-hour before each game at Ebbets Field, WOR-TV broadcast a live program called "Happy Felton's Knothole Gang." The heavyset Felton was a smiling host who dressed in a Dodgers uniform and wore a Dodgers cap. The program was aimed at the Brooklyn youth, sponsored in part by the Lincoln Savings Bank.

In the rightfield bullpen, a guest Dodger, like Jackie Robinson, Duke Snider or Gil Hodges would greet three boys, who wore their sandlot uniforms. The Dodger worked them out, throwing grounders and pop flies. He would pick the best of the three. The winner would return the next program and could choose the Dodger he wanted to meet. All three boys received a new bat and glove and were presented savings account books from the Lincoln Savings Bank. The sponsor was cleverly developing its future customers.

The last segment of the Knothole Gang show involved the previous winner asking baseball questions of his favorite Dodger, near their dugout. Then, as Happy Felton said his cheerful goodbye, the boy and his Dodger walked into the team's dugout to get autographs from the rest of the players. Most youngsters in Brooklyn yearned to appear on "Happy Felton's Knothole Gang."

My favorite player was Gil Hodges, the quiet but strong first baseman who knocked in runs and won fans with a gentlemanly demeanor. Gil served in the U.S. Marines during World War II in Okinawa, like my dad. He married a Brooklyn girl named Joan Lombardi and they made their home in Flatbush. I experienced the highs of #14's home runs and the lows of his batting slumps. In the 1952 World Series, against the Yankees, Hodges went hitless in 21 at-bats. The slump carried over into the next season, but Dodgers fans loved him. He received hundreds of letters of support. One Sunday, a Brooklyn priest dismissed his parishioners, saying, "Stay out of mischief and pray for Gil Hodges to end his slump." 1953 was the first season Hodges improved to hit .300.

Mets Manager Gil Hodges at Shea Stadium, NYC, July 1971.

Hodges was the manager of the New York Mets in 1969 and I interviewed him several times. One day in St. Louis, we were alone together on an elevator, in the Chase Plaza Hotel, and Gil asked me why I was so nervous around him. I told him, when I was a boy in Brooklyn, he was "my guy." I kept notebooks on all of Gil's at-bats. After we exited the elevator, Gil told me to relax around him. The tall, handsome and sure-handed first baseman was one of the renowned "Boys of Summer," as beat writer Roger Kahn called them decades later in his seminal book about them.

Brooklyn's team leader was Captain Pee Wee Reese, but Jackie Robinson was the most fiery competitor. The other core players were Duke Snider, Carl Furillo, Roy Campanella, Junior Gilliam, Billy Cox, Don Hoak, Andy Pafko, Gene Hermanski, and pitchers Ralph Branca, Hugh Casey, Don Newcombe, Carl Erskine, Preacher Roe, Clem Labine, Billy Loes, Joe Black, Roger Craig, Don Bessent, Ed Roebuck and a wild-throwing "bonus baby" named Sandy Koufax whose erractic pitches were dangerous even in batting practice. Duke Snider said he was hit by Koufax so many times on his butt, he folded his fielding glove and stuffed it in his hip pocket for protection.

During their post-war run, they were managed by the fiery Leo Durocher who ended up with the rival Giants and then three organization men, the reserved Burt Shotton, the insecure Charlie Dressen and the bland but strong Walter Alston who was wise enough not to mettle with a set lineup of veterans.

I was six years old, in 1947, when Robinson was the first black to play in the major leagues and the Dodgers became the first integrated team in all of sports. Jackie had the immense talent and strong personality to crack the color barrier and Brooklyn was the right place because of its multi-ethnic citizens. My dad took me to my first Dodgers game in 1949 when I was eight years old and I distinctly remember Jackie running on the basepaths. Little did I know I was watching social history by the Dodgers who pioneered the integration of blacks and whites in Major League Baseball.

Durocher feuded with Jackie while managing the Dodgers and traded insults with him as the manager of the Giants. But, Leo "The Lip" recognized Robinson's bulldog determination. Durocher quipped, "He doesn't come just to beat ya, he comes to beat ya and stick the bat up your ass!"

Every April on the eve of season home openers, those of us who proudly called ourselves "The Knothole Gang" eagerly attended the annual "Welcome Home" dinner for the Dodgers at the Hotel St. George, in Brooklyn. The players were accessible for autographs and photographs.

With Carl Furillo of the Dodgers, NYC 1953.

Because of my pre-occupation with the Dodgers, I listened to the radio a lot. That led to my interest in the broadcasts and the voices . . . . Red Barber, Vin Scully, Connie Desmond, and Al Helfer calling the games. Barber was the "Old Redhead" and he had a sweet sound from Dixie, telling us he was "Sitting in the catbird seat in the cool, cool, cool of the evening with the bases, FOB, full of Brooklyns . . . a base hit here and the Dodgers will be tearing up the pea patch."

The Dodgers main sponsor on radio and TV was Schaefer Beer (". . . The one beer to have when you're having more than one"). They sold an ocean of it, especially when neighborhood taverns had the only television sets. Before and after the radio broadcasts, on 1050 AM, WMGM ("The Call Letters of the Stars"), Ward Wilson, Marty Glickman and Bert Lee argued about the games and the teams on "Warm Up Time and "Sports Extra." Their caustic and sometimes, controversial, broadcasts had a profound effect on me and became the reason I wanted to be a sportscaster.

We saw the National League's best players a lot because they visited the Giants also. If the Braves were coming in, we saw the emerging slugger Hank Aaron who ended up baseball's alltime home run king. If the Cardinals were in, we were amazed by the smooth swinging Stan Musial. He got his nickname "The Man" by Brooklyn fans who watched him tattoo the Ebbets

Field rightfield wall. There were other future Hall of Famers, including Ralph Kiner of the Pirates, Robin Roberts of the Phillies. Warren Spahn of the Braves, Ernie Banks of the Cubs and the best of the them, the greatest player I ever saw, Willie Mays of the Giants.

In 1954, I was at a Dodgers-Giants game at Ebbets Field on a bright Saturday afternoon. Roy Campanella slugged a 3-run home run off Sal Maglie in the first inning. The Giants righthander was a head hunter. His nickname was "The Barber" for his close shaves. The next batter was Carl Furillo. Maglie's first pitch was heaved onto the screen of the backstop. The next pitch was high and tight and Furillo went down to avoid a beaning. The third pitch was swung at and purposely missed by Furillo who slung his bat at Maglie's shins. Sal jumped to avoid the bat. The Dodgers batboy collected the bat and returned it to Furillo. The game continued without a fistfight. Two years later, Maglie became a Dodger and newspaper reports indicated he made peace with Furillo. Thirty years later, I asked Vin Scully if my facts were right and he said yes and remembered the incident which was so indicative of the rivalry between the two teams.

October 3, 1951, remains a day of infamy in Brooklyn. At the Polo Grounds, at 3:58 PM, Bobby Thomson of the Giants beat the Dodgers 5-4 with a 9th-inning, three-run home run off Ralph Branca on an 0-1 pitch in the third and deciding game of a playoff for the National League championship. The line drive landed in the lower deck in leftfield about three or four rows up with leftfielder Andy Pafko looking up from the base of the wall. It was the ultimate "walk-off homer," before it became fashionable to describe such a game-deciding swing.

I can remember watching that devastating moment on our black and white television set in the living room, while wearing my blue Dodgers cap. Brooklyn had blown a 4-1 lead in the 9th inning to lose the pennant to the hated Giants who had trailed us by 13 games in mid-August. Although I was stunned, I walked to church for an altar boys' meeting and I was mocked along the way by Giants fans because I defiantly wore my blue Dodgers cap, as if my reluctance to accept reality would somehow erase it.

In the ensuing decades, I experienced much and forgot a lot, but I remember October 3, 1951, as a vivid shattering experience.

The black and white newsreel footage of Thomson's homer and Russ Hodges' high-pitched call "The Giants Win the Pennant . . . . the Giants Win the Pennant . . . ." is a reminder of that saddest day in Brooklyn history.

Years later, every time I saw Thomson at a social function, I said, "You're the only man who ever broke my heart." He always smiled and never acted arrogantly. Considering how much he hurt me, I found it ironic that the Staten Island native said he watched my sportscasts on TV regularly.

Through the years, I interviewed Branca and Thomson several times. I developed a warm friendship with Branca, talking about contemporary baseball, avoiding discussion of his date with destiny. Ralph is one of the finest men I've ever met, gracious and kind. His ability to succeed at life, despite the pitch to Thomson, is testament to his strong character. In 1951, he asked a Jesuit priest, who was a relative, "Why me?" The response was, "Because God knows you can handle it."

At many charitable events and golf tournaments, I often chatted with Sal Yvars, the backup catcher on the 1951 Giants. He confirmed the longtime suspicion that Giants manager Leo Durocher had a spy with binoculars in the team's centerfield clubhouse window stealing catchers' signs to the opposing pitchers and relaying the knowledge to the Giants right field bullpen which was in open view. Yvars told me of his role beyond being a bullpen catcher. If there was no buzz sound, it was a fastball and in the bullpen, he stood and did nothing. Yvars added, if there was a buzz sound from the clubhouse, it was a curve, and he tossed a ball in his right hand to himself for the batter to see.

The beginning of the summer of 1951 was delightful for Dodgers fans. The second half was a nightmare. The double-digit first place lead melted away as the Giants went 37 and 7 with a 16-game winning streak. The Giants stole the pennant. Sal Yvars, the man who relayed the swiped signals, told me so.

Thomson's historic home run cast a pall on the borough of Brooklyn, but what happened six years later was a bomb.

After the 1957 season, the Dodgers left Brooklyn for Los Angeles, despite leading the National League in home attendance for 5 of the previous 10 years, totaling over 14 million paid customers in a stadium that seated about 34,000 for each game. The Dodgers were offered the keys to the California kingdom and Gil, PeeWee, Newk, Skoonj and the Duke left us with only memories that linger till today.

For any Dodgers fan, it was traumatic and we cursed Walter O'Malley, the team's owner. He realized Brooklyn was suffering "white flight" to the suburbs in the 1950's because more blacks were moving in from the south and more Hispanics from the Caribbean. The daily newspaper, the Brooklyn Eagle, had ceased publishing because of a lack of advertising and readership. At the same time, the Brooklyn Navy Yard was closed, laying off thousands of workers. The large department stores and movie theaters on Fulton Street in downtown Brooklyn were emptier. Apartment dwellers all over Brooklyn were moving beyond the city limits to cheap, newly built detached homes with patches of grass lawns and shade trees. Only the prestigious Heights section, close by the Brooklyn Bridge, stayed upscale because many of its inhabitants were Wall Street types who enjoyed living only a subway stop or two away from their desks.

O'Malley wanted Robert Moses, who had federal governmental power to condemn land and build apartment projects and highways, to discount a parcel of land known as the Fort Greene meat market at the corners of Atlantic and Flatbush Avenues above a Long Island Railroad station and major subway station. Adjacent parking for cars was a critical issue for a new stadium because Moses' parkways tunnels and bridges were arterial connectors for the entire metropolitan area.

Instead, Moses offered a site in the decaying Bedford Stuyvesant section. The impasse wasn't resolved because O'Malley had a trump card. He was arguing for the railroad/subway complex site and they were offering a dump in the ghetto and all the while, the fat man with the cigar was humming to himself "California, Here I Come."

The city of Los Angeles offered O'Malley 300 acres and a new stadium at Chavez Ravine for his Dodgers to become the first major league team in California. The deal was too good to turn down. Lots of sunshine and lots of jobs were attracting a steady stream of transients and consumers. California's population was growing significantly and the state was prospering. The high speed freeway system linked everyone and O'Malley's new customers didn't need the subway.

There was plenty of room for parking spaces at Chavez Ravine near downtown Los Angeles alongside the Pasadena Freeway. The state symbol for California should not have been a bear, it should have been an automobile. No wonder, the stagnant New York Giants were lured from upper Manhattan to San Francisco at the same time the Dodgers moved to southern California. The Dodgers and Giants resumed their fierce rivalry on the West coast, 3 time zones away and faded from our interest. A gouge was taken out of Brooklyn's heart and our beloved Ebbets Field was rendered meaningless. Nothing significant was ever built at either of the sites that were offered by Moses to O'Malley.

Many of our relatives, friends and neighbors vacated their longtime city apartments for homes on Long Island, Westchester county and New Jersey.

In 1960, my parents bought a home in Bergenfield, New Jersey, and I commuted by car to Fordham University. Brooklyn's cheap but crowded housing and the degenerating public school system were no longer acceptable for first and second generation descendants of immigrants.

As the 1957 major league schedule was played out, Brooklyn could not hold its National League franchise. I was among 6,700 diehards at their last game in Ebbets Field. On the night of September 24, 1957, I was in the leftfield lower stands and saw Brooklyn shut out Pittsburgh 2-0 behind lefty Danny McDevitt. Before the last inning, I moved to a box-seat behind home plate. After the very last out and the Brooklyn Dodgers walked into the dugout runway forever, I didn't move until the ushers ordered me to leave. To this day when I see film of Ebbets Field and the players, I examine every detail. It's like looking at an ancient ruin. I spent so much happy time there. "Wait Till Next Year" was the slogan for Dodgers fans, that's why we were so optimistic. But, after the lights went out at Ebbets Field for the last time, there was no next year. Ebbets Field stood empty and silent as a tomb until demolition began on February 23, 1960. The same wrecking ball, painted like a baseball, was used in upper Manhattan to bring down the Polo Grounds which the Giants had vacated for San Francisco. Where Brooklyn's shrine to baseball stood, high rise apartments were erected, housing 450 low income families.

After the 1957 season, while the Milwaukee Braves were beating the Yankees in the World Series, the Dodgers and Giants left New York with one-way tickets to the West coast. Dodgers fans endured the emotional strain and learned a life lesson. As there will always be another woman and another job, there will always be another team and they were the Mets, born in baseball's expansion of 1962. Within the decade, the last-to-first place Mets of 1969 and their championship fanned the emotional embers of many old Dodgers and Giants fans.

In 1987, when the Mets were about to be eliminated from the National League playoffs by the Dodgers in Los Angeles, I was behind home plate with my WNBC-TV tape crew in the field-level luxury suite at Dodgers Stadium. Instead of waiting to celebrate their season, with three outs to go for the National League pennant, the fancy Los Angeles Dodgers fans in that suite left for the parking lot to beat traffic, like it was just another game in mid-summer. That says it all for the difference between Brooklyn and Hollywood.

My first visit as a reporter to L.A.'s Dodgers Stadium, I walked into the press room and complained about the black-and-white still photographs of the Brooklyn Dodgers. Those photos were Brooklyn's history, not Los Angeles.

Broadcaster Vin Scully, who went West with the team, stopped eating his lunch with a hearty laugh.

During my high school years at St. John's Prep in Brooklyn, at night I listened on WMGM to Marty Glickman describing Knicks games and Bert Lee calling the Rangers games. Marty described a basket as "Good . . . like Nedicks" Lee had a gravel-voice and his signature line was, ". . . The crowd is electric." Madison Square Garden on 8th Avenue between 49th and 50th Streets became my home away from home. I went there by subway from Brooklyn to Manhattan to attend Knicks and Rangers games. The "G.O." (General Organization) card, provided a discount for students. The cost was only for seventy-five cents, if we presented our "G-O" card, we sat on the side balconies which were close to the hardwood court and the ice.

Rooting for the Knicks and the Rangers in the '50s was more futile than rooting for the Dodgers. I admired the slick ball handling and passing of Knicks guard Dick McGuire. I liked the roughhouse style of Rangers defenseman "Leaping" Louie Fontinato. The hapless Rangers of the six-team National Hockey League may have been perennial doormats, but the games were fun because the opposing teams were packed with all-stars and future Hall of Famers like Maurice "The Rocket" Richard of Montreal, Gordie Howe of Detroit, Bobby Hull of Chicago and Frank Mahavolich of Toronto.

I was a fan of the six-team National Hockey League in the midst of its 25 year "Golden Era" run, from 1942 to 1967, when expansion proved that more doesn't necessarily mean better. In the 50's, most of us at Rangers games could name every player on all six teams and their familiarity was why we loved the rivalries so much.

My favorite visiting team was Montreal. The Canadians won five straight Stanley Cups in the late '50s. In addition to the Rocket, they had eight future Hall of Famers in their lineup, including the classy center Jean Beliveau, setting up Boom Boom Geoffrion on right wing, and Dickie Moore on left wing. Doug Harvey was rock solid on defense and a wizard playing the point on the most lethal power play in the NHL. Jacques Plante was an acrobat in goal, passing the puck like no one else before.

We Rangers fans cheered for wingers Andy Bathgate and Dean Prentice, defenseman Harry Howell and goalie Gump Worsley. We loved our Rangers, but they couldn't match up with the very talented "Flying Frenchmen" from Quebec.

I also attended college basketball games, fights, track meets and the rodeo at the Garden. Not once was I mugged while riding the subway. In those days, parents weren't at risk allowing a teenager to travel on the city's subway system.

I spent autumn Sundays with the football Giants when you could still buy a ticket. I never took pro wrestling seriously, even when it was the rage on television, the new sensation, in 1950. Those phony wrestling "exhibitions" celebrate violence and the message is negative, profane and vulgar.

In 1958, my senior year at St. John's Prep in Brooklyn, I worked evenings as a sports intern at WNTA-TV, Newark, New Jersey. At that time, Channel-13 was a commercial station. Sportscaster Bert Lee Jr. strongly influenced me because of his opinionated style.

I opted for Fordham University because it had a Communication Arts Department and a radio station, WFUV-FM. My boyhood broadcasting hero, Vin Scully, had graduated from Fordham. He did the play-by-play of the Fordham Rams baseball games and went on to the Brooklyn Dodgers broadcast booth. I was told Scully joined the glee club to help him develop his voice. Frankie Frisch, the New York Giants and St. Louis Cardinals fiery second baseman was called the "The Fordham Flash" and Scully became "The Fordham Thrush."

At the time, like others before me and after me, I underestimated the classic Jesuit education. I spoke for the first time "on the air" hosting sportscasts and doing the play-by-play of Fordham Rams basketball. Once a week on WFUV-FM, I also played jazz records for an hour. After daytime classes, I worked nights in Manhattan at WMGM as a production assistant in the sports department and programming. After the evening sportscasts, hosted by Marty Glickman, I picked the music for most of the hours the next day. Because of a change in ownership, WMGM became WHN and the format went from rock n' roll to American standards to elevator music.

Saturdays and Sundays, I earned $1.25 an hour, on a 12-hour shift, as a newscaster and disk jockey on WFYI-AM in Hempstead, Long Island. The 1000-watt daytimer was in the Roosevelt Field Shopping Center and our broadcast studio and control room could be seen by passersby. WFYI could be heard in Brooklyn and I sneaked in dedications to my girlfriend Bernadette. They were always Johnny Mathis love songs, the "makeout" music of the time.

Julie Ross was the music director at WMGM and hosted Friday night card-playing parties at his apartment in Queens. A guy who lived upstairs with his wife asked us to listen to some songs he wrote. He figured we were in the music business and invited us to his apartment and piano. He played and sang his songs and we liked them. Julie made a couple of telephone calls on his behalf. He was Neil Diamond.

During my school year, I was working at WMGM during the week and WFYI on weekends. I thrived on the workload. I was ambitious because of my parents' determination. My degree from Fordham University was a big deal because I was the first college graduate in the family.

All through Fordham, my classmate was John Halligan and after school we traveled downtown. I worked at WHN and he worked at Associated Press. Later on, John became the Rangers Director of Publicity which was his dream job and he stayed for years. John is now an executive with the National Hockey league.

Ray Siller was also a Fordham buddy. He hosted a daily program on WFUV-FM, mixing his humor with recorded music. Ray worked nights as a page at ABC television. He handed Dick Cavett some of his jokes which the late night TV host bought and used. After graduating Fordham, Ray skyrocketed as a comedy writer, also working for Bob Hope and Johnny Carson. For more than 15 years, Ray Siller was the head comedy writer on the Tonight Show and stayed with Carson until the program ended.

WFUV-FM, NYC, 1959.

In later years, three very talented sportscasters came out of Fordham University. Mike Breen, Michael Kay and Bob Papa are enjoying outstanding broadcasting careers, nationally, as well as in New York, the toughest market. Former Rams basketball player John Andariese has been analyzing Knicks games on radio and television for nearly three decades.

Part of my passion is music of all kinds. Because of my love for jazz, I listened to "Symphony Sid" Torin, starting at midnight on WEVD-FM. He played classic jazz recordings, sprinkled with Latin jazz, until 5:45 AM. I usually fell asleep before one AM. His live broadcasts from Birdland, originally on WJZ, were heard in thirty states. Not only was the music the hippest of hip, Sid's no nonsense "street talk" approach gave the program a certain authenticity.

Symphony Sid got his nickname when he was a salesman in a music store called the Symphony Shop. He had a deep, raspy voice and colored his comments with jazz musicians' lingo. Besides his music related sponsors, some others were offbeat including a hangover remedy, a meat cutting school, a pawn shop, a "zoot suit" pants shop and the Sunshine Funeral Parlor.

I was an avid listener of jazz disc jockey Les Davis on WBAI-FM and later on WEVD-FM. We became buddies in 1960 and have been like brothers ever since. Les taught me much about life and behavior and I treasure his friendship. He spent forty years on New York radio spinning jazz tracks and telling his insider stories. He is so identified with jazz, he came out of retirement in 2003 to host jazz programming on the satellite radio service Sirius. In his 70s, Les is still talking jazz into a microphone and playing prime cuts from the den in his Nevada home.

Birdland was the mecca for anyone who appreciated jazz. Broadway and 52nd Street was known as "The Jazz Corner of the World." The greatest musicians and vocalists were only a subway ride away. Manhattan was across the East River, but it was another mindset away. With a fake draft card that falsely listed me as 18 years old, I went to Birdland regularly on Saturday nights, coaxing bottles of beer in the side bleachers called The Peanut Gallery. Birdland's greeter was a wisecracking black midget named Pee Wee. He introduced the acts and made announcements in a squeaky voice. Jazz producer and promoter Lenny Triolo recalls that Pee Wee expected a few bucks from the musicians, otherwise he'd mispronounce their names. Legendary saxophonist Lester Young called Pee Wee, "A half a mother fucker."

Birdland was a smoke-filled low-ceiling room in the basement of the building. The sound was compact and always swinging. There was occasional laughter while cocktail glasses tinkled and customers' feet kept the beat.

My favorite attraction was the Count Basie Orchestra with singer Joe Williams. Other Birdland headliners included Miles Davis, Dizzy Gillespie, Maynard Ferguson, Buddy Rich, Errol Garner, Lester Young, John Coltrane, Billy Eckstine, Max Roach, George Shearing, Chris Connor, Carmen McRae,

Anita O'Day, Sarah Vaughn, June Christy and Dinah Washington who was the first black woman I ever saw wearing a blonde wig.

At the entrance of Birdland, at Broadway and 52nd Street, this greeting to all: "The Bopster's Creed" . . . . 'I think that I shall never dig/The Music of the moldy fig.'

The Dave Brubeck Quartet and the Modern Jazz Quartet were my favorites, too. I went to Greenwich Village for Art Blakey and his Jazz Messengers, Stan Getz, Charlie Mingus, Thelonious Monk, Horace Silver and Zoot Sims.

At the Hickory House on 52nd Street, the Marian McPartland Trio was solid for a decade. Downtown, The Five Spot and the Half Note had late sets and Sunday jazz brunches at the Village Vanguard were pleasant. I met jazz fans from all over the country and the world. I was a big admirer of the sweet but hip Beverly Kenney who appeared regularly at the Vanguard. She looked like your subsititute teacher and sang in a girlish manner but she had a no nonsense adherance to the meaning of the lyrics in any song whether it was a moody ballad or uptempo flagwaver. Kenney had immense vocal talent and would have been one of the enduring bigtime jazz artists but in 1960 she committed suicide at age 28.

I collected Django Reinhardt records. The French gypsy's recorded guitar work in the '30s and '40s with violinist Stephane Grappelli and their Quintette du Hot Club de France were masterpieces of music. He was said to be inspired by Louie Armstrong's New Orleans style jazz.

I was fortunate to hear the never-before-heard riffs of controversial downtown comedian, Lenny Bruce. At Carnegie Hall and Town Hall appearances, I heard him shock date-night audiences with his new riff entitled "Tits and Asses." I enjoyed Frank Sinatra, Ella Fitzgerald, and Tony Bennett in their Carnegie Hall concerts. In a one-of-a kind evening, I saw Sammy Davis Jr. perform tirelessly and enthusiastically for more than two hours at the Copacabana. I remember Bill Cosby downtown at the Limelight, breaking new ground as a black comedian. In his own right, like Jackie Robinson, the brilliant Cos was "The First." One night at the Blue Angel, I heard a new singer named Barbra Streisand and the next day when she delivered her new record to WMGM, I complimented her extraordinary singing while she waited in the reception area. She was very sweet. Her high leather boots with a short fur jacket was a new look and provocative. We both were from Brooklyn and she spoke with me easily. She had gone to Erasmus High School and she was definitely a Manhattan girl with a lot of gypsy in her, what we used to call "Bohemian." In 1964, at only 21 years of age, she was thrilling in her blockbuster performance in "Funny Girl" on Broadway. Streisand's "No One's Gonna Rain on My Parade" was inspiring and an epic moment for me.

There were lots of Broadway musical hits in the '60s and I enjoyed Zero Mostel in "Fiddler on the Roof" and "A Funny Thing Happened On The Way to the Forum," Carol Channing in "Hello Dolly," Anthony Newley in "Stop the World," Robert Morse in "How to Succeed . . . . ," Georgia Brown in "Oliver" and Julie Andrews in "The Sound of Music." The quintessential tap-dancing ensemble extravaganzas, "A Chorus Line" and "42nd Street," are my all time favorites.

In 1964, I tried to hear the Beatles' raucous concert at Shea Stadium. Thirty eight years later in 2002, in Hartford, Connecticut, Paul McCartney in concert was the single greatest musical performance I have ever witnessed.

In 1971, at Madison Square Garden, I saw ZZ Top as a warm up act for Sly and the Family Stone. In 1972, I was in the photographer's well in front of the stage at Madison Square Garden for the Rolling Stones. I also heard Joe Cocker, The Who, Grand Funk Railroad, Eric Clapton and Elton John at the Garden. Billy Joel singing and playing in a one and only concert at Yankee Stadium was a treat.

In Las Vegas, my all-time favorites were Louis Prima and Keely Smith, backed by Sam Butera and the Witnesses. Other Las Vegas headliners I enjoyed included Elvis, Dean Martin, Steve Lawrence and Eydie Gorme, Peggy Lee, and Don Rickles. In New Orleans, I had a front table for Jerry Lee Lewis and I went to see Santana at the Forum in Los Angeles. On California trips, I caught Howard Rumsey and his Lighthouse All Stars at Hermosa Beach, south of Los Angeles. In San Francisco, I went to the Blackhawk jazz club. In Chicago, I heard Sarah Vaughn at Mr. Kelly's.

In 1998, one of the most thrilling musical nights I ever experienced, happened in San Juan, Puerto Rico, where the 15-member Fania All Stars came out of retirement for an Hispanic "Oldies But Goodies" concert by the sea. Well-dressed Latino couples of my generation danced to the hot salsa beat. It reminded me of those church dances in Brooklyn in the '50s when we were teenagers and we knew how to mambo, cha-cha and meringue. Those were the days of ONLY touch dancing.

So much of my youth was spent on my love of the Dodgers and I admit to a mid-life pilgrimage to Dodgertown in Vero Beach, Florida. I arranged a profile on manager Tommy Lasorda during spring training for WNBC-TV. He drove me in a golf cart over Jackie Robinson Avenue and Roy Campanella Boulevard. But, everyone wore LA caps. I got past the Los Angeles part of it.

I treated the grounds, the buildings and pictures on the walls, as Brooklyn shrines and relics. I kept imagining this is where PeeWee and the boys spent February and March. I remembered eagerly awaiting those newspaper black and white photographs of them posing and squinting in sunny Vero Beach, promising "This will be the year."

Tiny Holman Stadium has no shade and no dugouts. The stands are close to the field and visitors are allowed to stroll the open fields. The Dodgers, always in their home white uniforms, are easily accessible for talk and autographs. While Lasorda drove me around the grounds in his golf cart, everywhere I looked there were Dodgers, but none of them were familiar. Thirty years had passed and my Dodgers were still a memory. However, later in the Dodgertown lunchroom, I spotted Duke Snider across the room. Tommy Valenti, an advertising executive involved with the Dodgers of my youth, asked me if I'd like to meet the Duke. I didn't dare interrupt no. 4 while he was eating.

While I was at Fordham University, I met and fell in love with Bernadette Mazzone, a beautiful and vivacious Brooklyn girl also of Sicilian descent. She was 16 years old and a cheerleader at Lafayette High School. We were married four years later. During the next 25 years we lived in Manhattan and Westport Connecticut. Besides being a wonderful mother, she went on to a successful career in the fashion modeling business as an agent and executive. We were blessed with a daughter.

For some reason, as a kid I was nicknamed "Sam." Bernadette knew me as Sam. So, we named our daughter Susan Ann Marchiano, so that the initials were S.A.M. Our daughter grew up on Manhattan's Yorkville section, on the Upper East Side and she graduated from Stuyvesant High School, where she was sports editor of the school newspaper. She interned with leading hockey writer Stan Fischler who taught her much about covering a team. Sam matriculated to Columbia University where she was the sports editor of the Spectator. While at Columbia, Sam interned at Newsday. After graduation, she became a sports writer, in San Diego, Los Angeles and San Francisco, before working as a beat sportswriter for the New York Daily News. Then, Sam went into television as a segment producer for "Inside Edition," a syndicated news magazine program. She moved on to my old stomping grounds, ESPN, as a sports producer. She made the transition easily to on-the-air reporter at Sportschannel, FOX Sports, and now a supervising producer at Major League Baseball.com. Watching and listening to my daughter report live from an NFL game and the World Series is a bonus I never anticipated. Sam is her own woman and our pride and joy. When the three of us crossed the Brooklyn

Bridge to Manhattan, we stretched our horizons. It's all about striving and for her mother and me, our joy has been watching our daughter evolve as a person and mother. In 2004, she gave birth to Frances, another girl who took my heart.

Like other Americans in the second half of the past century, we endured the Cuban missile crisis, Vietnam, the assassinations of President John Kennedy and his brother Robert and Dr. Martin Luther King, along with the Watergate scandal and the Persian Gulf War. Our lives were changed forever more by the terrorists' attacks on the World Trade Center and the Pentagon on September 11, 2001 and the subsequent War on Terror and conflict in Iraq.

Adding up my good health, my happy days growing up in Brooklyn, my family, and succeeding in radio and television in New York, I'm thankful to the Good Lord.

An often asked question of me is, "Which team do you root for?" I haven't been passionate about a team since the Dodgers left Brooklyn, but I have rooted for compelling stories. Over the past forty-plus years, there have been friendships made, jobs won and lost, and colorful characters met at exciting events. I eyeballed a lot of hot stuff in sports and I am grateful and still wide-eyed. From 1967 on, I reported for all three of the local network owned and operated TV stations in New York, WCBS, WABC and WNBC, and now WPIX.

In the '70s, the people who ran ABC's Wide World of Sports were the most talented and imaginative I ever encountered. Those assignments were my most interesting and rewarding.

I was fortunate my ancestors from Italy settled in Brooklyn, within two miles of Ellis Island where they had to register after disembarking like other immigrants from the ships that carried them and their dreams from "the old country." The New York harbor was only a couple of city blocks away from our brownstone. It's a cliché in films, but I can remember hearing the lonely wails of ships' foghorns in the darkness of night. In 2004, when I was presented with the Ellis Island Medal of Honor, I accepted in the names of my grandparents who had the courage and strength to change their lives and the family benefited for generations.

Brooklyn in the '40s and '50s seems like a paradise now. Those were simpler times. My generation was raised more responsibly, with more interpersonal attention at home. My family and friends succeeded within the law. We validated ourselves through education and labor.

There have been a couple of reunions of my Brooklyn buddies. Among the ten of us, there wasn't one guy who spent time in prison or ruined his life. Sitting in a Brooklyn Park Slope Bar one night in 2005, we reminisced and agreed that the cultural changes during our lifetime were numerous and profound. The Majestics had become grandfathers and, for the most part, content that the trip was very interesting and to be cherished like the fine wine in our glasses.

With Joe DiMaggio at Yankee Stadium, NYC, June 1969.

What were the odds against a kid, fifty years ago, sitting in the bleachers at Ebbets Field, making his dream come true and becoming a sportscaster? And, I never left my home town, the greatest city on earth. The long shot proved to be possible.

Working in sports has been a delight and the bonus has been meeting so many interesting people and being an eyewitness to great moments in sports.

I interviewed Casey Stengel, Joe DiMaggio, Mickey Mantle, Willie Mays, Ted Williams, Hank Aaron, Muhammad Ali, Rocky Marciano, Vince Lombardi, Joe Namath, Wilt Chamberlain, Bill Bradley, Billie Jean King, Jack Nicklaus, Arnold Palmer, Frank Sinatra and (for UPI Audio) Ferderico Fellini.

Most importantly, I didn't have to leave my family and friends to work elsewhere. While I've enjoyed every moment of my broadcasting career, my greatest joy has been my daughter Susan who has been a delight for her mother and me her whole life.

From those early years listening on the radio to anchoring sportscasts, on television, what has New York sports meant to me?

The Yankee Clipper, Yogi and the Scooter, Pee Wee, Campy, Newk and "Oisk." The "Say Hey Kid" and Sal "The Barber" . . . . Mel Allen's "How about that ". . . . Red Barber "sitting in the catbird seat" . . . . Russ Hodges screaming "The Giants win the pennant, the Giants win the pennant" . . . . Fred Capposella chirping "It is now post time" . . . . Jimmy Cannon, Red Smith, Milton Gross and Dick Young writing about Graziano and Lamotta, Gifford and Rote, Mantle and Maris . . . . Marty Glickman's "Good as Nedicks" . . . Howard Cosell "telling it like it is" . . . . the bar at Toots Shor's . . . . the back rooms at Mr. Laffs . . . . Captain Willis, Dollar Bill and Clyde . . . Hit the sign and win a suit . . . . a Ballantine Blast . . . . the monuments in centerfield and Gladys Gooding at the organ . . . . Larsen's Perfect game . . . . Brooklyn's only championship in '55 . . . Broadway Joe's Super Bowl III guarantee . . . . the Miracle Mets of '69 . . . . the Knicks first Championship in '70 . . . . Ali and Frazier at the Garden . . . . when the Nets won it all with Doctor J . . . . The Gag line with Gilbert, Hadfield and Ratelle . . . . Secretariat by 31 lengths in the Belmont Stakes . . . . Tom Terrific . . . Koos . . . Cleon and Agee . . . Big Orange and Tug's "Ya Gotta Believe . . . . Four straight Cups by the Islanders . . . . Mr. October, the Gator and Donnie Baseball . . . . Big Tuna's Super Bowl Giants . . . . L.T.'s "nut cracking time," Bavaro refusing to go down and Simms' Super Sunday in Pasadena . . . . Looie's sweaters and Mookie's dribbler . . . . the all-time thrill of the '93-'94 Rangers ending the Curse of 1940 . . . Jumbo's TD catch . . . Derek, Jorge, Bernie and Mo . . . and . . . the whole Torre story.

I saw "Willie, Mickey and the Duke" in the flesh and the greatest pre game meal was a Nedick's hotdog and orange drink at the old Garden, waiting for my friends under the marquee on 8th Avenue, before college basketball doubleheaders, and Knicks and Rangers games. After the big fights we talked and argued about them, till the wee hours in the back room at P.J. Clarke's. There were nights at Mr. Laffs when youth was joyously unrestrained. In those gentler times, big-time athletes felt comfortable to socialize with the media. Their prominence wasn't about their salaries, it reflected their athletic abilities. For the most part, that relaxed social life and its public interplay of jocks and women, no longer exists because the gossip industry has turned leading athletes into tabloid stars and targets of litigation. Today's superstars hire bodyguards for their social rounds. It was a sign of the times in 2006 when National Basketball Association Commissioner David Stern said he preferred his players leave their firearms at home. As for self-centered millionaire athletes, former World Middleweight Champion Marvin Hagler said it best: "It's tough to get up in the morning and run to stay in shape when you're wearing silk pajamas."

Working in the capitol of the world among my friends and relatives has been a privilege. After marriages to Bernadette and Thayer, the next big thrill is my granddaughter Frances. "Frankie" doesn't know it yet but what preceded her was so interesting, mostly sweet, sometimes bitter, but never dull.

BIOGRAPHY (2007)

Sal Marchiano, the sports anchor of the CW-11 News at Ten, has been reporting Sports on New York television for forty years. He began his TV sportscasting career in May of 1967 at WCBS-TV, following four years on the radio with the Mutual Network. WNEW-AM and WJRZ-AM. Sal joined WPIX-TV in 1994, after a ten-year stint at WNBC-TV, three years at ESPN, two years at WCBS-TV, ten years at WABC-TV and his original three years at WCBS-TV.

In the seventies, Sal hosted daily network radio sportscasts for ABC. He described boxing matches, collegiate football games and major league baseball for ABC Sports and was a regular contributor to ABC's weekly Wide World of Sports.

Sal was born in Brooklyn, New York, and resides in Fairfield, Connecticut. He earned a Bachelor of Social Science Degree in Communication Arts from Fordham University. He was the recipient of an Ellis Island Medal of Honor and two Emmy awards for excellence in broadcast news. His daughter, Sam, is a television anchor and correspondent with Major League Baseball.

Printed in the United States
101170LV00003B/118-126/A